Socialism and British Literature

Socialism and British Literature

A People to Come

Roberto del Valle Alcalá

LIVERPOOL UNIVERSITY PRESS

First published 2025 by
Liverpool University Press
4 Cambridge Street
Liverpool
L69 7ZU

British Library Cataloguing-in-Publication data
A British Library CIP record is available

ISBN 978-1-83624-489-9

Typeset by Carnegie Book Production, Lancaster

This one, too, is for Naia and Sol

Contents

Acknowledgements   ix

Introduction: A People to Come   1

Chapter One: From Utopia to Hegemony   15

Chapter Two: The People Are Missing   51

Chapter Three: Realism without Guarantees   99

Chapter Four: The Anarchic Trace   137

Coda: A Politics of Heterogeneity   181

Bibliography   185

Index   195

Acknowledgements

I wish to thank my editor at Liverpool University Press, Christabel Scaife, for her initial expression of interest in this project and for her help throughout the publication process. The anonymous reviewers, who commented on the book proposal and final draft, have been a model of intellectual rigour and generosity. My sincere gratitude to them.

The first and second sections of Chapter One have appeared, respectively, as 'Specters of Utopia in *Mary Barton*', *Studies in the Novel* 55:3 (2023) and, in a slightly different version, as 'Writing a Class to Come: Social Fiction, Heterogeneity, and the Political', in *The Routledge Companion to Working-Class Literature*, edited by Ben Clarke (2024). Portions of my discussion of *Border Country* in Chapter Three were originally published as 'Utopia Against Abstraction: Raymond Williams, Communication, and the Desire of the Common', *Rethinking Marxism* 34:2 (2022). I thank the editors and peer reviewers at those venues for their invaluable feedback.

Finally, this book has been made possible by a generous sabbatical grant from the Bank of Sweden Tercentenary Foundation (*Riksbankens Jubileumsfond*).

Introduction

A People to Come

My point of departure in this book is a questioning of the long-held assumption in studies of British radical literature and culture that socialism (and more generally, left-wing politics) is indissociable from the notion of class. Socialist writing and other forms of oppositional cultural and artistic creation have usually been read as more or less autonomous manifestations of class 'consciousness', operating as an outgrowth – at the level of 'experience' and in the particular realm of aesthetic expression – of an objective social foundation rooted in the binary logic of capitalist relations of production. For example, in the introduction to a classic collection of essays on the topic, we read that 'A socialist novel, by being written in the historical interests of the working class, reveals a standpoint consistent with that of the class-conscious sections of this class'.[1] What is immediately apparent in this definition is its identification of the 'historical interests of the working class' as an objective and presumably homogeneous entity, and its correlation of a particular form of literary expression with a subjective standpoint that is ultimately reducible to such an objective reality. If not a passive reflex (or reflection) of socio-economic reality, socialist writing is nevertheless presented as a *necessary* product of the historical development of that class – a sign of its objective journey towards consciousness. The fundamentally flawed analysis implicit in such definitions is not only the result of a simplistic understanding of the relationship between cultural activity and socio-economic reality (an understanding that was for the most part abandoned long ago) but also, specifically, a function of the historical account of socialist ideas that this type of analysis presupposes.[2] For the suggestion that socialism entertains an internal or immanent relation with the working class, understood as an objective entity in history, is also one that does not necessarily hold up to historical scrutiny.

---

[1] H. Gustav Klaus, 'Introduction', in *The Socialist Novel in Britain: Towards the Recovery of a Tradition* (Brighton: Edward Everett, 2018), p. 1. The first edition of this collection was published in 1982.

[2] See, for example, Raymond Williams's discussion in *Marxism and Literature* (Oxford: Oxford University Press, 1977), especially pp. 75–100.

As Mark Bevir observes in his influential study of British socialism in the late nineteenth century, the ascription of political ideas to given socio-economic developments is less appealing to historians today than it once was: 'Today ... socialism often appears less as the natural outcome of workers' reacting to the prior formation of capitalism and more as a contingent and variegated cluster of political theories'.[3] This historiographic reorientation was pioneered in the 1980s by scholars of nineteenth-century radicalism such as Gareth Stedman Jones, for whom the phenomenon of Chartism enjoyed a considerable degree of discursive autonomy with regard to structural developments in society and the economy. Thus, according to Stedman Jones, while the discontents addressed by the Chartists largely corresponded to those of a socially recognisable class of waged workers, 'the form in which these discontents were addressed cannot be understood in terms of the consciousness of a particular social class, since the form pre-existed any independent action by such a class and did not significantly change in response to it'.[4] The linguistic and cultural construction of radical identities in the nineteenth century was thus a heterogeneous phenomenon which often stressed continuity with previous discursive formations (such as particular traditions of eighteenth-century radicalism) and which, consequently, is hardly reducible to any narrow sociological category or explanation. As a result, there is now a tendency among historians to accept that a populist idea of 'the people', rather than the working class, 'provided the main frame of collective identity for workers throughout the nineteenth century'.[5] This is something that scholars of nineteenth-century literature have also identified, not only among the less ideologically advanced modulations of radical sentiment which proliferated at mid-century but also in the more recognisably socialistic interventions of late Victorian writers such as George Gissing.[6] Thus, in *The Political Unconscious*, his classic work of Marxist criticism, Fredric Jameson observes, apropos of Gissing's most famous novel of the 1880s, *The Nether World*, that

[It] cannot be said to be a proletarian novel, in spite of the nominal occupations – die-sinking, the manufacturing of jewelry or artificial flowers – of some of its characters. Its conceptual and organizational

---

[3] Mark Bevir, *The Making of British Socialism* (Princeton, NJ: Princeton University Press, 2011), p. 6.

[4] Gareth Stedman Jones, *Languages of Class: Studies in English Working Class History* (Cambridge: Cambridge University Press, 1983), p. 95.

[5] Bevir, *The Making*, p. 8.

[6] See, for example, Sally Ledger's study of Dickens's populist politics, *Dickens and the Popular Radical Imagination* (Cambridge: Cambridge University Press, 2007).

framework is not that of social class but rather that very different nineteenth-century ideological concept which is the notion of 'the people', as a kind of general grouping of the poor and 'underprivileged' of all kinds, from which one can recoil in revulsion, but to which one can also, as in some political populisms, nostalgically 'return' as to some telluric source of strength.[7]

Without specifically delving into Gissing's fiction here, we may effectively move beyond the binary alternative between 'revulsion and fascination', or horror and nostalgia, that Jameson mentions by stressing the specific political operation at stake in this logic of populism, especially in so far as it concerns the possibility of recasting socialist politics in a less deterministic manner.[8]

For precisely what *Socialism and British Literature* suggests is that the discursively open and historically contingent language of 'the people', where 'the people' is understood as a political subject without necessary determinations or objective guarantees (and thus, as a people which needs to be assembled or imagined, a people that is always yet to come), is at the heart of literary engagements with the idea of socialism in Britain.[9] In fictional and creative explorations of left-wing politics, from the nineteenth-century ideological contexts which eventually gave rise to mass socialist movements at the beginning of the twentieth century to early twenty-first-century recreations of radical politics, what transpires is an impulse to expand the discursive forms and identities of 'socialism' and to disengage them from any given or fixed socio-economic position. In embracing a notion of the people that evades objectivist reductionisms, and in accepting it (without necessarily naming it at all times) as the basic constituency of a literary-socialist imagination whose discursive forms are – as Gareth Stedman Jones says in relation to Chartism – in excess of any particular social group with whom its individual claims may be identified, I subscribe in this book to the revisionist definition of socialism proposed by Mark Bevir in *The Making of British Socialism*. As Bevir points out, the 'old historiography typically gave socialism stable content and then projected that content back through history'.[10] Yet it is essential to insist that socialism 'has no necessary core'; indeed, '[t]here are no ideas and actions such

---

[7] Fredric Jameson, *The Political Unconscious* (London: Methuen, 1981), p. 189.

[8] Jameson, *The Political Unconscious*, p. 189.

[9] Stuart Hall's proposal, in his important theoretical interventions of the 1980s, of '*a socialism which is without guarantees*, that is to say a socialism which does not believe that the motor of history is inevitably on its side', is directly relevant to this book's definition of socialism, *The Hard Road to Renewal: Thatcherism and the Crisis of the Left* (London: Verso, 2021), p. 195.

[10] Bevir, *The Making*, p. 13.

that when they are present, we have an instance of socialism, and when they are absent, we do not have an instance of socialism. On the contrary, socialism is a fluid set of beliefs and practices that people are constantly making and remaking and in which no one idea or action has a fixed or necessary place'.[11]

Relying on such a definition, the key assumption that informs my investigation in this book could be summarised in the following terms: socialism, as imagined in British literature, is, at bottom, a populism in the sense that its central subject is a heterogeneous people. This people lacks ontological positivity (it is a 'missing people'), since any attempt to actualise it is primarily discursive rather than social or economic.[12] Moreover, the lack of a transhistorical (or necessary) ideological core implies that the people has to be constantly reimagined. Any doctrinal stabilisation of its content is thus provisional and contingent.[13] Following Jacques Derrida, we could say that this notion of socialism, like that of democracy, is 'autoimmune' in the sense that it lacks the possibility of a full and self-stabilising presence. Its people – unlike the class whose 'consciousness' corresponds to an objectively determinable state of development – is defined by a 'lack of the proper and the selfsame. And so it is defined only by turns, by tropes, by tropism'.[14] With his concept of 'democracy to come', Derrida suggests, in this sense, that there is 'no absolutely intelligible idea, no *eidos* ... of democracy'.[15] If, analogously, the redefinition of British socialism that historians such as Mark Bevir propose implies discursive openness and fluidity, that is because its political subject resists integration into (or reduction to) any logic of objective fullness. In other words, the people of socialism that British literature imagines is a people to come.

A key theoretical reference in this book is the work of the Argentine political philosopher Ernesto Laclau. Laclau's thought has revolutionised our understanding of populism and, in its specifically leftist decantation,

---

[11] Bevir, *The Making*, p. 13.

[12] The phrase a 'missing people' is one I borrow from Gilles Deleuze, to whom I return later in this Introduction.

[13] Patrick Joyce offers a similar theorisation of the people in nineteenth-century England as an eminently autonomous imaginary. As he writes, 'everyone speaks in the name of "the people", yet the people are nowhere to be found outside the imagining of the people. This imagined people takes on a colossal force as the source of all sorts of claims for authority and legitimacy', *Democratic Subjects: The Self and the Social in Nineteenth-Century England* (Cambridge: Cambridge University Press, 1994), p. 19.

[14] Jacques Derrida, *Rogues: Two Essays on Reason*, trans. by Pascale-Anne Brault and Michael Naas (Stanford, CA: Stanford University Press, 2005), p. 37.

[15] Derrida, *Rogues*, p. 37.

its identification with a post-Marxist and radical-democratic definition of socialism.[16] I do not wish to offer here a comprehensive account of the ways in which Laclau's ideas inform the literary investigation that follows (for these will be explained below), but I want to highlight the centrality of a notion I have already mentioned in passing and which plays an important role in his theory of populism. This is the notion of 'heterogeneity'. Laclau's post-Marxism rests on his rejection of dialectics as a legitimate way of accounting for the constitution of social identities precisely because there is no room for heterogeneity in dialectics. As he points out, 'dialectical transitions are not only compatible with contradiction, but have to rely on contradiction as the condition of their unity within a homogeneous space. There is nothing heterogeneous in a dialectical contradiction'.[17] As in the conception of class that contains the resources of its own self-cancelling and liberation (the Hegelian *Aufhebung*), a dialectical understanding of social conflict is guided by a logic of necessity from which '[a]ny remnant of a contingent empiricity' has to be removed.[18] From this point of view, socio-historic reality, however punctuated by negativity and dislocation in its conjunctural unfolding, is a saturated and homogenous space, an expression of what Derrida describes as the 'metaphysics of presence'. The logic which heterogeneity introduces is very different, for '[h]eterogeneity only enters the game if it can be shown that the very logic of totality … fails at some point as a result of an aporia that cannot be resolved within that totality's structuring principles'.[19] In other words, heterogeneity signals the irreducibility of a given political identity to an underlying objective – and necessary – logic, affirming instead the constitutive nature of its contingency. To say that the people of socialism is yet to come is thus to affirm that its empirical presence in a given antagonistic relation is not logically deducible from its history. Or, to say it with Laclau, that '[t]here is no Absolute Spirit that can assign to it an objectively determinable content'.[20] The irreducibility of contingency and heterogeneity does not preclude the emergence of homogeneity in the realm of the social, but the key point to emphasise is that '[h]omogeneity is always achieved, never given'.[21]

This notion of heterogeneity is particularly important to my discussion in this book of a first-stage literary-socialist discourse. I will show how the opening to a logic of radical otherness in the social (the affirmation of a

---

[16] See also Chantal Mouffe, *For a Left Populism* (London: Verso, 2018).

[17] Ernesto Laclau, *The Rhetorical Foundations of Society* (London: Verso, 2014), p. 161.

[18] Laclau, *Rhetorical Foundations*, p. 161.

[19] Laclau, *Rhetorical Foundations*, p. 162.

[20] Laclau, *Rhetorical Foundations*, p. 165.

[21] Laclau, *Rhetorical Foundations*, p. 169.

radical absence of 'ipseity', as Derrida says) that we find in mid-century social-problem fiction (my case study will be Elizabeth Gaskell's *Mary Barton*) is followed by a breakdown in the assumption of historico-political necessity as working-class experience is focalised and examined, now in properly socialist terms, from within.[22] My discussion of Robert Tressell's seminal novel, *The Ragged Trousered Philanthropists*, rests to a large extent on the constitutive role of heterogeneity and its particular conceptual expression in Marxist theory: the notion of the lumpenproletariat.[23] I will return to this concept (on which Laclau bases a significant part of his analysis) and its significance to the literary identification of a people at the heart of British socialism in this Introduction, but first I want to address, briefly, one of the key theoretical sources of Laclau's notion of heterogeneity: the work of Georges Bataille.

In his essay 'The Psychological Structure of Fascism', Bataille argues that '[p]roduction is the basis of a social *homogeneity*. *Homogeneous* society is productive society, namely, useful society. Every useless element is excluded, not from all of society, but from its homogeneous part'.[24] The contradictions which define the capitalist mode of production are not stages in a logical unfolding from which a new – full and totalising – homogeneity will arise (as in the dialectical conception of history), but an irreducible pressure upon the system, leading to 'a tendential dissociation of *homogeneous* social existence'.[25] According to Bataille, heterogeneity is no more reducible to social homogeneity than, in psychoanalytic theory, the unconscious is capable of full integration into consciousness.[26] While homogeneity is accessible in the form of objectivity ('basically, it is the specific reality of solid objects'), heterogeneity is that which disrupts the possibility of the full constitution and self-closure of such objectivity, for '[*h*]eterogeneous reality is that of a force or shock' and,

---

[22] Derrida, *Rogues*, p. 37.

[23] For a systematic investigation of this concept in Marxist theory, see Clyde W. Barrow, *The Dangerous Class: The Concept of the Lumpenproletariat* (Ann Arbor: University of Michigan Press, 2020).

[24] Georges Bataille, 'The Psychological Structure of Fascism', in *Visions of Excess: Selected Writings, 1927–1939*, ed. by Allan Stoekl, trans. by Allan Stoekl, with Carl R. Lovitt and Donald M. Leslie, Jr. (Minneapolis: University of Minnesota Press), p. 137.

[25] Bataille, 'Psychological Structure', p. 139.

[26] 'The exclusion of *heterogeneous* elements from the *homogeneous* realm of consciousness formally recalls the exclusion of the elements, described (by psychoanalysis) as *unconscious*, which censorship excludes from the conscious ego. The difficulties opposing the revelation of *unconscious* forms of existence are of the same order as those opposing the knowledge of *heterogeneous* forms', Bataille, 'Psychological Structure', p. 141.

consequently, that which renders social homogeneity 'a precarious form, at the mercy of violence and even internal dissent'.[27]

The theoretical status of the heterogeneous in Bataille is analogous to the notion of the Real in Lacan, another concept on which Laclau's theorisation of politics rests.[28] In Lacanian discourse, the Real alludes to that moment or element of psychic life which resists symbolisation: it is the point of failure of the Symbolic (the order of language) and thus the residue confronting the subject with an ineradicable exposure to the impossible (because never truly accessible, and thus always traumatic) fullness.[29] The heterogeneous/ Real is, according to Laclau, that which short-circuits the endogenous logic of dialectical development: the point at which the totalising order meets its internal limit, thereby preventing the attainment of immanent fullness. In his debate with Marxism, and in his substitution of the concept of the people for that of class, this is the critical role Laclau assigns to the notion of the lumpenproletariat. The latter is the heterogeneous (or Real) element that threatens to disrupt the logical integration of the dialectical conception of History.[30] As Laclau explains, 'History, for Marx, insofar as it is a coherent story, is a history of production ... So occupying a precise location within the relations of production offers, for Marx, the only possible claim to being a historical actor. But this location is precisely what the *lumpenproletariat* does not have'.[31] Laclau argues that the introduction of the notion of the lumpenproletariat confronted Marx with a major theoretical problem. While the immediate empirical referent of the lumpenproletariat was the marginal sector of the urban population (the 'rabble of the city'), the conceptual elaboration implicit in this notion of a class fraction defined by its distance from the process of production entailed its potential reemergence in different guises and at multiple locations within society, which in turn threatened the homogeneous conception of 'history as the history of production' (with its 'defence requir[ing] the most unlikely contortions').[32]

The socially heterogeneous status of the lumpenproletariat features prominently in the literary history of British socialism. One of the best-known

---

[27] Bataille, 'Psychological Structure', pp. 142, 139.

[28] 'Heterogeneity is another name for the Real', Laclau, *Rhetorical Foundations*, p. 165.

[29] I will return to some of these concepts in my discussion of James Kelman in Chapter Four.

[30] Laclau compares the status of the lumpenproletariat in Marx and Engels to that of the 'peoples without history' in Hegel. See Ernesto Laclau, *On Populist Reason* (London: Verso, 2005), p. 142.

[31] Laclau, *Rhetorical Foundations*, p. 163.

[32] Laclau, *Rhetorical Foundations*, p. 164.

documents in this history, as well as in that of Marxist literary theory, concerns precisely this issue, through its examination of the problematic presence of the unproductive and parasitic London lumpenproletariat in the work of Margaret Harkness, one of the leading practitioners of naturalism in late nineteenth-century England.[33] Friedrich Engels's famous 1888 letter to Harkness criticised her first novel, *A City Girl*, for its alleged lack of realism; indeed, his central observation therein would mark a standard point of reference for subsequent Marxist polemics in defence of realism and typicality, from Georg Lukács's classic indictment of anti-realist experiments in late nineteenth and early twentieth-century European literature to the more dogmatic expressions of Soviet-style 'socialist realism' in the 1930s and 40s.[34] Engels writes, 'Realism, to my mind, implies, besides truth of detail, the truthful reproduction of typical characters under typical circumstances'.[35] The problem with Harkness's characters, according to Engels, is that they are set in social circumstances that cannot be said to be typical of the stage of historical development: 'the

---

[33] See Glyn Salton-Cox, 'Uncivil Society: Margaret Harkness, Engels and the Lumpenproletariat', *Key Words: A Journal of Cultural Materialism* 16 (2018), pp. 23–40.

[34] According to Lukács, the central aesthetic limitation of both naturalism and modernism lies in their alleged failure to connect surface phenomena to the underlying objective reality in a dialectical gesture that would adequately express a full understanding of the social totality: 'The modern literary schools of the imperialist era, from Naturalism to Surrealism, which have followed each other in such swift succession, all have one feature in common. They all take reality exactly as it manifests itself to the writer and the characters he creates ... But both emotionally and intellectually they all remain frozen in their own immediacy; they fail to pierce the surface to discover the underlying essence, i.e. the real factors that relate their experiences to the hidden social forces that produce them', 'Realism in the Balance', in Theodor Adorno et al., *Aesthetics and Politics*, trans. by Rodney Livingstone (London: Verso, 1980), pp. 36–37. For a classic discussion of the socialist realist novel, see Katerina Clark, *The Soviet Novel: History as Ritual* (Bloomington: Indiana University Press, 2000).

[35] Frederick Engels, 'Engels to Margaret Harkness', in Karl Marx and Frederick Engels, *Marx and Engels Collected Works, Vol. 48* (London: Lawrence & Wishart/Electric Book, 2010), p. 167. Carolyn Lesjak has recently offered a persuasive account of the continuing relevance of the concept of 'type' to our understanding of nineteenth-century realism and its radical political possibilities. See *The Afterlife of Enclosure: British Realism, Character, and the Commons* (Stanford, CA: Stanford University Press, 2021). For a similarly politicised recent vindication of realism, see Anna Kornbluh, *The Order of Forms: Realism, Formalism, and Social Space* (Chicago, IL: The University of Chicago Press, 2019).

working class figures are a passive mass, unable to help itself and not even showing (making) any attempt at striving to help itself'.[36] While this may have been a fitting account of the labouring masses of an earlier period, he adds, it was certainly not the case in the 1880s. Engels nevertheless concedes, in a final remark that highlights the real conceptual difficulty introduced by the empirical presence of this heterogenous other, that 'nowhere in the civilised world are the working people less actively resistant, more passively submitting to fate, more *hébétés* than in the East End of London'.[37] The irruption of this inassimilable and traumatic other in the very midst of the presumed historical agent of change does not merely point to the existence of a sociological exception to the logic of capitalist development but rather underscores the irreducibility of a heterogeneous conception of social identities (and potentially suggests the impossibility of a homogenising conception of social reality).[38] Thus, the identity of the working class is inhabited, or haunted, by an excess that cannot be integrated or dissolved into a homogenous conception of productive labour.[39] In other words, there is something absent, something missing, in this identity, whose functional constitution as an empirical agent in social antagonisms is always, in one way or another, provisional and contingent.[40]

Let me briefly return at this point to Fredric Jameson's Marxist reading of populism in late nineteenth-century fiction. In his discussion of Gissing, Jameson suggests that this political strategy 'represents the solution (or attempted solution) to a specifically formal and narrative problem, what the younger Lukács would have called the crisis of narrative *totality*'.[41] Ultimately, however, this is a failed solution, according to Jameson, insofar as it merely reproduces, on a formal level, the limits and contradictions that define the stage of development of the capitalist mode of production in the late nineteenth century: 'the crisis of the social totality is the result of the same phenomena

---

[36] Engels, 'Engels to Margaret Harkness', p. 167.

[37] Engels, 'Engels to Margaret Harkness', p. 168.

[38] Raymond Williams's theoretical understanding of realism points precisely in this direction. According to Williams, any account of the novel as a totalising form, as a 'knowable community', must be offset against the experience of 'unknowability' that characterises modern social reality. See *The English Novel from Dickens to Lawrence* (London: The Hogarth Press, 1987), pp. 9–27.

[39] Again, this is the precise status of the Real in Lacanian theory.

[40] As Laclau puts it, 'Heterogeneity inhabits the very heart of a homogeneous space. History is not a self-determined process. The opaqueness of an irretrievable "outside" will always tarnish the very categories that define the "inside"', *On Populist Reason*, p. 152.

[41] Jameson, *The Political Unconscious*, pp. 189–190.

– reification, social fragmentation, the division of labor, Taylorization – which dictate the terms of the naturalist organizational strategy'.[42] In such a context, the 'conception of a novel about "the people"' functions as a sign of the depoliticising impulse which would logically follow from the disaggregation of social homogeneity. Naturalist conventions of 'specialization' – according to the insurmountable logic of the capitalist division of labour – would mobilise the idea of the people as 'a merely classificatory concept' (offering a repertoire of occupations and subject positions in a fractured totality) or, alternatively, reinscribe it as a class identity 'in spite of itself': 'Yet this too would amount to a transcendence of the initial framework, and something like an autocritique of the very concept of the "people", as well as a bursting of the narrative seams'.[43] But, however apposite to the particular narrative problems raised by Gissing's *The Nether World*, this is not a conclusion we can generally accept if we take the notion of the people as a non-totalisable and heterogeneous alternative to class and privilege it, following Mark Bevir and others, in a historical perspective on British socialism.

My literary investigation below begins not by locating the symptoms of a crisis in the objective social totality but by reconstructing the terms of an opening (or a breakdown in the imagination of social homogeneity, which social-problem British fiction began to register in the 1840s) that would ultimately inscribe heterogeneity as the insurmountable social logic out of which a recognisable literary socialism could emerge at the turn of the century. An important dimension of this opening concerns the status assigned to utopianism in this context. For, as Mark A. Allison has shown in a book whose central refrain is not unrelated to my own – namely, the idea that socialism remains 'a *goal to be imagined*, rather than an ideological program to be instantiated' – a key aspect of nineteenth-century prefigurations of literary socialism was their anti-political drive.[44] Thus, 'Many socialists hoped to liberate humankind from the morass of politics, by shifting the gravity of collective life away from the state – or by transcending traditional political practices and logics altogether'.[45] This was a powerful impulse among utopian socialists in the first half of the century, from Robert Owen to Saint-Simon.[46]

---

[42] Jameson, *The Political Unconscious*, p. 190.

[43] Jameson, *The Political Unconscious*, p. 191.

[44] Mark A. Allison, *Imagining Socialism: Aesthetics, Anti-Politics, and Literature in Britain, 1817–1918* (Oxford: Oxford University Press, 2021), p. 2.

[45] Allison, *Imagining Socialism*, p. 10.

[46] As Allison continues, 'Perhaps the most widely known catchphrase for this widely held ambition is the Saint-Simonian prophecy that the "government of men" would soon be supplanted by the "administration of things"', *Imagining Socialism*, p. 10.

But the echoes of a decidedly anti-political orientation in socialism would be clearly heard again at the *fin de siècle* in the neo-utopianism of, for example, William Morris's *News from Nowhere*.[47] My investigation of the constitutive heterogeneity of literary socialism in this book traces its effects in both political and anti-political directions, from the radical 'discovery' of articulatory practices by writers such as Tressell and Wilkinson to the anarchic impulse which animates the socialist imagination of novelists like Lessing and Kelman.

The thought of Gilles Deleuze provides another key point of reference for my investigation and another theoretical resource for my privileging of heterogeneity in the constitution of socialist discourse. The breakdown of homogeneous imaginaries which I trace in my analysis is consistent with Deleuze and Guattari's announcement in *Anti-Oedipus* that 'We no longer believe in a primordial totality that once existed, or in a final totality that awaits us at some future date. We no longer believe in the dull gray outlines of a dreary, colorless dialectic of evolution, aimed at forming a harmonious whole out of heterogeneous bits by rounding off their rough edges'.[48] If the dialectical notion of totality is irrecuperable, the logic of the people cannot be a surface symptom of its crisis but a contingent departure from its assumed homogeneity. In this sense, Deleuze goes on to claim, in his second book on cinema, that '[t]here will no longer be conquest of power by a proletariat, or by a united or unified people'.[49] This does not imply defeatism but rather, once again, the reaffirmation of contingency and heterogeneity as the premises from which any emancipatory politics may arise.[50] Crucial here is

---

[47] Allison cites a famous passage in Morris's novel where the utopian host informs his time-travelling 'Guest' that, in this new England of the future, '"politics" have ... been superseded, because disagreements no longer "crystallize people into parties permanently hostile to one another, with different theories as to the build of the universe and the progress of time. Isn't that what politics used to mean?" (86). While impressed, Guest confesses that he is "not so sure of that" (86). Both Guest's favorable reaction and his ambivalence would seem well founded', *Imagining Socialism*, p. 10.

[48] Gilles Deleuze and Félix Guattari, *Anti-Oedipus* (London: Continuum, 2011), pp. 45–46.

[49] Gilles Deleuze, *Cinema 2: The Time-Image*, trans. by Hugh Tomlinson and Robert Galatea (Minneapolis: University of Minnesota Press, 1997), pp. 219–220.

[50] Michael Hardt and Antonio Negri's concept of the multitude offers an influential theoretical development of this post-Marxist conception of the revolutionary subject. It also resonates with Laclau's notion of the people as the product of a contingent 'process of political constitution', even if the multitude points to a mode of articulation 'without hegemony', *Commonwealth* (Cambridge, MA: The Belknap Press of Harvard University Press, 2009), p. 169.

the 'consciousness that there were no people, but always several peoples, an infinity of peoples, who remained to be united, or should not be united, in order for the problem to change'.[51] For Deleuze, the people are missing in the sense that their existence is never a given but rather, as demonstrated by the Third World film-makers he studies in this book, an aesthetic-political intervention – that is, a creation – without guarantees.[52] The radical content of art thus lies, according to Deleuze (and Guattari), in the way that it 'summon[s] forth' a 'people to come'.[53]

This idea of the 'people to come' and, more generally, of the politics to come that the heterogeneous and contingent subject of socialism presupposes is a conceptual refrain to which my book returns from different angles and in a variety of literary contexts. As I have already signalled, the first context I examine is that of mid-nineteenth-century social-problem fiction. Chapter One thus begins with a reading of Elizabeth Gaskell's *Mary Barton* as a text in which the pressures of a consolidated class dynamic are negotiated at an irreducible distance. Against an ideological – and already dated – injunction of paternalist utopianism, the perceived spectacle of proletarian agency in industrial England prompts an ontological dislocation, an opening towards radical heterogeneity in the form of spectral solidarities and the uncertain possibility of a different kind of utopia. I then analyse the place assigned to heterogeneity – that key discovery of nineteenth-century social discourse – in the emergence of a distinctive literary socialism at the beginning of the twentieth century through Robert Tressell's *The Ragged Trousered Philanthropists*. The – at first sight paradoxical – insistence on negativity, the meticulous and often devastatingly pessimistic reconstruction of a working-class experience defined by precariousness and internal contradiction provides the co-ordinates within which socialism becomes aesthetically and politically imaginable. The chapter concludes with a discussion of Ellen Wilkinson's 1929 novel *Clash* as a limit-text poised between the fictional imagination of socialism in terms of heterogeneity and political mediation characteristic of early twentieth-century

---

[51] Deleuze, *Cinema 2*, p. 220.

[52] For a discussion of the political compatibility between Deleuze and Laclau, see Clayton Crockett, *Deleuze Beyond Badiou: Ontology, Multiplicity, and Event* (New York: Columbia University Press, 2013). Crockett points out that Laclau's critique of Deleuze (and of Deleuze-inspired political philosophy) obscures the fact of their affinity regarding the question of populism: 'I think that Laclau fails to appreciate the heterogeneity of Deleuze's philosophy in his critique', *Deleuze Beyond Badiou*, p. 182.

[53] Gilles Deleuze and Félix Guattari, *What is Philosophy?* (London: Verso, 1994), p. 218.

developments on the one hand and an essentialist retrenchment around notions of class which in turn announces the more doctrinaire versions of 1930s proletarian realism on the other.

Chapter Two begins by considering the relevance of Deleuze's theorisation of the missing people, as outlined above, to one of the key fictional works of the interwar period: Lewis Grassic Gibbon's monumental trilogy *A Scots Quair*. This cycle of novels offers one of the most penetrating accounts of class formation and historical change in British literature. Yet, crucially, Gibbon's perspective is one that privileges heterogeneity and contingency – through an emphasis on the idea of transformation – over the teleological assumptions which proliferated among practitioners of socialist realism. Through his mobilisation of an aesthetic-political strategy of fabulation (a concept I borrow from Deleuze), Gibbon unfolds a wealth of possibilities for literary socialism beyond any dogmatic identification of its class subject or (inter) national context. This discussion is followed by a reading of George Orwell's own ambivalent elaborations on the relationship between class and politics, through a theoretical assessment of his affinity with notions of sensation, form of life, and flight, as well as a consideration of his turn, at the outbreak of the Second World War, to an idiosyncratic form of radical populism. A discussion of J. B. Priestley's more canonical version of wartime populism – still woven around the productive tensions of a 'missing people' – completes the chapter.

In Chapter Three, I begin by examining a British iteration of socialist realism in the contested ideological landscape of the 1950s. Through a reading of Jack Lindsay's novel *Betrayed Spring*, I trace the semantic instabilities – and hegemonic possibilities – accruing to the signifier 'socialism' in the post-war period, especially in relation to the political constellation associated with the 1945–1951 Labour government. The bulk of this chapter, however, is devoted to the towering figure of Raymond Williams and to his theoretical and, more importantly, practical contributions (as a leading novelist) to the rehabilitation of a realism committed to socialist transformation. In keeping with my central contention throughout the book, this emerges – with a renewed and perhaps hitherto unmatched emphasis – as a socialism without necessary outcomes or fixed ideological contents resulting in turn from a representational politics 'without guarantees'.

In the fourth and final chapter, I turn to the 1960s writing of Doris Lessing and the specific context of post-Communist and New Leftist elaborations on the metapolitical (and, as I argue, *anarchic*) possibilities of a socialism 'to come', in the Derridean sense I have referred to above. This is followed by a brief discussion of the 'antinomian' horizon imagined by Lessing's friend and comrade, the historian and polemicist E. P. Thompson, in his sole incursion into fiction (*The Sykaos Papers*). I conclude the chapter with an investigation of

James Kelman's innovative explorations of class and antagonism as a negative foundation for the fictional reimagination, in the twenty-first century, of a socialist politics defined by heterogeneity and contingency.

Chapter One

From Utopia to Hegemony

1.1 Spectres of Utopia: Elizabeth Gaskell's *Mary Barton*

Towards the end of Elizabeth Gaskell's 1848 novel *Mary Barton*, following the death of its ill-fated anti-hero and father to the eponymous character, we come across a conversation in which the industrialist Mr Carson suggests a link between John Barton's class grievance (which is also the motive behind his recent assassination of Carson's son) and Owenism: 'You mean he was an Owenite; all for equality and community of goods, and that kind of absurdity'.[1] His interlocutor quickly – and emphatically – corrects Carson: 'No, no! John Barton was no fool. No need to tell him that were all men equal to-night, some would get the start by rising an hour earlier to-morrow'.[2] What had moved Barton, according to Job Legh, was no naïve fantasy of equality but rather the painful recognition that 'those who wore finer clothes, and eat better food, and had more money in their pockets ... cared not whether his heart was sorry or glad'.[3] In other words, what had prompted him to crime in the first place was his sense of the moral crisis engulfing society rather than a political determination to transform it. This denial of radical politics and the substitution of a range of ideologically obfuscating discursive strategies (including, most notoriously, the shift from social realism to melodrama in the second half of the novel) has of course been an analytical staple for generations of critics.[4] And yet, in

---

[1] Elizabeth Gaskell, *Mary Barton*, ed. by Shirley Foster (Oxford: Oxford University Press, 2008), p. 370.

[2] Gaskell, *Mary Barton*, p. 370.

[3] Gaskell, *Mary Barton*, p. 370.

[4] Famously, Raymond Williams reads the novel's abandonment of its realist approach in the earlier chapters in favour of melodrama as an ideologically determined retreat from its subject matter, *Culture and Society 1780–1950* (Harmondsworth: Penguin, 1961), pp. 99–103. Carolyn Lesjak explains this retreat in the following terms: 'Was it possible to depict working-class conditions of life realistically without inspiring class conflict? What was the best way of generating interest in the working class on the part of a middle-class reading public? In short, *Mary*

light of this emphatic disavowal of Owenism and what could more generally be described as the 'utopianism' of radical social change, it may be worth asking whether a significant amount of this utopian content is not actually metabolised by the novel as it races towards closure. It is striking to read, for example, that Mr Carson, long (and, by implication, unjustly) 'considered hard and cold', was in fact deeply committed to 'a perfect understanding, and complete confidence and love ... between masters and men', consequently believing that 'it was most desirable to have educated workers, capable of judging, not mere machines of ignorant men'.[5] To which the narrator triumphantly adds, 'Many of the improvements now in practice in the system of employment in Manchester, owe their origin to short earnest sentences spoken by Mr. Carson. Many and many yet to be carried out into execution, take their birth from that stern, thoughtful mind, which submitted to be taught by suffering'.[6] The suffering alludes, of course, to the death of the young Carson, that cavalier capitalist whose callous treatment of striking workers had led to his assassination by the trade unionist Barton. Indeed, there is something remarkable in the suggested transformation, as if this loss of the personal son had been constitutive of the public, social father. What is at stake in this sequence, and in the reformist content of Carson's vision, is the rise of paternalism as an ideological position and functional programme beyond the emotive rhetoric of Christian reconciliation through which Barton's own death (in Carson's arms, no less) is narrated in an earlier chapter. It would seem, ironically, that by the end of the novel the true Owenite, albeit a conservative and admittedly anti-political one, is Carson himself.[7] But the connection between this change of heart, or,

Barton and the industrial novel more generally found itself in something of a Catch-22: if it fulfilled its realist criterion it ran the "wicked" risk of "exciting class against class" and consequently losing its middle-class audience and its moral authority as a cultural force of class conciliation', *Working Fictions: A Genealogy of the Victorian Novel* (Durham, NC: Duke University Press, 2006), pp. 30–31.

[5] Gaskell, *Mary Barton*, p. 374.

[6] Gaskell, *Mary Barton*, p. 374.

[7] As the great historian of Owenism Gregory Claeys has noted, the overarching anti-political emphasis of Owen's ideas has tended to obscure the actual democratic content of the various Owenite experiments and organisations: 'Owen did intend to abolish "politics", but in so doing it was precisely arbitrary, "irrational" and unwarranted power which he sought most to replace. But the schemes he advanced to substitute for existing political processes were in fact much more an integral part of traditional republican and democratic theory than has been recognised previously. Even Owen's wish to supersede politics, therefore, took place within a language and conceptual framework which was recognisably a part of contemporary political debate', *Citizens and Saints: Politics and Anti-Politics in Early*

more precisely, the specific nature of what the novel endorses in Carson as his – and its own – reformist programme, and the experience of loss is not to be glossed over. For this is a novel that abounds in death and loss, as well as in the traces and returns they conjure up. I want to argue that the two primary aspects of loss and utopianism (understood, as we will see, in precisely delimited ideological terms) are intimately related and mutually constitutive. I claim that the paternalist programme advocated by the novel in its efforts to disassociate itself from the monstrous reality of class conflict is articulated spectrally, that is, as the kind of presence that only an absence can enable and register. This will necessarily be an untimely programme in the Derridean sense, out of joint and ultimately devoid of ontological positivity (i.e. 'hauntological', as Derrida puts it), but no less persuaded of its remedial urgency in the context of a riven industrial society.[8] Robert Owen's early paternalist-utopian ideas, as formulated in his treatise *A New View of Society* (published between 1813 and 1816) can furnish, I suggest, a fine approximation of the reformist ideal that this novel spectralises – that is, invokes while bemoaning its loss, ultimately committing its social imaginary to a transcendence that remains displaced and to come.[9]

Critics such as Patsy Stoneman and Lisa Surridge have argued that *Mary Barton* can be read as a novel about fathers and fatherhood and, in a more general political sense, about competing definitions of paternalism. According to Surridge, 'the novel goes far towards establishing working-class men as exemplars of a new model of fatherly care' and, by extension, of an ideal yet eminently vulnerable paradigm of nurturing masculinity.[10] The shortcoming that the novel identifies in the social vision of the bourgeoisie

British Socialism (Cambridge: Cambridge University Press, 2002), p. 66. For his part, Mark A. Allison has shown how Owen's ambivalent relationship to politics is rooted in the fact that 'his socialism's ultimate coherence was aesthetic, rather than philosophical or metaphysical, in nature', *Imagining Socialism*, p. 37.

[8] In *Specters of Marx*, Derrida reads the famous opening of *The Communist Manifesto* through Shakespeare's spectral figurations in *Hamlet*, suggesting that the spectre represents a 'furtive and untimely' temporal logic, 'a moment that no longer belongs to time, if one understands by this word the linking of modalized presents (past present, actual present: "now", future present)', *Specters of Marx*, trans. by Peggy Kamuf (New York: Routledge, 1994), p. xix.

[9] It is worth emphasising here, given my overarching preoccupation with socialism in this book, that the Owen of *A New View of Society* is not yet socialist. It is nevertheless essential to situate the utopian socialism Owen's name would become associated with in a discursive continuum whose first logical manifestation is this early industrial paternalism.

[10] Lisa Surridge, 'Working-Class Masculinities in *Mary Barton*', *Victorian Literature and Culture* 28:2 (2000), p. 341.

has less to do with the exploitative nature of its position in the class structure than with an initial (pre-loss, we might say) failure to extend, as Stoneman writes, 'the same sort of paternal care' to the 'workers that they show for one another'.[11] Native to a world of endless misery and suffering, and defined by personal and collective histories of loss, the proletarian fathers epitomised by John Barton are forced to extend their paternal role often beyond the limits of the natural family. Barton thus becomes a temporary father to friends and neighbours, for example nursing the fever-stricken Davenports in their hour of need. This is a paternalism, as Stoneman suggests, that 'is not only nurturing rather than authoritative' but also 'functional rather than innate'.[12] It is, we might add, a paternalism produced by the mutuality of loss rather than the verticality of class distance. As a practical, if always temporary and provisional, logic of paternal care, it can therefore, as Stoneman writes, 'easily [pass] into the principle of co-operation'.[13] Although this is, of course, a principle that the narrative denounces for its monstrous potentiality when conceived of as an expression of antagonistic intra-class solidarity, it is also a central component of the ideological absence which the novel's economy of loss and spectral restitution seeks to salvage – a co-operation restoring and elevating paternal care as the promissory horizon of every missed opportunity in industrial capitalism's young history of inter-class relations.[14] I want to argue that what is at stake here is a pressing alternative between the recuperation of lost futures as ghostly presences, with their spatio-temporally displaced baggage of individual and collective hopes, and the irruption of a (potential) positivity of irrecuperable, because politically secessionist, working-class difference. The co-operation *Mary Barton* spectralises is thus not just a function of its strident melodrama or wishful ideological resolution but a serious attempt to initiate the reimagination of the paternalist programme in the midst of a social universe defined by the immanence of antagonistic division. In this respect, the 'ghost' of

---

[11] Patsy Stoneman, *Elizabeth Gaskell* (Bloomington: Indiana University Press, 1987), pp. 71–72.

[12] Stoneman, *Elizabeth Gaskell*, p. 72.

[13] Stoneman, *Elizabeth Gaskell*, p. 72.

[14] Talia Schaffer has insisted on the centrality of care communities to Victorian fiction. It is indeed notable, as she points out, that '[n]obody yearned for those communities more than Victorian subjects, because they were enduring the great shift [...] toward the modern paradigm of an institutional, medical, professional form of care, and the process made them think deeply about what was lost as well as what was gained', *Communities of Care: The Social Ethics of Victorian Fiction* (Princeton, NJ: Princeton University Press, 2021), p. 59.

Owenism, with its fusion of a paternal-familial conception of society with practical experiments in co-operation, constitutes a significant, although always indirect, frame of reference for this novel.[15]

Indeed, *Mary Barton* begins with an anxious recognition of the realities of division in industrial society. As Gaskell announces in the preface, her writing responds to a deeply felt urge to redress the 'unhappy state of things between those so bound to each other by common interests, as the employers and the employed must ever be'.[16] However mistaken these two classes are in their judgement of each other, the fact remains for Gaskell that the division between them, at the level of lived experience and 'state of feeling', is such that a political unravelling of monstrous proportions (not dissimilar from 'the events which have so recently occurred among a similar class on the Continent' in that momentous year, 1848) appears increasingly plausible.[17] The feared outcome is not only implied by the stock characterisation of the working class as a 'dumb people' (a trope which, of course, reiterates standard figurations of the revolutionary multitude reaching back to Burke) but is also embedded in the moral and affective fracture from which the antagonism arises. Thus, bereft of a principle of co-ordination, Gaskell warns her readers, the classes have been left to drift apart upon a dense magma of resentment. A double monstrosity, then, will result from the compounding of the close, pressing reality of division with the terrifying spectacle of this 'dumb' collective subject becoming vocal. It is not long before the articulation of such an experience situates John Barton at the centre of this world's antagonistic ontology. As he puts it to his friend Wilson in one of the opening political salvos in the novel, 'Don't think to come over me with th' old tale, that the rich know nothing of the trials of the poor; I say, if they don't know, they ought to know. We're their slaves as long as we can

---

[15] It is important to remember that, by the 1830s and 40s, Owenism had evolved significantly from Owen's more conservative early ideas into a movement of working-class self-organisation. However, the opposition to partisan politics and the preference for a familial ideal of socio-political organisation remained central throughout its history. As Claeys writes, 'the model of politics which Owen settled upon was essentially that of the family, with the later Owenite organisations being primarily concerned to render this idea practicable', *Citizens and Saints*, p. 77. It is nevertheless also true, as Claeys explains, that the years after 1845 saw a significant convergence between an increasingly politicised Owenite movement (which had by now largely turned its back on Owen himself) and a socially radicalised incarnation of Chartism, *Citizens and Saints*, pp. 261–262.

[16] Gaskell, *Mary Barton*, p. 3.

[17] Gaskell, *Mary Barton*, p. 4.

work; we pile up their fortunes with the sweat of our brows, and yet we are to live as separate as if we were in two worlds; ay, as separate as Dives and Lazarus, with a great gulf betwixt us'.[18]

This imaginary of division in industrial society immediately displaces the fleeting evocation, in the opening pages, of the Bartons and Wilsons' holiday outing to the pastoral setting of Green Heys Fields, with its wistful echoes of natural and cyclic rhythms and the sort of experiential register associated with a bygone agrarian world that now can only be perceived by the industrial working classes as so many 'pleasant mysteries for townspeople to watch'. For, as the narrator informs us, 'here the artisan, deafened with noise of tongues and engines, may come to listen awhile to the delicious sounds of rural life: the lowing of cattle, the milkmaid's call, the clatter and cackle of poultry in the old farmyards'.[19] Mere fragments of a peripheral experience for the industrial worker, these 'pleasant mysteries' are soon contrasted with the rather more unpleasant ones resulting from an urban existence defined by disjunction and displacement. Perhaps the most significant mystery of this kind concerns Esther, John's disgraced sister-in-law, and the circumstances of her disappearance, since her symbolic status as the novel's fallen woman not only contributes a specifically gendered dimension to its ideological constellation but also names one of the central horrors of this divided society. For Esther is an example of precisely the sort of unsanctioned mobility across class and gender boundaries, norms, and identities that displaces any possibility of emotional co-ordination between employers and workers. Driven by the illicit desire to transgress her domestic role as a working-class woman and become a lady, Esther becomes instead an archetypal figure of Victorian exclusion – a streetwalker. As Barton relates to his friend Wilson,

> You see Esther spent her money in dress, thinking to set off her pretty face; and got to come home so late at night, that at last I told her my mind; my missis thinks I spoke crossly, but I meant right, for I loved Esther, if it was only for Mary's sake. Says I, 'Esther, I see what you'll

---

[18] Gaskell, *Mary Barton*, p. 11. According to Amy Mae King, Gaskell's agenda of social reform in the novel amounts to a call 'for the two classes to *see* each other and classify themselves as like species'. In this sense, only a fundamental 'reform of perception' can offer a way out of this deadlock of antagonistic division, 'Taxonomical Cures: The Politics of Natural History and Herbalist Medicine in Elizabeth Gaskell's *Mary Barton*', in Elizabeth Gaskell, *Mary Barton: A Norton Critical Edition*, ed. by Thomas Recchio (New York: W. W. Norton & Company, 2008), p. 619.

[19] Gaskell, *Mary Barton*, p. 5.

end at with your artificials, and your fly-away veils, and stopping out when honest women are in their beds; you'll be a street-walker'[20]

Deirdre D'Albertis observes, apropos of Barton's prophetic words in this passage, that 'The plot of the novel unfolds to fulfil this prediction, yet it is both Esther and John Barton who alienate themselves from the domestic sphere represented by Mary and her mother'.[21] In effect, what the novel codifies as Esther's 'fall' has a clear parallel in John's own drift towards trade-union radicalism and, ultimately, towards politically motivated assassination. According to D'Albertis, 'Barton and Esther, the most flamboyant characters in *Mary Barton*, flaunt their disaffection with the order of things – he rejects a system of political representation that recognizes workers only in the form of caricature, while she rebels against a standard of feminine conduct that rewards only self-abnegation'.[22] In both cases, what is at stake is the figuration of a monstrous (a heterogeneous, in Bataille's sense) development in working-class subjectivity, the articulation of a movement outside the sanctioned parameters of a society founded on productive and reproductive functional divisions. The streetwalker, defined by her 'disorderly vagrancy' and 'wild night wanderings', is a literal instantiation of the kind of threatening, nomadic mobility which capitalism historically seeks to contain.[23]

As Michel Foucault argues in his lectures on *The Punitive Society*, the rise of a fully-fledged industrial society in the nineteenth century entailed a redefinition of the 'illegalisms' threatening the productive apparatus of capitalism. The principal menace was no longer a direct attack on, or 'depredation' of, accumulated wealth (which defined the 'external' form of antagonism between the labouring classes and capital in a pre-industrial historical context) but rather the more general problem of 'dissipation', that 'illegalism [which] takes the form of absenteeism, lateness, laziness, festivity, debauchery, nomadism, in short, everything that smacks of irregularity, of mobility in space'.[24] According to Foucault, three of these are the 'major forms' in which this threat of dissipation is imagined by nineteenth-century social and economic thought: 'intemperance, as wasting the body; improvidence, as dispersion of time; and disorderliness, as mobility of the individual

[20] Gaskell, *Mary Barton*, p. 9.
[21] Deirdre D'Albertis, 'The Streetwalker and Urban Observations in *Mary Barton*', in Elizabeth Gaskell, *Mary Barton: A Norton Critical Edition*, ed. by Thomas Recchio (New York: W. W. Norton & Company, 2008), p. 584.
[22] D'Albertis, 'The Streetwalker', p. 584.
[23] Gaskell, *Mary Barton*, pp. 122, 154.
[24] Michel Foucault, *The Punitive Society: Lectures at the Collège de France 1972–1973*, trans. by Graham Burchell (Basingstoke: Palgrave Macmillan, 2015), p. 188.

in relation to the family, to work'.[25] All three inform *Mary Barton*'s exposé of working-class subjectivity. One of Gaskell's early narratorial interventions, designed to counter the potentially subversive weight of her own admission that 'the contrast [between the classes] is too great', offers a rather faithful iteration of the improvident workman stereotype: 'True, that with child-like improvidence, good times will often dissipate his grumbling, and make him forget all prudence and foresight'.[26] Likewise, figures of intemperance recur throughout the novel, with John the opium addict and Esther the alcoholic prostitute both leading the way to intemperate perdition and reminding the reader of their fundamental symbolic affinity as deviant working-class subjects. But the main threat in the novel's economy of dissipation is arguably that 'disorderliness' – that 'moral nomadism', as Foucault describes it – which entrenches the logic of antagonistic division as an internal property of the social body, dissolving it from within. What is at stake in this identification of proletarian disorderliness is a failure to 'fixate' behaviours, indeed to train subjectivity in a way that will prove conducive to the social co-ordination required by the productive apparatus. Ultimately, and this is the point where the paternalist-utopian contribution will become significant, what is at stake is the necessity of educating the working classes.

The French philosopher Miguel Abensour has famously argued that utopia concerns 'the education of desire'.[27] What the utopian tradition of the early nineteenth century brings to the domain of economic, social, and political transformations under industrial capitalism is a fresh preoccupation with the sphere of desire. According to Abensour, 'the displacement of the political' operated by thinkers such as Fourier, Saint-Simon, and Owen in their utopian projects of reform is not so much a privileging of the domestic over the political as 'the opening up of a new field of action' for politics, 'that of the ensemble of needs and desires of real men'.[28] And yet, in a society defined by division and separation, by the monstrous abstraction of labour from life – in other words, in a society characterised by the distortion of need and the corruption of desire – education becomes a matter of guidance and direction, of discipline and authority. This is the point of departure for Robert Owen in his seminal text *A New View of Society*. Reflecting on his pioneering experiences in the model

[25] Foucault, *The Punitive Society*, p. 192.

[26] Gaskell, *Mary Barton*, pp. 23–24.

[27] See, for example, Miguel Abensour, 'William Morris: The Politics of Romance', in *Revolutionary Romanticism*, ed. by Max Blechman (San Francisco: City Lights Books, 1999), pp. 125–162.

[28] Miguel Abensour, *Utopiques IV: L'histoire de l'utopie et le destin de sa critique* (Paris: Sens & Tonka, 2016), p. 54; my translation.

factory community of New Lanark at the turn of the century, Owen wants not only to offer an alternative programme of industrial development based on welfare and happiness for the workers but also to sketch out a diagnosis of the evils afflicting early industrial society and to prescribe a remedy for them. For Owen, the root of the problem lies in the fact that 'the poor and working classes ... are now permitted to be very generally formed without proper guidance or direction, and, in many cases, under circumstances which directly impel them to a course of extreme vice and misery'.[29] This speaks to a state of moral degradation amplified by the nature of inter-class relations. But for the young Owen of *A New View of Society*, whose overriding aim is, as Ophélie Siméon has pointed out, 'to harmonise class interests, ensure economic prosperity and reduce the risk of sedition', the crisis results from a failure to educate the working classes through 'a firm, well-directed kindness' and according to the principle of *'happiness of self, clearly understood and uniformly practiced'*.[30] Interestingly, the main obstacle to this reorientation of working-class conduct seems to be not an enduring unkind instinct on the part of the ruling classes or some intractable feature in the nature of the working classes, but the fateful pursuit of 'that *greatest of all errors, the notion that individuals form their own characters'*.[31] The high-pitched intensity with which Owen inveighs against this doctrine is greatly revealing, in a passage that is worth quoting at length:

> But destroy this hydra of human calamity, this immolator of every principle of rationality, this monster, which hitherto has effectually guarded every avenue that can lead to true benevolence and active kindness, and human happiness will be speedily established on a rock from whence it shall never more be removed. This enemy of humanity may now be most easily destroyed. Let it be dragged forth from beneath the dark mysterious veil by which till now it has been hid from the eyes of the world; expose it but for an instant to the clear light of intellectual day; and, as though conscious of its own deformity, it will instantaneously vanish, never to reappear.[32]

The Gothic imagery of Owen's invective is indeed notable. The 'error' in question is not just theoretical – a problem of failed pedagogical doctrine, as it were – but ontological. A deformed monster threatening the rational

---

[29] Robert Owen, *A New View of Society and Other Writings* (London: Penguin, 2001), p. 10.

[30] Ophélie Siméon, *Robert Owen's Experiment at New Lanark: From Paternalism to Socialism* (Cham: Palgrave Macmillan, 2017), p. 4; Owen, *A New View*, pp. 27, 14.

[31] Owen, *A New View*, p. 64.

[32] Owen, *A New View*, p. 65.

cognition of human nature itself, its 'dark mysterious veil' must be torn in such a definitive way that its implications may never return to haunt us. Of course, what this strident tone betrays is precisely the fear that an autonomous realm of working-class self-formation, an undirected education of desire for and by the working classes themselves, may continue to hinder the prospect of social harmony and 'human happiness', projecting its dark spectral returns against 'the clear light' of orderly class relations.

The ideological horror Owen identifies here is in direct continuity with that foundational fiction about monstrous self-formation, Mary Shelley's *Frankenstein*, published only a few years after Owen's text. In Shelley's novel, particularly in the confessional narrative offered by the creature, it is soon established that monstrosity, in so far as it is a social rather than a natural condition, is intimately linked to the free and unregulated acquisition of knowledge. Thus, upon learning about 'the strange system of human society' and its commitment to the 'division of property', to 'immense wealth and squalid poverty', to 'rank, descent, and noble blood', the reality of the creature's own wretchedness finally becomes apparent to him, prompting the desperate wish 'that I had for ever remained in my native wood, nor known or felt beyond the sensations of hunger, thirst, and heat!'[33] The truth that this revelation concerning human society imparts is not restricted to the creature's realisation of his plight but also concerns the 'strange nature' of knowledge itself, which 'clings to the mind, when it has once seized on it, like a lichen on the rock'.[34] The general implication in *Frankenstein* is that this strangeness is amplified to a monstrous level if the acquisition of knowledge takes the form of a Promethean, solitary, and indeed autonomous pursuit – a matter of self-formation. As Patrick Brantlinger has noted,

> *Frankenstein* is, among other things, a novel about two educations or, rather, *mis*educations, Victor's and the Monster's. To the extent that Victor pursues his course of reading and research in isolation and against the advice of his father and his professors, he is a sort of autodidact – wilfully so, because he chooses isolation. In contrast, the Monster is perforce an autodidact, in some respects similar to the working-class autodidacts whose autobiographies serve as a rich source of evidence in E.P. Thompson's *Making of the English Working Class*.[35]

---

[33] Mary Shelley, *Frankenstein*, ed. by J. Paul Hunter, 2nd edn (New York: W. W. Norton & Company, 2012), p. 83.

[34] Shelley, *Frankenstein*, p. 83.

[35] Patrick Brantlinger, *The Reading Lesson: The Threat of Mass Literacy in Nineteenth-Century British Fiction* (Bloomington: Indiana University Press, 1998), p. 60.

I would argue that Gaskell's elaboration on the Frankensteinian motif in *Mary Barton* is designed to respond, in very specific terms, to this suggestion of a proletarian autodidacticism rendered antagonistic and effectively self-sufficient, whole in its rebellious autonomy and therefore monstrous in its political irrecuperability. The prospect of working-class education – that is, the intellectual *and* affective formation of the working class – can thus only be contemplated in terms of the functional split which animates the novel's economy of loss and revenance (which in turn founds the possibility of its utopian pedagogy). Far from negating it, the narrative splits the vision of working-class self-education into two: on the one hand, an organic and conveniently peripheral version of proletarian enlightenment, epitomised by Job Legh, and on the other, the properly monstrous, because dissipative and ultimately politically destructive, acquisition of knowledge associated with John Barton (and, in a sense, also with Esther). The 'good' autodidacticism associated with Job is presented by the narrator as a residue of a bygone world, not too dissimilar in its nostalgic overtones from the pastoral scene at Green Heys Fields with which the novel opens:

> There is a class of men in Manchester, unknown even to many of the inhabitants, and whose existence will probably be doubted by many, who yet may claim kindred with all the noble names that science recognises … In the neighbourhood of Oldham there are weavers, common hand-loom weavers, who throw the shuttle with unceasing sound, though Newton's 'Principia' lies open on the loom, to be snatched at in work hours, but revelled over in meal times, or at night. Mathematical problems are received with interest, and studied with absorbing attention by many a broad-spoken, common-looking factory-hand … There are botanists among them … There are entomologists … practical, shrewd, hard-working men, who pore over every new specimen with real scientific delight.[36]

The encyclopaedic range of these learned, Renaissance-like but ultimately 'broad-spoken' and 'common-looking' proletarians is commensurate with their rough simplicity and is therefore, by implication, politically innocuous. For these exotic islands of perfectly inconsequential proletarian intellectualism are as indicative of historical developments in nineteenth-century England as the aforementioned mysteries of hay-making and ploughing.

And yet, in a context defined by the precariousness and instability of social relations, indeed by their potential for 'dissipation' in Foucault's sense, the production and circulation of knowledge remain fraught processes, forever

---

[36] Gaskell, *Mary Barton*, pp. 37–38.

subject to socially dangerous (either wasteful or strictly subversive) appropriations. There is, for example, the paradigmatically dissipative *and* gendered attraction of proletarian women to fanciful imaginings of class mobility. This is, of course, the cause of Esther's 'fall' and the foible which Mary manages to resist (before her own temporary 'fall' in the short-lived romance with the young Carson) with a display of 'practical shrewdness ... which contrasted very bewitchingly with the simple, foolish, unworldly ideas she had picked up from the romances which Miss Simmonds' young ladies were in the habit of recommending to each other'.[37] But far more ominously, the unregulated dispensation of knowledge to and by the working class can result in a politically uncontrollable reversal of that benign, romanticised, and ultimately ineffectual vision of proletarian autodidacticism suggested by Job Legh. When describing the spiral of class hatred, 'the hoards of vengeance', rising 'in [John Barton's] heart' following the loss of his job and, soon afterwards, of his son, the narrator issues an urgent warning against the inciting power of knowledge: 'For there are never wanting those who, either in speech or in print, find it in their interest to cherish such feelings in the working classes; who know how and when to rouse the dangerous power at their command; and who use their knowledge with unrelenting purpose to either party'.[38] Like the 'ghoul-like fever' that preys upon the malnourished Manchester poor, this kind of partisan 'knowledge' (the same knowledge about social inequality, incidentally, that dawns upon the wretched monster in *Frankenstein*) is putrid and highly contagious and finds its victims among poor 'uneducated' workers like Barton.[39] Suddenly, the experience and learning that had gradually transformed John into a 'chairman at many a Trades' Union meeting' and ultimately into a Chartist leader are reduced to a bout of 'monomania', an 'overpowering thought' defined by 'hatred to the one class, and keen sympathy with the other'.[40] What is the cause of this most general, most politically haunting fall? Surprisingly, the fact that '[n]o education had given him wisdom; and without wisdom, even love, with all its effects, too often works but harm'.[41] Thus, as the narrator announces, 'The actions of the uneducated seem to me typified in those of Frankenstein, that monster of many human qualities, ungifted with a soul, a knowledge of the difference between good and evil'.[42] A classic locus for critical accounts of *Mary Barton*, this famous misreading of Shelley's text is

---

[37] Gaskell, *Mary Barton*, pp. 78–79.

[38] Gaskell, *Mary Barton*, p. 25.

[39] Gaskell, *Mary Barton*, p. 72.

[40] Gaskell, *Mary Barton*, pp. 25, 164, 165.

[41] Gaskell, *Mary Barton*, p. 165.

[42] Gaskell, *Mary Barton*, p. 165.

without doubt a significant element of the rhetorical strategy of the novel. What we observe here is a hasty retreat from the problem the narrative has been building up to until this point: the possibility of a monstrous, because strictly autonomous and self-directed, learning steeped in the antagonistic immanence of class conflict. However, this is not just a cheap devaluation of the proletarian economy of knowledge but also a tactical shift – however rushed and formally awkward – to the paternalist end of the problem: 'The people rise up to life; they irritate us, they terrify us, and we become their enemies. Then, in the sorrowful moment of our triumphant power, their eyes gaze on us with mute reproach. Why have we made them what they are; a powerful monster, yet without the inner means for peace and happiness?'[43]

The monstrosity of immanence, the outpouring of anarchic working-class agency, now becomes the monstrosity of failed transcendence – of a verticality that neglects its duties and responsibilities. This is something that needs to be rebuilt if the truly monstrous outcome of revolution is to be eschewed. Gaskell transcribes here the essence of Owen's plea for 'a firm, well-directed kindness', suggesting that 'combination', that 'awful power' on which industrial capitalism rides, 'must work under the direction of a high and intelligent will'.[44] And yet it is evident that a strictly rational path (on the Owen model) is no longer available, since the very nature of this historical reality paints 'a sorrowful moment'.[45] The road to transcendence involves a jagged itinerary, perhaps a 'visionary' journey (for, as the narrator admits, 'being visionary is something. It shows a soul ... a creature who looks forward for others') through the painful suffering of loss.[46] However, this can no longer be an individualised loss, sealed off in the immanence of incommensurable social experiences. It will have to be a true pedagogy of grief, socialising in its affects and effects, across the gulf which *Mary Barton*'s opening chapters explore (that gulf which Disraeli's Condition-of-England novel *Sybil* had

---

[43] As Chris Baldick writes, 'The working class now becomes "the uneducated"; at the moment when it tries to overcome its subordination it has to be told that its actions are based upon a fundamental ignorance of Manchester Political Economy and its eternal truths', *In Frankenstein's Shadow: Myth, Monstrosity, and Nineteenth-Century Writing* (Oxford: Clarendon Press, 1987), p. 86; Gaskell, *Mary Barton*, p. 165.

[44] Owen, *A New View*, p. 27; Gaskell, *Mary Barton*, p. 168.

[45] Gaskell, *Mary Barton*, p. 165. The irony, as briefly noted above, is that by the time *Mary Barton* was published the Owenite movement had largely abandoned Owen, turning instead to a 'monstrous' fusion of social and political radicalism. As Claeys observes, 'It required the European revolutions of 1848 finally to instigate a major commitment to political reform from much of the old Owenite leadership', *Citizens and Saints*, pp. 265–266.

[46] Gaskell, *Mary Barton*, p. 165.

recently described as 'impassable').[47] Gaskell's paternalist programme is thus woven around the rather special *éducation sentimentale* brought about by the young Carson's assassination. This is not simply the reactivation of a positive utopia of social integration 'under the direction of a high and intelligent will' but a more fundamental opening beyond what *is* or *has been* in the history of class relations.[48] The grim presentation – 'on the dinner-table' – of Harry Carson's remains ('*The remains!*', as the narrator emphatically puts it) prompts a split across the opposing factions and their protagonists, not in the sense that any particular ideological position is disavowed by either party but in the more ontological – or hauntological – sense that their subjective coherence as immanent forces in the field of class antagonisms is suddenly disrupted and displaced by 'unspeakable terrors' and 'unquiet slumbers'.[49]

Thus, Mary, upon learning of her father's culpability, and faced with the horror of Jem's trial after being wrongfully accused of the crime, becomes unbearably 'haunted with memories and foreshadowings' before collapsing into 'a state of complete delirium'.[50] During her frenzied journey to Liverpool in search of an alibi for Jem, she even contemplates the 'spectral thought' of suicide.[51] Jem, for his part, while anxiously awaiting the proceedings, is filled with 'the phantoms of what life with her might be'.[52] When John finally reappears following a prolonged disappearance after the crime (thus mirroring the apparitional economy established by Esther at the beginning of the novel), it is only as a vacant and thoroughly spectral figure, a long way from that energetic monster of class antagonism described in the first part of the novel: 'No haunting ghost could have had less of the energy of life in its involuntary motions than he'.[53] The novel's central political agent is thus decentred and recast as the 'phantom likeness of John Barton – himself yet not himself'.[54]

Yet the ontological split extends across the class divide as well, giving us a Mr Carson who is not only haunted by suffering but is a true other to his

---

[47] '"Oh, sir!" said Sybil, haughtily; "I am one of those who believe the gulf is impassable. Yes," she added, slightly but with singular grace waving her hands, and somewhat turning away her head, "utterly impassable"', Benjamin Disraeli, *Sybil; or The Two Nations*, ed. by Nicholas Shrimpton (Oxford: Oxford University Press, 2017), p. 212.

[48] Gaskell, *Mary Barton*, p. 168.

[49] Gaskell, *Mary Barton*, pp. 202, 260, 305.

[50] Gaskell, *Mary Barton*, pp. 257, 260.

[51] Gaskell, *Mary Barton*, p. 290.

[52] Gaskell, *Mary Barton*, p. 321.

[53] Gaskell, *Mary Barton*, p. 333.

[54] Gaskell, *Mary Barton*, p. 335.

former self: 'Have I no inward suffering to blanch these hairs? Have not I toiled and struggled even to these years with hopes in my heart that all centred in my boy? I did not speak of them, but were they not there? I seemed hard and cold; and so I might be to others, but not to him!'[55] The spectacle of grief that this puts on display is, therefore, both a device enabling narrative and ideological closure and a genuine operation of spectralisation from which personal and collective identities, and especially their functional enlistment in the class war, emerge irreparably distorted and split. Thus the 'hard and cold' capitalist Mr Carson can even seem to lose the solidity of his bourgeois identity, projecting the spectre of a 'childhood and youth' 'accustomed to poverty', even if 'it was honest, decent poverty' and 'not the grinding squalid misery he had remarked in every part of John Barton's house'.[56]

Beyond the figure of Christian reconciliation to which the affective homology between Barton and Carson leads in the climax of this scene, what is implied here is a displacement of those immanent forms of identification and being on which, for Gaskell, modern social relations are founded: forms which thrive on the negation of otherness and the resulting closure upon the self. *Mary Barton*'s commitment to the paternalist reform of social relations is spectral in the sense that its central emphasis is not on the production of disciplined working-class and benevolent middle-class subjects, but on the articulation of a response to otherness – on the recognition of the other as other. The notion of spectrality, as theorised by Derrida, points in this precise direction. As he observes in a conversation with Bernard Stiegler, 'our relation to another origin of the world or to another gaze, to the gaze of the other, implies a kind of spectrality. Respect for the alterity of the other dictates respect for the ghost [*le revenant*]'.[57] Notions of identity and identification predicated on closure and coherence are therefore incompatible with the opening to otherness implied by spectrality.[58] And what is really at stake in this opening, both for Derrida and Gaskell, is the question of justice. In this

---

[55] Gaskell, *Mary Barton*, p. 352.

[56] Gaskell, *Mary Barton*, p. 356.

[57] Jacques Derrida and Bernard Stiegler, 'Spectrographies', in *The Spectralities Reader: Ghosts and Haunting in Contemporary Cultural Theory*, ed. by María del Pilar Blanco and Esther Peeren, trans. by Jennifer Bajorek (London: Bloomsbury Academic, 2013), p. 42.

[58] As Julian Wolfreys has written, 'Epistemological modes of enquiry implicitly or explicitly dependent in their trajectories and procedures on the apparent finality and closure of identification cannot account for the idea of the spectral', *Victorian Hauntings: Spectrality, Gothic, the Uncanny and Literature* (Basingstoke: Palgrave, 2002), p. x.

sense, the judicial subplot in the final part of the novel is of great significance. The sequence running from Jem's trial up until Mr Carson's initial confrontation with Barton offers a rather conventional identification of justice with punishment.[59] But this is an identification that the multiple hauntings and openings set in motion by the novel in its final chapters render inoperative. However inadequate from a strictly narrative point of view (for, yes, Barton's death *does* register as a contrived device), this is a significant move in terms of the novel's utopian vocation, insofar as it introduces a notion of justice which cannot be contained within the epistemological and ontological bounds of hitherto available forms of identification *and* measurement. Thus, the problem of justice is a problem beyond measure, though not in the sense that adjudication between two incommensurable social experiences defined by division and estrangement is impossible (which is the central problematic contemplated in the first part of *Mary Barton*) but rather in the sense, which any viable utopianism of transcendence must explore, that the unconditional opening to the other imposes an excess that cannot be quantified or measured. As Derrida puts it in *Specters of Marx*, this is not a plea for 'a *rendering justice* that would be limited to sanctioning, to restituting, and to *doing right*, but for justice as incalculability of the gift and singularity of the an-economic ex-position to others. "The relation to others – that is to say, justice", writes Lévinas'.[60]

Perhaps what remains truly problematic in *Mary Barton*'s utopian vision is not so much what John Lucas has described as its 'grotesquely inadequate hope' for Christian reconciliation, while 'know[ing] that such a resolution is impossible' (a knowledge which is of course imparted by the fact that 'at the very end of *Mary Barton* all the main characters are sent off to Canada'), as it is the coexistence of these two modes of utopian displacement: the spectral and what we might call the strictly spatial.[61] While Carson's paradoxical conversion to a certain form of Owenism in the penultimate chapter culminates the novel's spectral opening to a redemptive to-come beyond the abyss of division and antagonism, the final chapter appears anxious to contain this openness by reducing it to a geographical location. After bringing Esther's nomadic and eminently spectral trajectory through the novel to a close, by having her

---

[59] Stoneman reads this in terms of the gendered contrast between the nurturing and 'feminised' ethics of the working class and a bourgeois system defined by 'single-minded masculinity' which 'finds appropriate articulation in [the] aggressive use of the forces of law and order', *Elizabeth Gaskell*, p. 69.

[60] Derrida, *Specters of Marx*, p. 26.

[61] John Lucas, 'Carson's Murder and the Inadequacy of Hope in *Mary Barton*', in Elizabeth Gaskell, *Mary Barton: A Norton Critical Edition*, ed. by Thomas Recchio (New York: W. W. Norton & Company, 2008), p. 504.

return to the long forsaken family home, 'as a wounded deer drags its heavy limbs once more to the green coolness of the lair in which it was born, there to die', and subsequently laying to rest her and Barton's haunting presence in an apparent gesture of definitive erasure (they are both buried in the same grave 'without name, or initial, or date'), the novel seems to prepare itself for a different kind of utopian vision from which a more stable form of narrative and ideological closure may be derived.[62] Canada embodies in this sense the kind of 'constitutive secessionism' which, according to Fredric Jameson, defines the utopian tradition beginning with Thomas More's seminal text. For, Jameson writes, 'the modification of reality' which utopia proposes is expressed first and foremost in that 'geopolitical secession of the Utopian space itself from the world of empirical or historical reality' that More imagined in 1516: 'the great trench which King Utopus causes to be dug in order to "delink" from the world, and to change his promontory into an island'.[63] Thus, topologically separate, the 'no place' of utopia (*ou-topia*) can also become the 'good place' (*eu-topia*) pursued by social reformers and dreamers. The novel undoubtedly concludes on such a note of both *ou-* and *eu-*topian displacement, with the narrator offering us a vision of Mary and Jem's future in Canada:

> I see a long wooden house, with room enough to spare. The old primeval trees are felled and gone for many a mile around; one alone remains to overshadow the gable-end of the cottage. There is a garden around the dwelling, and far beyond that stretches an orchard. The glory of an Indian summer is over all, making the heart leap at the sight of its gorgeous beauty.[64]

But this secessionist articulation of the utopian imagination is really a final iteration of those rather insular figurations of residual and defensive comfort, from the pastoral scenes with which the novel opens to the various accounts of natural history and travel in distant lands – so many exotic islands of hope which, as the novel otherwise makes abundantly clear, industrial capitalism has rendered increasingly irrelevant. What this unconvincing embrace of a flatly spatial utopianism offers, however, is an enlightening contrast with the ambivalent yet far more suggestive trajectory of haunting through which the spectre of utopianism, in the form of a desired – if never fully resolved – transcendence, is called back to life. Thus, *Mary Barton*'s true utopian displacement lies in those fractal openings, in those discontinuous articulations

[62] Gaskell, *Mary Barton*, p. 378.

[63] Fredric Jameson, *Archaeologies of the Future: The Desire Called Utopia and Other Science Fictions* (London: Verso, 2005), p. 39.

[64] Gaskell, *Mary Barton*, p. 378.

of a renewed paternalist challenge to the immanence of class conflict that blur and distort the positive contours of increasingly monstrous identities, replacing them with so many ghostly wanderings in search of a new social relationality.

1.2 Heterogeneity and Articulation: Robert Tressell's *The Ragged Trousered Philanthropists*

If in *Mary Barton* the theme of social division is rehearsed in terms of an impossible restitution of disciplined and benevolent class subjectivities, especially through a spectral elaboration on the absent link between them, it is also true that its neo-paternalist and utopian imaginaries presuppose a relatively simple social cartography. The division in industrial society is total, but it is also straightforward: two class positions and a mutual estrangement predicated, in Amy Mae King's words, on a 'failure of perception'.[65] It is worth noting the contrast between this neat geography of moral and social division in industrial Manchester and the spectacle of dissolution presented by London in the novel. Although only briefly alluded to in connection with John Barton's southward journey to present the Chartist petition in Parliament, I would argue that the fleeting experience of the great metropolis plays a significant role, first, in the way that it marks a turning point for the development of the character (from morally outraged to 'monstrously' political) and, second, in the way that it establishes an opposition between reformable and unreformable social spaces. For London is the place where the promise of reform – the Charter – is defeated, a place that symbolises the ruling-class refusal to know, to see, and to acknowledge the plight of the working class, but also a place that cannot be easily known, explained, or redeemed, and which, therefore, lies beyond the possibility of spectral-utopian redemption.[66] This becomes immediately apparent in John Barton's brief account of the capital upon his return home: 'It's as big as six Manchesters, they told me. One-sixth may be made up o' grand palaces, and three-sixth's o' the middling kind, and th' rest o' holes o' iniquity and filth, such as Manchester knows nought on, I'm glad to say'.[67] There is an impenetrability here that makes Gaskell's London a far more ominous and derelict urban setting than Manchester. The dereliction of London's urban landscape is architectural as much as moral, since, as Barton explains (again in a way that puts Manchester ahead of London), 'the houses are many on 'em

---

[65] King, 'Taxonomical Cures', p. 629.

[66] Parliament's refusal 'to listen to the working men' (Gaskell, *Mary Barton*, p. 88) is ultimately the event that precipitates John Barton's transformation into a radicalised, working-class anti-hero.

[67] Gaskell, *Mary Barton*, p. 90.

built without any proper shape for a body to live in'; it is the incommensurable multiplicity of this space, its monstrous lack of uniformity and 'shape' (even that which a clean social division grants) that ultimately grounds its 'iniquity'.[68] In London, the tragedy of class conflict and mutual estrangement is replaced by the spectacle of heterogeneity, by the blurring of clear social borders and forms.

As Peter Stallybrass argues in a classic article, social heterogeneity 'was the obsessive site/sight of the representable' in mid-nineteenth-century discourse.[69] In fiction, journalism, and social commentary, the spectacle of urban poverty was constructed as something that was immediately apparent to the 'vision of the bourgeois spectator' and yet, at the same time, as a 'nameless thing' dissolving all categories and social distinctions. Paradoxically, 'the more it was proclaimed to be unrepresentable, the more it was represented', leading to 'a veritable hysteria of naming'.[70] In his article, Stallybrass discusses a famous passage in 'The Eighteenth Brumaire of Louis Bonaparte' where Marx indulges this nineteenth-century compulsion in the middle of an analysis of the political intrigue leading up to the establishment of the Second French Empire. Marx here focuses on the creation of the Society of 10 December, a cover used by 'the Paris lumpenproletariat' in the guise of 'a charitable organization' to advance the Bonapartist cause.[71] The passage in question amounts to a notorious catalogue of social others:

> Alongside decayed roués of doubtful origin and uncertain means of subsistence, alongside ruined and adventurous scions of the bourgeoisie, there were vagabonds, discharged soldiers, discharged criminals, escaped galley slaves, swindlers, confidence tricksters, *lazzarone*, pickpockets, sleight-of-hand experts, gamblers, *maquereaux*, brothel-keepers, porters, pen-pushers, organ-grinders, rag-and-bone merchants, knife-grinders, tinkers and beggars: in short, the whole indeterminate fragmented mass, tossed backwards and forwards, which the French call *la bohème*[72]

This 'whole indeterminate fragmented mass' is characteristically contradictory in that it combines a quality of obtrusive visibility, an irreducible spectacularity, as it were, from which the observer's gaze cannot turn away, with the

---

[68] Gaskell, *Mary Barton*, p. 90.

[69] Peter Stallybrass, 'Marx and Heterogeneity: Thinking the Lumpenproletariat', *Representations* 31 (1990), p. 72.

[70] Stallybrass, 'Marx and Heterogeneity', pp. 72–73.

[71] Karl Marx, 'The Eighteenth Brumaire of Louis Bonaparte', in *The Political Writings* (London: Verso, 2019), p. 531.

[72] Marx, 'The Eighteenth Brumaire', p. 531. This translation is slightly different from the one Stallybrass uses in his article.

elusiveness that accompanies discursive proliferation.[73] The lumpenproletariat, for Marx, is at once an inescapably material entity (as suggested by the sartorial reference of its root *Lumpen*, which, as Stallybrass reminds us, means 'rags and tatters') and a threat to the social homogeneity associated with the working class. According to Stallybrass, Marx's analysis of the lumpenproletariat in 'The Eighteenth Brumaire' opens up a new way of thinking about the political and about class itself. For what this heterogeneous social group (whose contribution to the formation of the Bonapartist State is revealed to be central) announces is the possibility that class may actually be the result rather than the precondition of politics. In other words, that politics, no longer understood as a superstructure but as a 'formative process', may be the point of departure and constitutive instance of the social. In this sense, class would emerge 'as an unstable yoking together, through political rhetoric, of heterogeneous groups'; it would be 'shaped and transformed by state processes'.[74] For Stallybrass, 'the real scandal of the lumpenproletariat in Marxist theory' is the fact that it presents social heterogeneity not as 'the antithesis of political unification but [as] the very condition of possibility of that unification'.[75]

Theoretically, what is at stake here is the envisioning of the social totality as a failed, incomplete, or impossible entity, and the construction of the political as a space of articulation, rather than historical necessity, that may restore, in the provisional and contingent manner that defines rhetorical and discursive operations, a functional illusion of social fullness. The work of Ernesto Laclau and Chantal Mouffe provides the key reference point for this discussion. As they write in *Hegemony and Socialist Strategy*, 'The incomplete character of every totality necessarily leads us to abandon, as a terrain of analysis, the premise of "*society*" as a sutured and self-defined totality. "Society" is not a valid object of discourse. There is no single underlying principle fixing – and hence constituting – the whole field of differences'.[76] This absence of an underlying principle is

---

[73] Jacques Rancière observes that, for Marx, '[t]he *lumpen* is not a class but a myth – the myth of a bad history that comes to parasitize the good. In that sense it is inscribed in an already constituted political mythology: bourgeois denunciations of thieves, prostitutes and "escaped galley-slaves" as the hidden force behind all worker and republican disturbances; worker denunciations of self-interested confusions between the truly laboring, militant people and the equivocal fauna of Parisian streets and barriers', *The Philosopher and His Poor*, trans. by John Drury, Corinne Oster, and Andrew Parker (Durham, NC: Duke University Press, 2003), p. 96.

[74] Stallybrass, 'Marx and Heterogeneity', p. 70.

[75] Stallybrass, 'Marx and Heterogeneity', p. 88.

[76] Ernesto Laclau and Chantal Mouffe, *Hegemony and Socialist Strategy: Towards a Radical Democratic Politics* (London: Verso, 2001), p. 111.

what accords the political pre-eminence over the social for, as Laclau observes in *On Populist Reason*, 'the *sine qua non* requirements of the political are the constitution of antagonistic frontiers within the social and the appeal to new subjects of social change'.[77] Crucially for his theory, the antagonistic basis on which politics is predicated 'presupposes heterogeneity because the resistance of the antagonized force cannot be logically derived from the form of the antagonizing one'.[78] From this point of view, then, class ceases to be an expression of the dialectical motion of history and becomes an ontologically dislocated function of political (or, in Laclau's post-Gramscian language, hegemonic) articulation.

My aim in what follows is to show how a seminal text of English working-class literature, Robert Tressell's *The Ragged Trousered Philanthropists*, a novel that has often been regarded as problematic, not least due to its oblique relationship to the industrial norm of working-class experience in the nineteenth and early twentieth century, can be read as engaging with this logic of heterogeneity and political articulation. I want to argue that it is precisely by confronting (often unwillingly and even despairingly) an experience of social fragmentation and disorganisation at the heart of the working class that politics – and specifically socialist politics – can be imagined by the novel as an open discursive and temporal horizon.

The peculiar status of Tressell's novel in the literary canon of the British working class is in no small measure determined by its relatively marginal setting with respect to the main centres of industrial capitalism in Britain and by the general social and ideological situation surrounding this marginal location. It is surprising, as Raymond Williams observes, that the first 'internal English working-class' and properly socialist novel 'is set in the small-scale provincial building trade', in a 'community which did not, so to say, deliver class consciousness, but actually obstructed and confused it'.[79] Set and written in Hastings (the novel's Mugsborough) between 1906 and 1910 by the Irish-born signwriter and decorator Robert Noonan (under the pen name Robert Tressell), *The Ragged Trousered Philanthropists* is an extraordinary reconstruction of the horror and suffering endured by an early twentieth-century hyper-exploited working class permanently poised on the brink of starvation, but it is also an often haughty indictment of the position of ideological incorporation of this class fraction. While no ambiguity surrounds

---

[77] Ernesto Laclau, *On Populist Reason* (London: Verso, 2005), p. 154.

[78] Laclau, *On Populist Reason*, p. 150.

[79] Raymond Williams, 'The Welsh Industrial Novel', in *Who Speaks for Wales? Nation, Culture, Identity*, ed. by Daniel Williams (Cardiff: University of Wales Press, 2003), p. 99 and 'The Ragged-Arsed Philanthropists', in *Writing in Society* (London: Verso, 1991), p. 246.

the moral characterisation of the capitalist class as a veritable caste of parasites (their names, for one thing, are immediate transcriptions of their structural position as archetypal exploiters: Rushton, Sweater, Didlum, Grinder, Starvem, and so on), the weight of the blame tends to fall on the gormless workers themselves, that class of 'philanthropists' whose 'unselfish' work in exchange for starvation wages creates the obscene wealth of the bourgeoisie.

The novel opens with this cast of alienated characters at work in 'The Cave', the house which Rushton's company is decorating for Adam Sweater, a local businessman, politician, and leading member of the corrupt network of colluding interests in Mugsborough that the novel refers to as 'The Forty Thieves'.[80] While subject to all kinds of indignities and abuses at the hands of Hunter, their brutal yet piously Christian foreman (whom the men usually refer to behind his back as 'Nimrod' or 'Misery'), they reproduce a variety of illusions often derived from their avid reading of bourgeois newspapers such as *The Obscurer* and *The Daily Chloroform*, which in turn leads to their political self-identification as Liberals or Tories. The characteristic inanity of figures like the sub-foreman Crass is compounded by misplaced ideas about resistance to the routine exploitation they endure. Thus, a common practice is to 'get some of our own back' whenever Hunter is not looking. But the resistance typically amounts to petty pilfering and, more commonly, in the dismissive phonetic rendition Tressell reserves for the alienated philanthropists, 'proceed[ing] to "hinjoy" a quiet smoke'.[81] The novel is adamant about the self-defeating nature of these actions, which the men carry out in a total absence of political consciousness. Thus, for example, it is precisely while enjoying a smoke that Jack Linden, an older worker who 'called himself a Conservative and was very patriotic' even after losing a son in the Anglo-Boer War, is caught and immediately fired by Hunter.[82] Resigned to his fate (which is destitution for his family, including his orphaned grandchildren), he makes 'no attempt to defend himself: he knew it was of no use'.[83]

The sarcasm of Tressell's rhetorical strategy is further punctuated by the downright bitterness of his protagonist's conclusions. For Frank Owen, the

---

[80] As Peter Miles explains, 'The house is so named because it belongs to one of the Forty Thieves – and, in the pantomime *Ali Baba*, the Thieves hide their riches in a cave. To consolidate the point, "The Cave" also has a "Moorish" room at its heart. (The pantomime was a popular one and, for example, in December 1905 was playing at the Palace Theatre, Plymouth.)', 'Introduction', in Robert Tressell, *The Ragged Trousered Philanthropists* (Oxford: Oxford University Press, 2005), p. xx.

[81] Tressell, *The Ragged Trousered Philanthropists*, p. 32.

[82] Tressell, *The Ragged Trousered Philanthropists*, p. 34.

[83] Tressell, *The Ragged Trousered Philanthropists*, p. 41.

enlightened socialist whose despair and frustration at the reactionary idiocy of his fellow workers offers the main ideological frame of the novel, '*They were the enemy*. Those who not only quietly submitted like so many cattle to the existing state of things, but defended it, and opposed and ridiculed any suggestion to alter it [...] No wonder the rich despised them and looked upon them as dirt. They *were* despicable. They *were* dirt. They admitted it and gloried in it'.[84] This absence of consciousness, reinterpreted in such a harsh manner through the novel's own affirmative instantiation of political consciousness, is however not only a general failure of the class under certain historical conditions but also an implicit statement about the nature of political intervention, about that socialist revolution that is yet to come and which is no longer a necessary outcome of the socio-economic structure – logically deducible from its contradictions, as it were – but an external, heterogeneous, and contingent function of articulation. This will ultimately become apparent in 'The Great Oration', the chapter where Barrington, the bourgeois socialist in proletarian disguise who is both Owen's ultimate ally in the novel and the device through which political despair is rearticulated as the possible beginning of a new political consciousness, explicitly outlines the socialist programme that the novel endorses.

For Barrington, socialism distinguishes itself from capitalism in that it does not presuppose 'a wild dream of Superhuman Unselfishness': 'No one will be asked to sacrifice himself for the benefit of others or to love his neighbours better than himself as is the case under the present system, which demands that the majority shall unselfishly be content to labour and live in wretchedness for the benefit of a few'.[85] Socialism, rather, 'simply means that even as all industries are now owned by shareholders, and organised and directed by committees and officers elected by the shareholders, so shall they in future belong to the State, that is, the whole people—and they shall be organised and directed by committees and officers elected by the community'.[86] As various commentators have remarked, despite its nominal alignment with revolutionary socialism, Barrington's agenda is all too moderate and evolutionary. According to Dave Harker, for example, 'Barrington *sounds* revolutionary ... yet he has no understanding of the class character of the state. So he ignores the ruling-class backlash which Marx was sure would occur if a revolutionary programme was enacted by a parliamentary majority'.[87] The monopolistic concentration of capital would lead to the smooth intervention of public ownership and then

---

[84] Tressell, *The Ragged Trousered Philanthropists*, p. 40.
[85] Tressell, *The Ragged Trousered Philanthropists*, p. 493.
[86] Tressell, *The Ragged Trousered Philanthropists*, pp. 493–494.
[87] Dave Harker, *Tressell: The Real Story of* The Ragged Trousered Philanthropists (London: Zed Books, 2003), p. 66.

'automatically and inevitably to the defeat of private capitalists, without running the risk of imperialist war'.[88] This is, for Harker, a quietist and naïve politics that 'owes most to Bellamy's *Looking Backward*' and stays true to Robert Blatchford's emphasis on ideological persuasion regarding the abstract 'merits of socialism' while essentially disregarding the role of agency and revolutionary practice.[89] There is little doubt that the novel privileges the terrain of ideas and a generally elitist understanding of theoretical struggle, but this does not necessarily imply that the representation of socialist politics in the narrative is 'monologic', as Harker puts it.[90] On the contrary, what stands out in 'The Great Oration', as Williams notes, is its multi-layered discursive construction:

> The chairman, the interrupters and the general scene reproduce just that consciousness which is resistant to sustained serious talk, and this is not for light relief; indeed it shows both the need and the problem of that kind of serious discourse. So there is this innovation of inserting (it would now be done more often in avant-garde fiction) levels of discourse which do not cancel each other, and both teaching and the problems of teaching are there. It is done because experience alone will not teach, as, in a way, it does or is supposed to do in the positive kind of working-class novel.[91]

Any intended monologism would thus be effectively subverted by a formal strategy which may be compared, as Williams suggests, to modernist avant-gardism.[92] The crucial point, however, is that the absence of a full experiential positivity in the sense that Williams indicates here is precisely what makes political discourse necessary – and indeed possible. But this is not only or primarily the absence of that industrial context out of which 'the positive kind of working-class novel' is supposed to emerge, that archetypal saturated social space of proletarian imaginaries, with its corresponding forms of consciousness,

---

[88] Harker, *Tressell*, p. 66.

[89] Harker, *Tressell*, pp. 66, 67.

[90] Harker, *Tressell*, p. 66. Another critic, Pamela Fox, has noted that what is important in this respect is not so much 'to place Tressell on a political continuum (Fabian vs. Marxist) as to pinpoint the type of resistance valued in the novel: ideological, rather than bloody, upheaval', *Class Fictions: Shame and Resistance in the British Working-Class Novel, 1890–1945* (Durham, NC: Duke University Press, 1994), p. 68.

[91] Williams, 'Ragged-Arsed Philanthropists', p. 251.

[92] For a more recent investigation of this novel's affinities with modernism, see Deaglán Ó Donghaile, 'Modernism, Class and Colonialism in Robert Noonan's *The Ragged Trousered Philanthropists*', *Irish Studies Review* 26:3 (2018), pp. 374–389.

but actually the absence (or the active blurring) of solid material boundaries within which the class itself may be *objectively* apprehended.

Owen's characterisation is instructive in this respect. He is emphatically described as a superior kind of craftsman, a decorator and signwriter committed to the more artistic aspects of his work and instinctively averse to the capitalist obsession with 'cheapness and profit' prevailing in the trade.[93] But for all his outstanding qualities as a worker, Owen and his family are condemned to 'a wretched existence on the very verge of starvation', more often than not joining the great mass of people – skilled or unskilled, employed or unemployed – whose 'life was one long struggle against poverty'.[94] In this sense, Frank Owen represents not only the formation of a resistant if largely pessimistic political consciousness at the heart of the novel but also the concrete breakdown of objective or qualitative criteria for the introduction of class distinctions into this great mass of the poor. In a context where labour, however qualified or productive of value, may be suddenly rendered inoperative and effectively dissolved into that passive and undifferentiated state of life 'on the very verge of starvation', the notion of class is stripped of any solidity. What remains, in its place, and against the objective determinations of labour as such, is the bottomless abyss of poverty. Rather than a form of stratification definable in terms of class, this is an expression of social entropy, an abyss that dismantles social identities and divisions. Not even wealth is protected from its destructive pull:

> Why, even those who were successful or wealthy could not be sure that they would not eventually die of want. In every workhouse might be found people who had at one time occupied good positions; and their downfall was not in every case their own fault.
>
> No matter how prosperous a man might be, he could not be certain that his children would never want for bread. There were thousands living in misery on starvation wages whose parents had been wealthy people.[95]

The workhouse becomes here a specific symbol for the lack of objective guarantees defining this social universe. This is no longer a place reserved for a particular subclass of the excluded, a natural habitat for the 'undeserving' lumpenproletariat, as it were, but rather the symbolic marker of a downfall whose causes are not strictly determinable and a sign of the dissolution of work and class into the visual spectacle of destitution. Jack Linden ends up

---

[93] Tressell, *The Ragged Trousered Philanthropists*, p. 60.
[94] Tressell, *The Ragged Trousered Philanthropists*, p. 61.
[95] Tressell, *The Ragged Trousered Philanthropists*, p. 62.

in the workhouse after being evicted from his home, following a long period of unemployment. There is also the case of Latham, a venetian blind maker fallen on hard times whose presence in the novel is essentially reduced to a sartorial performance of poverty: 'His boots were patched, broken, and down at heel, and the knees and bottoms of the legs of his trousers were in the same condition as the sleeves of his coat'.[96] This character in a sense literalises the lumpen horizon awaiting workers in this world. Indeed, this is the very essence of the 'ragged trousered' class which the novel invokes. But what is particularly significant here is that the lumpen nature of characters like these is not determined by their exteriority to the universe of labour. On the contrary, Latham 'had been "in business" – as he called it – for about forty years working, working, always working'.[97] His is, like Linden's, unquestionably a lifetime of 'hard labour' resulting in bottomless poverty and the workhouse. What this announces is a radical disconnection between the materiality of production and any sense of solid and homogeneous identification in society – in other words, a true *lumpenproletarianisation* of the working class.

It is curious that, as the novel works towards this characterisation of the social as eminently heterogeneous in its processes and effects, a rather emphatic commitment to homogeneous divisions and classifications is one of the defining features of Owen's discourse. His 'lectures', in particular the chapter entitled 'The Oblong', betray a traditional Marxist understanding of class predicated on a rigid conception of productive labour and on a revealing exclusion of 'tramps' and 'beggars', the poorest among the poor, from the ranks of the working class, as they are grouped with 'the "Aristocracy", "Society" people, great landowners, and generally all those possessed of hereditary wealth'.[98] Indeed, Owen goes on to explain that 'that's the proper place for them. They belong to the loafer class. They are no better mentally or morally than any of the other loafers in that division; neither are they of any more use'.[99] This characterisation of the lumpenproletariat as idle and parasitical is consistent with Marx's own account, as we have seen. But in the context of *The Ragged Trousered Philanthropists*, what this would amount to if it were to express the novel's stance on this question would be a negation of the very experience of social heterogeneity with which Owen's and his fellow workers' lives are so deeply and inescapably entwined. The fact is, however, that this cannot be said to represent the novel's final position concerning the lumpenproletariat. Later on, commenting on the hunger marches of the town's poor, the narrator offers

---

[96] Tressell, *The Ragged Trousered Philanthropists*, p. 241.
[97] Tressell, *The Ragged Trousered Philanthropists*, p. 242.
[98] Tressell, *The Ragged Trousered Philanthropists*, p. 275.
[99] Tressell, *The Ragged Trousered Philanthropists*, p. 282.

a revealingly different emphasis in his characterisation of 'those unfortunate outcasts of society – tramps and destitute, drunken loafers', admonishing 'the self-righteous hypocrites who despise these poor wretches' and inviting them to consider that, under similar circumstances, they too may have found themselves in a similar condition.[100] But even more significant is Barrington's return to the problematic status of tramps in 'The Great Oration':

> I don't wish to speak disrespectfully of these tramps at all. Some of them are such simply because they would rather starve than submit to the degrading conditions that we submit to, they do not see the force of being bullied and chased, and driven about in order to gain semi-starvation and rags. They are able to get those without working; and I sometimes think that they are more worthy of respect and are altogether a nobler type of beings than a lot of broken spirited wretches like ourselves, who are always at the mercy of our masters, and always in dread of the sack.[101]

This is indeed a significant shift from Owen's overhasty condemnation and even a step beyond the charitable sympathy expressed by the narrator. But what are the political implications of this reversal of the standard symbolic construction of the lumpenproletariat? Where does it lead to in terms of the novel's construction of a socialist strategy? First, it is worth noting that what Barrington observes in the lumpenproletariat is not a parasitical subcaste of loafers but a position of radical exteriority (indeed, of heterogeneity) with respect to the dual system of labour and poverty.[102] This exteriority, rather than featuring as a mere moral defect, may actually be recognised as an alternative, and possibly a 'nobler', way of enacting class resistance. In other words, the exteriority of the lumpenproletariat offers an insight into the heterogeneous

---

[100] Tressell, *The Ragged Trousered Philanthropists*, p. 296.

[101] Tressell, *The Ragged Trousered Philanthropists*, p. 517.

[102] This condition of radical exteriority to the system of capitalist production is one of the elements differentiating the concept of the lumpenproletariat from that of the 'industrial reserve army'. As Laclau points out, the latter concept is an index of Marxism's privileging of homogeneity and thus an insufficient category to account for the heterogenous contingency of social identities: 'although the temporarily unemployed are not part of the capitalist relations of production, they are still functional to capitalism because they help to increase the rate of profit. Although they are formally outsiders, this is a different "outside" from that of the *lumpenproletariat*, because it has a functionality within the system and, as a result, these people are still part of a "history of production"', *On Populist Reason*, pp. 146–147.

nature of political action in relation to any 'objective' class conditions. Thus, with Barrington's admission, the novel's socialist strategy implicitly becomes also a matter of exteriority, something which is defined by the contingency and indeterminacy of a discursive and temporally dislocated intervention. What is at stake, then, is the centrality of articulation as Laclau and Mouffe define it: 'a *political construction* from dissimilar elements'.[103]

My claim is that dissimilarity of elements, and their ultimate (re) construction as an articulated whole, is precisely the condition that undergirds an otherwise emphatic focus on class exploitation and socialism in Tressell's novel. For example, the forms of oppression affecting the English working class and the Indian victims of colonisation are dissimilar, yet Barrington links these two elements together in what might be described, again following Laclau and Mouffe, as a 'chain of equivalence'.[104] Then there is, of course, a fundamental dissimilarity in the subjective effects of the objective condition of exploitation endured by Tressell's 'philanthropists' (ranging from total incorporation to varying degrees of oppositionality). And there is also, as we have seen, a telling dissimilarity between the socialist narratives or subject positions represented by Owen and Barrington. It may be argued that Owen represents a still relatively internal position, immanent to the plane of production and fundamentally invested in a substantialist understanding of labour (based on use value and quality as opposed to exchange value and quantity), where socialism operates, first, as the unveiling of a pre-existing truth (exploitation) and, second, as a narcotic of sorts, not unlike 'what drink was to some of the others – the thing that enabled [him] to forget and tolerate the conditions under which [he was] forced to exist'.[105] Barrington, on the other hand, represents the introduction of an external position (external to the working class but allied

---

[103] Laclau and Mouffe, *Hegemony and Socialist Strategy*, p. 85.

[104] Laclau and Mouffe, *Hegemony and Socialist Strategy*, p. 127. This important moment in Barrington's 'Great Oration' offers a significant corrective to what is otherwise perceived as Tressell's relative neglect of the realities of imperialism in the novel: 'India is a rich, productive country. Every year millions of pounds worth of wealth are produced by her people, only to be stolen from them by means of the Money Trick by the capitalist and official class. Her industrious sons and daughters, who are nearly all total abstainers live in abject poverty, and their misery is not caused by laziness or want of thrift, or by Intemperance. They are poor for the same reason that we are poor – Because we are Robbed', Tressell, *Philanthropists*, pp. 494–495. For an assessment of Tressell's mixed attitudes towards imperialist ideology, see Julie Cairnie, 'Imperial Poverty in Robert Tressell's *The Ragged Trousered Philanthropists*', *Journal of Commonwealth Literature* 37:2 (2002), pp. 175–194.

[105] Tressell, *The Ragged Trousered Philanthropists*, p. 443.

to it) as well as the establishment of exteriority as a general principle for the definition of socialist politics.

In a sense, Barrington is symptomatic of the crisis which assailed Marxist theory at the turn of the century and which would eventually result, as Laclau and Mouffe explain in *Hegemony and Socialist Strategy*, in the consolidation of a logic of political articulation at the heart of Marxism in the twentieth century (whose culminating point, as they argue, would be the thought of Antonio Gramsci). While Tressell's novel is undoubtedly far from the theoretical refinement involved in the latter's theory of hegemony, it is not difficult to observe in the role assigned to Barrington elements of the ideological crisis analysed by Laclau and Mouffe. The general historical background to this debate was the end of the 'long depression' of 1873–1896 and the failure to materialise of capitalism's anticipated terminal crisis:

> The transition to 'organized capitalism', and the ensuing boom that lasted until 1914, made uncertain the prospect of a 'general crisis of capitalism'. Under the new conditions, a wave of successful trade union economic struggles enabled the workers to consolidate their organizational power and influence within Social Democracy. But at this point, a steady tension began to assert itself between the trade unions and the political leadership within the party, so that the unity and socialist determination of the working class became increasingly problematic. In all areas of society, an *autonomization of spheres* was taking place – which implied that any type of unity could only be attained through unstable and complex forms of rearticulation.[106]

As Laclau and Mouffe point out, Marxist orthodoxy emerges in this context, not as a mere systematisation of the ideas of Marx and Engels but as a specific development characterised by the strategic role assigned to theory and to the intellectuals. The paradox at the heart of this orthodox codification of Marxism, as carried out by thinkers such as Kautsky and Plekhanov, lies in the fact that the more deterministic its analysis of the economic contradictions of capitalism becomes, the more central is the role accorded to the interpretative function of socialist intellectuals.[107] This entails 'the emergence

---

[106] Laclau and Mouffe, *Hegemony and Socialist Strategy*, pp. 17–18.

[107] The more rigid and vulgar echoes of this orthodoxy defined the position of the leader of the Social Democratic Federation (SDF), Henry Mayers Hyndman, who liked to repeat, in a characteristic disparagement of working-class self-organisation (and especially of the role of the trade unions) that 'no slave class ever emancipated itself', quoted in Keith Laybourn and Dylan Murphy, *Under the Red Flag: A History of Communism in Britain* (Stroud: Sutton Publishing,

of an articulating nexus' that cannot be dissolved into the logic of historical necessity.[108] This emphasis can help us understand not only the centrality and dual/dialogic nature of socialist consciousness to Tressell's novel but also its crucial orientation towards a logic of heterogeneity and exteriority that introduces articulation as the 'secret' of political action. However peripheral to the main theoretical developments of Marxism in the early twentieth century, therefore, Tressell's text can be linked to this general strategic turn.[109] This was a turn that was, according to Laclau and Mouffe, founded upon the knowledge 'that the socialist determination of the working class does not arise spontaneously but depends upon the political mediation of intellectuals'.[110] Even if the novel's ending is notoriously eschatological in its anticipation of the inevitable collapse of 'that atrocious system ... which was now fast crumbling into ruin' and the advent of the 'Co-Operative Commonwealth', complete with a strictly utopian vision of 'the gilded domes and glittering pinnacles of the beautiful cities of the future', the primacy of political intervention as a temporally distended project of articulation and hegemony – as the construction of *a class to come* – offers the true moment of provisional closure.[111] It is Barrington's promise to return to Mugsborough in the spring with 'a Socialist Van', and his announcement to Owen that 'We'll have some of the best speakers in the movement; we'll hold meetings every night; we'll drench the town with literature, and we'll start a branch of the party', that truly concludes the narrative, offering both a corrective

---

1999), p. 11. This led to numerous factional splits and the growing isolation and irrelevance of the SDF.

[108] Laclau and Mouffe, *Hegemony and Socialist Strategy*, p. 20.

[109] Harker points out that the novel 'was close to the cutting edge of British socialist thought in 1910' and that 'To some extent, Noonan was moving beyond Blatchford and Hyndman, and towards a Marxist theory of ideology', *Tressell*, pp. 69, 64. It is nevertheless clear that, theoretically, it was hardly in sync with the main Marxist debates of its time.

[110] Laclau and Mouffe, *Hegemony and Socialist Strategy*, p. 85.

[111] Tressell, *The Ragged Trousered Philanthropists*, p. 611. As I have already noted, the temporal structure of that which is 'to come' is at the centre of Derrida's theoretical engagement with ethics and politics in his later work, most notably in *Specters of Marx*. Addressing the notion of a 'democracy to come', Derrida writes, 'the effectivity or actuality of the democratic promise, like that of the communist promise, will always keep within it, and it must do so, this absolutely undetermined messianic hope at its heart, this eschatological relation to the to-come of an event *and* of a singularity, of an alterity that cannot be anticipated', *Specters of Marx*, p. 81. For Derrida, this temporal logic is 'spectral', 'out of joint', in the sense that it implies 'awaiting what one does not expect yet or any longer', p. 81.

to Owen's immanentist pessimism (insofar as he remains entangled in the 'internal' contradictions of exploitation) and a continuing vector of political articulation for the working class.[112]

One of the key difficulties of *The Ragged Trousered Philanthropists* stems from its engagement with a social situation defined not only by brutal capitalist exploitation but also by heterogeneity and fragmentation – indeed, by a logic of class that offers no objective guarantees, a class that is absent and remains to be constructed. This is not to say, however, that fatalism is the inevitable ideological inference that the novel invites. On the contrary, as I have been arguing, it is precisely by uncovering the centrality of articulation as the type of political intervention adequate to social heterogeneity that its socialist programme becomes imaginable and that the idea of class, as a contingent and properly political entity, becomes thinkable in the novel.[113]

1.3 Articulation or Reductionism? Ellen Wilkinson's *Clash*

Tressell's novel is situated at the cusp of a process of deep social and political transformation in turn-of-the-century Britain. As Stuart Hall and Bill Schwarz have summarised it, this specifically British conjuncture is broadly defined by a shift from mid-Victorian laissez-faire liberalism to a 'democratic-interventionist "solution"'.[114] What, according to these authors, is notable about this historical transition is the 'necessarily contingent' nature of the political dynamics and 'forces' involved in the process.[115] This points to the inadequacy of those historical accounts which stress a 'fundamental continuity' between the mid-nineteenth and early twentieth century and which, in for example 'seeing the Labour Party as the natural successor to the Liberals, or the "growth" of the welfare state', effectively 'fail to grasp the immediate determinations which impelled a change of course and the desperate attempts to organize new solutions'.[116] This is, then, an institutional and ideological context marked by

---

[112] Tressell, *The Ragged Trousered Philanthropists*, p. 602. This promise is combined, in a more traditional and conservative gesture, with a Dickensian invocation of Christmas. Barrington even becomes a Santa Claus figure of sorts, pretending to be his assistant before the children, then giving them presents and later on cash to Owen, Mrs Linden, and Bert White's mother.

[113] See Bevir, *The Making*, p. 298.

[114] Stuart Hall and Bill Schwarz, 'State and Society, 1880–1930', in Stuart Hall, *The Hard Road to Renewal: Thatcherism and the Crisis of the Left* (London: Verso, 2021), p. 95.

[115] Hall and Schwarz, 'State and Society', p. 95.

[116] Hall and Schwarz, 'State and Society', p. 97.

openness and contingency, and one to which the articulatory approach which Tressell's novel tentatively embraces would seem particularly suited.

I want to conclude the chapter by exploring the ongoing relevance of this contingent political logic to the formation of a specifically literary-socialist discourse, but also by highlighting the growing tension to which this logic was subjected in the 1920s, at the tail end of this transitional period. Ellen Wilkinson's 1929 novel *Clash* is a significant development in that its basic premise is the practical as well as theoretical gulf lying between prominent democratic demands such as those expressed by the socialist and feminist movements in this period. There is a symptomatic sense of the radical hetero-geneity and yet mutually inciting radicalism of these ideological positions in the novel. As Hall and Schwarz argue, the cross-fertilisation of these movements in the early decades of the twentieth century is not to be understood as 'a spontaneous alliance' – which did not occur – but rather in terms of the activation of 'new sources of contention and antagonism, as well as new *potentialities* for alliances'.[117] Wilkinson herself was an emblematic product of such potentialities. Born in Manchester in 1891, her political career began at an early age with a dual commitment to labour politics and suffragism. A member of the Independent Labour Party since 1907, she joined the Manchester Society for Women's Suffrage, a local branch of the National Union of Women's Suffrage Societies (NUWSS), in 1912 while a student at Manchester University and was soon employed by it. As Paula Bartley observes, while '[t]emperamentally she seemed more suited' to the insurgent methods of the suffragettes than to the constitutional approach of the more moderate suffragists, the latter's willingness to take the Labour Party up on its pledge in 1912 to support votes for women, and to actively collaborate with it, was key.[118] From that point onwards, Wilkinson's political engagement was to be defined by a complex articulation of radical-democratic positions. Thus, after the First World War, she 'continued to hone her organising skills in the trade union movement, helped to found the Communist Party, campaigned for peace and promoted the rights of women' while formally belonging to a multiplicity of organisations in a layering of militant identities that was often contradictory and conflicted.[119] This multifaceted involvement would

---

[117] Hall and Schwarz, 'State and Society', p. 103; my emphasis.

[118] Paula Bartley, *Ellen Wilkinson: From Red Suffragist to Government Minister* (London: Pluto Press, 2014), p. 7.

[119] Bartley, *Ellen Wilkinson*, p. 14. For example, her departure from the Communist Party in 1924 did not, as Matt Perry points out, 'entail a conversion to mainstream Labourism', *'Red Ellen' Wilkinson: Her Ideas, Movements and World* (Manchester: Manchester University Press, 2014), p. 41. On the contrary, she remained a

consolidate her 'expansive' socialism, as Ian Haywood and Maroula Joannou describe it, in the 1920s and directly inform her first novel.[120]

Clash follows Joan Craig, a young working-class woman and trade union organiser, through her involvement in the 1926 General Strike and its immediate aftermath. Yet the most distinctive aspect of the novel concerns Joan's personal and political interactions with a group of bourgeois Londoners gathered around her unlikely friend, the former suffragette and mine-owning Bloomsbury socialite Mary Maud Meadowes. In a sense, the point of departure for Wilkinson's fictional investigation of complex political alliances is a displacement of class, not as the primary experiential anchor in the social reality of 1926, but as the exclusive and deterministic form of radical identification. As Joan travels to London with her union boss William Royd to attend the Trades Union Congress (TUC) conference that will eventually declare the strike, she also commences a journey of self-distancing from the immanent experience of working-class life granted by her trade union job – an experience, as the novel's opening emphasises, defined by disappointment and tiredness after eight years working as a labour organiser: 'that kind of tiredness known only to those who set out to organize their fellow men'.[121]

Pamela Fox describes Joan's travelogue, documenting her engagement with the world of the Bloomsbury intelligentsia, as a 'journey of temptation' in which 'bourgeois London emerges (at times too pointedly) as Joan's Garden of Eden', while the writer Anthony Dacre, with whom she becomes romantically involved, 'is her demon'.[122] At the heart of this novel lies what Haywood and Joannou have described as 'Wilkinson's attempt to politicise literary romance' and indeed to deploy it as a form of discursive mediation, with precise political effects, as we will see, on the experiential immediacy attributed to proletarian life.[123] The emphasis on distance and separation from the realities of class is indeed central to the novel's initial impulse. Joan's friendship with Mary Maud is key in so far as it renders imaginable the possibility of an inter-class personal *and* political relationship at a remove from the social homogeneity of

---

critical Marxist committed to 'transform[ing] the Labour Party, via the Left-Wing Movement', p. 42. Moreover – her radical socialism notwithstanding – once an MP, Wilkinson became a close friend and collaborator of the Conservative Nancy Astor in the fight to secure the extension of the franchise to all women over the age of 21, which 'made her an uncomfortable colleague', Bartley, *Ellen Wilkinson*, p. 33.

[120] Ian Haywood and Maroula Joannou, 'Introduction', in Ellen Wilkinson, *Clash* (Nottingham: Trent Editions, 2004), p. viii.

[121] Wilkinson, *Clash*, p. 3.

[122] Fox, *Class Fictions*, p. 170.

[123] Haywood and Joannou, 'Introduction', p. xiv.

the industrial north. Driven by her desire 'for contacts with hard life', we read that Mary Maud was initially attracted to 'Joan's uncompromising realism'.[124] Yet beyond the sense of personal loyalty and affection which develops between the two, and despite the tinge of anxiety which Joan's militant socialism occasionally triggers in Mary Maud, the latter's radical feminism remains a defining aspect and driving force throughout the narrative. Thus, as she discusses the prospect of Joan's marriage to Tony with their friend Gerry Blain, the political core of her objection – along with her lingering sense of militancy, which offers a revealing contrast to her more frivolous moments – becomes apparent: 'You know I was a keen suffragist—went to prison and all that [...] Well, the Women's Movement has been the only thing I ever really cared about. I've had too much money of my own, too many love affairs to get any work done myself, but always I've dreamed that some day there would arise a woman leader who would carry on the tradition'.[125] Mary Maud insistently defends the idea that Joan is a 'most unusual girl' who may become 'an heiress of the work those women did' and thus a leader, 'a rallying point', for future feminists.[126]

The novel's romantic plot is a central conduit for the negotiation of complex allegiances and indeed visions of the political. For ultimately what is at stake in the relationship between Joan and Tony is the choice between competing definitions of feminism, as well as their possible interaction with other forms of radicalism and personal and collective ways of life. If Mary Maud's feminist credentials are straightforward and pure, Tony's are far more ambivalent. Despite his declared commitment to equality, he demands from Joan that she renounce her job in order to marry him once he has secured a divorce from his wife Helen. This clash between an ultimately rhetorical embrace of feminism and the attempt to construct, in practice, a truly feminist life through the development of Joan's 'professional identity' amounts, according to Laura Beers, to the 'crucial conflict' in the novel.[127] But it is also the main source of pressure on the very possibility of articulating a viable politics of complexity through the construction of a simultaneously personal and political radical identity.[128]

[124] Wilkinson, *Clash*, p. 10.

[125] Wilkinson, *Clash*, p. 57.

[126] Wilkinson, *Clash*, pp. 58, 57.

[127] Laura Beers, 'Feminism and Sexuality in Ellen Wilkinson's Fiction', *Parliamentary Affairs* 64:2 (2011), p. 251.

[128] Here it is important to reiterate that 'Long before the women's movement of the 1970s had pinpointed and publicised the connection, *Clash* insists that the personal is political', Haywood and Joannou, 'Introduction', p. xix.

For the articulation of this complexity – this heterogeneity – of demands and positions into a radical project after all forms the novel's opening vision as Joan arrives in London at the beginning of the narrative. The inaugural scene at the Memorial Hall in London where the TUC holds its conference is crucially described as 'a beehive' of radical types and demands: 'Communists, single-taxers, credit-reformers ... Unemployed sandwich-men paraded in front of the hall ... The inevitable mild middle-class lady gave out leaflets on birth-control. A little apart from the hubbub a typical group of London workers looked on with their usual air of cheerful detachment. A taxi-man, wearing his union button, surveyed the scene with immense benevolence'.[129] This, we could argue, is indeed the formative vision of radical politics in the novel: an open 'discursive' space towards which working-class and middle-class radicals gravitate with their heterogeneous claims and identities. This vision, which offers a dynamic counterpoint to the exhausted backdrop of labourist monotony with which the novel begins, and which runs through the rehearsal of feminist positions throughout the narrative, is not sustained after the crisis in its romantic plot becomes explicit. For as Tony's opportunism is gradually exposed, Joan begins to gravitate towards a very different – and much less complex – political imaginary. As a new horizon of realignment around her proletarian identity is announced, Gerry Blain – a disabled war veteran of stern socialist convictions – emerges as an increasingly likely replacement for the unreliable Tony Dacre. Gerry's idealisation of the working class is symmetrical to his hatred for the bourgeois background that is his own and the traces of whose betrayal (in that great act of class deceit that the Great War had been) are indelibly etched in his broken body. The 'struggle to control' the 'giant industries' of Britain 'seemed the biggest thing in life to him' and the General Strike represents precisely the long-awaited opportunity to 'take them out of the hands of men like his father, the men to whom they represented only percentages and dividends'.[130]

Significantly, what drives Blain through visions such as these is a very private – indeed, Oedipal – notion of politics, one according to which 'the Hidden God' incarnated by the proletariat will redress the injustice of his personal suffering. This is a version of the political that does not suddenly take over in the novel, but which rather competes with the more open and less reductive *possibility* (for it never amounts to more than a possibility) of a complex political identity. Paradoxically, the farther the narrative advances towards a romantic denouement securing Joan's integration of personal independence and collective commitment, the more strictly its ideological

[129] Wilkinson, *Clash*, p. 15.
[130] Wilkinson, *Clash*, p. 50.

co-ordinates are narrowed down to this class-essentialist frame of reference. Thus, Tony is at one point described as 'essentially middle-class' and lacking in 'that rigid, working-class patriotism which was Joan's inspiration and which Blain had so wholeheartedly adopted'.[131] This ultimately leads to the conclusion that their Bloomsbury friends' unreliability is necessarily determined by their class position. As Gerry sums it up, 'Sympathetic with the workers, yes, but it's all a show to them, an interesting exhibition of unusual types. They are bored with their own crowd, so they stand outside the struggle, like keen spectators at a boxing match, and cheer the workers on to victory. But they are never *in* the fight. And if you go with that crowd, Joan, you will be out of the fight too'.[132]

For all its promise of a complex articulation of feminist and socialist identities, Wilkinson's *Clash* ultimately offers a retreat into class essentialism as the basis for socialist politics in the following decade. As Joan concedes in her final exchange with Gerry, for all the difficulties posed by 'the fine shades between class and class' (difficulties posed, that is, by the tenuous but also, at an earlier point in the novel, attractive possibility of a socialism without sharp class boundaries), it is now finally apparent to her that 'the big broad issue is there' and that this is 'the issue that this century will be occupied in fighting out'.[133] The authors I consider in the next chapter – beginning with Lewis Grassic Gibbon and his monumental contribution in *A Scots Quair* – start from the opposite conclusion: namely, the realisation that no socialism 'this century' can rest on a simplification of the social as an ultimately homogeneous and objective entity, for politics itself is inseparable from the logic of contingency and transformation that also informs artistic creation.

[131] Wilkinson, *Clash*, p. 92.
[132] Wilkinson, *Clash*, p. 181.
[133] Wilkinson, *Clash*, p. 189.

Chapter Two

The People Are Missing

2.2 A Politics of Fabulation: On Lewis Grassic Gibbon

Lewis Grassic Gibbon's trilogy *A Scots Quair* offers one of the key fictional accounts of working-class life in early twentieth-century Britain. Gibbon's cycle of novels, beginning with the publication of *Sunset Song* in 1932, followed by *Cloud Howe* in 1933 and *Grey Granite* in 1934, charts the decline of a peasant community in the Mearns region of north-east Scotland and its eventual transformation into an urban proletariat. While the historical remit of these novels is undeniable, their approach to the matter of time calls into question any assumption of homogeneity, any potential complicity with teleology or historical necessity. As I will argue in this section, the idea of transformation, understood as the mobilisation of heterogeneity against 'the stable, the eternal, the identical, the constant', is central to Gibbon's temporal politics of contingency and to the specific narrative strategy that the trilogy deploys.[1]

The first novel, *Sunset Song*, introduces its heroine Chris Guthrie and follows her development through childhood and early womanhood in the years immediately prior to the First World War, before climaxing in the great catastrophe of the war itself, with its direct toll on the local community, and the ultimate loss of this old rural people and way of life. The idea of historical development as tragic decline is a key theme in Gibbon's writing and is generally informed by a brand of historical anthropology known as diffusionism that was popular in the early twentieth century. Morag Shiach notes that diffusionism 'advanced the view that all civilisations across the globe had developed from one original civilisation. For the Diffusionists this was ancient Egypt. They argued that crucial developments, like the working of metal, the development of agriculture and even eventually industrialisation, could all be traced to ancient Egypt'.[2] Jeremy Idle in turn argues that '[c]ivilization for Gibbon is an evil: originally man was free, without Gods or

---

[1] Gilles Deleuze and Félix Guattari, *A Thousand Plateaus*, trans. by Brian Massumi (London: Continuum, 2011), p. 398.

[2] Morag Shiach, 'Lewis Grassic Gibbon and Modernism', in *The International*

the state, without sexual inhibitions or war. Man existed like this for untold centuries; he should have continued existence indefinitely in such a fashion'.[3] According to Gibbon, then, if Egypt is the ancient heartland from where civilisation 'diffused', it is in that sense also 'where man's downfall occurred' and therefore 'where history was born'.[4] An enduring feature of Gibbon's writing is precisely the tension between history as the collective and social temporality that renders the process of change (and, from a diffusionist perspective, decline) intelligible and, given history's ultimately destructive nature, those temporalities pertaining to 'the shape and rhythm of individual lives' that account for transformation in a historically resistant and ontologically open manner.[5] Shiach summarises this 'concern [running] across the three novels of *A Scots Quair*' as a strategy of '[s]etting history in play without being paralysed by its nightmarish qualities'.[6] She further suggests that this 'concern drives Gibbon to a series of innovative fictional devices', including 'the formal structuring of *Sunset Song* through the cyclical rhythms of agricultural labour' and the 'very particular use of the pronoun "you" by a narrative voice seeking constantly to move between individual and collective uses of that pronoun'.[7] But we can also add, as a reading of the prelude to this first novel will show, a more radical intermixing of unorthodox temporal modalities – of myth and legend, of folk memory and family history – pushing beyond and prising open the formal logic of historical time. What is fundamentally in question here is the teleology of so much historicism in the wider context of Gibbon's cultural and political milieu, and what is perhaps on offer, as I want to suggest, is an untimely politics of contingency, of becoming and heterogeneity, whose proper narrative strategy may be described, following Gilles Deleuze, as fabulation.[8]

Companion to Lewis Grassic Gibbon, ed. by Scott Lyall (Glasgow: Scottish Literature International, 2015), p. 10.

[3] Jeremy Idle, 'Lewis Grassic Gibbon and the Urgency of the Modern', *Studies in Scottish Literature* 31:1 (1999), p. 258.

[4] Idle, 'Urgency of the Modern', p. 258.

[5] Shiach, 'Lewis Grassic Gibbon', p. 10.

[6] Shiach, 'Lewis Grassic Gibbon', p. 13.

[7] Shiach, 'Lewis Grassic Gibbon', p. 13.

[8] A key aspect of Gibbon's political and artistic trajectory was his commitment to anarchism. Thus, for example, he writes in 1934, 'I am a Scotsman, an artist, and – an integral part of my being – an anarchist. My art is implicit anarchy', quoted in William K. Malcolm, 'Art for Politics' Sake: The Sardonic Principle of James Leslie Mitchell (Lewis Grassic Gibbon)', in *'To Hell with Culture': Anarchism and Twentieth-Century British Literature*, ed. by H. Gustav Klaus and Stephen Knight (Cardiff: University of Wales Press, 2005), p. 35. As Malcolm notes, Gibbon's anarchism 'was typically eclectic and idiosyncratic', opening up to 'hard-line revolutionary Marxism'

The latter is a concept Deleuze borrows from the philosopher Henri Bergson, for whom it fundamentally refers to the production of religious imaginaries in closed, traditional societies. As Ronald Bogue has explained, fabulation, as originally conceptualised by Bergson, 'has as its goal the creation of hallucinatory fictions that regulate behaviour and reinforce social cohesion'.[9] In Deleuze's adaptation of the notion, this 'visionary faculty' that 'consists in creating gods and giants', and is 'exercised first of all in religions', is also 'freely developed in art and literature'.[10] For Deleuze, as he shows in *Cinema 2: The Time-Image*, there is a significant connection between this notion and the Nietzschean critique of truth. For example, in a discussion of the Québécois documentary film-maker Pierre Perrault, Deleuze argues that Perrault's purpose, when addressing 'real characters', 'is not simply to eliminate fiction but to free it from the model of truth which penetrates it'.[11] For '[w]hat is opposed to fiction is not the real; it is not the truth which is always that of the masters or colonizers' but rather the 'fabulating function of the poor, in so far as it gives the false the power which makes it into a memory, a legend, a monster'.[12] Deleuze here takes up the visionary or hallucinatory logic of fabulation described by Bergson – the 'fabrication of giants' that is its proper task – and inscribes it within Nietzsche's genealogical project.[13] As he argues in his earlier discussion of the cinema of Orson Welles – to whom he ascribes 'an authentic or a spontaneous Nietzscheanism' – the critique of truth is central to the project of liberating life from morality and opening it up to its proper, affirmative being (that is, transformation or becoming).[14] For 'it is not a matter of judging life in the name of a higher authority which would be the good, the true; it is a matter, on the contrary, of evaluating

towards the end of his life in the admission that his desired primitivist-libertarian utopia may not be attained 'without the preliminary conditioning of communism', 'Art for Politics' Sake', pp. 35, 40. However, this tactical qualification of Gibbon's politics should not be mistaken for an acceptance of orthodox Marxist accounts of history. It is precisely in his rejection of historico-revolutionary teleologies that Gibbon's anarchism can be apprehended at its most principled.

[9] Ronald Bogue, *Deleuzian Fabulation and the Scars of History* (Edinburgh: Edinburgh University Press, 2010), p. 16.

[10] Gilles Deleuze and Félix Guattari, *What is Philosophy?*, trans. by Hugh Tomlinson and Graham Burchill (London: Verso, 1994), p. 230.

[11] Gilles Deleuze, *Cinema 2: The Time-Image*, trans. by Hugh Tomlinson and Robert Galatea (Minneapolis: University of Minnesota Press, 1997), p. 150.

[12] Deleuze, *Cinema 2*, p. 150. Deleuze's '*fonction de fabulation*' is translated by Tomlinson and Galatea as 'story-telling function'. I have here modified that translation.

[13] Deleuze and Guattari, *What is Philosophy?*, p. 171.

[14] Deleuze, *Cinema 2*, p. 142.

every being, every action and passion, even every value, in relation to the life which they involve. Affect as immanent evaluation, instead of judgement as transcendent value'.[15] The genealogical critique of morals and the resulting transmutation of all values invoked by Nietzsche amount to a positive evaluation and search for the good life, rather than the life of the good and truthful, where the former is 'the kind which knows how to transform itself, to metamorphose itself according to the forces it encounters'.[16] And if artistic (including literary) creation is the highest and the most vital expression, that is because 'the creative artist takes the power of the false to a degree which is realized, not in form, but in transformation'.[17]

In the light of this theoretical discussion, I want to argue that *A Scots Quair*, Gibbon's great literary creation and signal contribution to modernism generally and to the Scottish Renaissance in particular, is thoroughly invested in this dual project of critique and transformation, of vital affirmation and creative 'invention of a people', in which history does not suffice and instead poses a moral, temporal, and political limit – indeed, is an obstacle to the emergent possibility of becoming.[18] This commitment is already apparent in the striking opening of the novel's prelude, entitled 'The Unfurrowed Field':

> Kinraddie lands had been won by a Norman childe, Cospatric de Gondeshil, in the days of William the Lyon, when gryphons and such-like beasts still roamed the Scots countryside and folk would waken in their beds to hear the children screaming, with a great wolf-beast, come through the hide window, tearing at their throats. In the Den of Kinraddie one such beast had its lair and by day it lay about the woods and the stench of it was awful to smell all over the countryside, and at gloaming a shepherd would see it, with its great wings half-folded across the great belly of it and its head, like the head of meikle cock, but with the ears of a lion, poked over a fir tree, watching. And it ate up sheep and men and women and was a fair terror, and the King had his heralds cry a reward to whatever knight would ride and end the mischieving of the beast.[19]

Timothy C. Baker has noted that this peculiar combination of history and myth, punctuated as it is by the 'heightened diction' of its 'pseudo-medieval

---

[15] Deleuze, *Cinema 2*, p. 141.

[16] Deleuze, *Cinema 2*, p. 141.

[17] Deleuze, *Cinema 2*, p. 146.

[18] Deleuze, *Cinema 2*, p. 150.

[19] Lewis Grassic Gibbon, *A Scots Quair*, ed. by Ian Campbell (Edinburgh: Polygon, 2006), p. 11.

tone', 'suggests the complexity of Gibbon's view of history'.[20] It may also be argued, somewhat more emphatically, that there is, in this playful invocation of a decidedly unhistorical past (complete with ferocious gryphons and knights in armour), a determination to situate temporality on the side of fabulation and against history understood as objective linearity – indeed, to invoke the 'powers of the false' as a vital resource for transformation, which is ultimately the ontological and political axis around which the novel is organised. Thus, the *sui generis* pseudo-history (or anti-history) with which 'The Unfurrowed Field' begins not only privileges a sense of place that will ultimately define the novel (for Kinraddie, as much as Chris Guthrie, is a protagonist in its own right) but also crucially roots it in a notion of time beyond or outside history.[21] The native people of this place, as we read, are 'common folk' of 'the old Pict stock' whose main defining trait is, once again, the fact that 'they had no history'.[22] What transpires from this succession of episodes semi-myth-ically rendered by the prelude is the alternative continuity of the land, which no historical narrative of continuity can properly capture. This is the land as lived and living setting, as place, but also as condition of possibility for the temporal and experiential violence of history, and therefore for the reality of transformation that accompanies it at every turn. Quite emphatically, across the arc of development that follows Chris Guthrie and the other characters in her fading peasant world, the land is the fulcrum and anchoring point of life, a life whose defining characteristic is precisely its untimeliness, its precariousness and mutability. Thus, Chris's mother, who tragically takes her own life as well as that of her baby twins early on, confides at one point: '*Oh, Chris, my lass, there are better things than your books or studies or loving or bedding, there's the countryside your own, you its, in the days when you're neither bairn nor woman*'.[23]

For Chris Guthrie, the founding contradiction is that between the unhistorical Scots tongue of the land, 'known and used' but also now 'forgotten in the far-off youngness' of a missing people, and the 'sharp and clean and true' English language of 'her reading and schooling'.[24] This is the

---

[20] Timothy C. Baker, '*A Scots Quair* and History', in *International Companion to Lewis Grassic Gibbon*, ed. by Scott Lyall (Glasgow: Scottish Literature International, 2015), p. 47.

[21] The novel's epilude, in a notable instantiation of the Nietzschean motif of the eternal return, also bears the title 'The Unfurrowed Field', which further underscores Gibbon's commitment to non-linear and anti-historical temporal structures, as well as a general privileging of space over time.

[22] Gibbon, *A Scots Quair*, p. 14.

[23] Gibbon, *A Scots Quair*, p. 37.

[24] Gibbon, *A Scots Quair*, p. 41.

conflict between a fixity that transcends the closeness, the affective density, of experience (and is thereby integrated into history) and a fluidity that may not be actual, that may indeed be missing, but that precisely for that reason inscribes its 'beauty' and 'sweetness' (those of the 'Scottish lands and skies', no less) with a higher degree of continuity and endurance than any linear-historical sense of time and identity.[25] Thus, the loss of the mother announces the loss of a universe of naïve and childish perceptions, a sense of permanence and at the same time an imaginary transcendence of the here and now. The truth that Chris learns with this death is not only, as the narrator puts it, that 'you'd never be the same again' but, crucially, that 'the world went on and you went with it'.[26] While the diffusionist narrative underpinning Gibbon's favoured interpretation of temporality naturally emphasises a thematic of decline at the heart of this experience of loss (it is worth noting that this 'world' that 'went on' is also, from the viewpoint of peasants like Chris's father, a 'world [that] was rolling fast to a hell of riches' in which 'the day of the crofter was fell near finished'), the deeper and more radical implication of her realisation, of her abrupt transition into adulthood, is precisely the idea that life, that being itself, *is* becoming.[27] And herein lies, perhaps, the crux of the novel's political ontology. It is interesting that this idea is framed (and, we could say, almost explicitly theorised) with a reference to the Greek philosopher Heraclitus's famous (and apocryphal) dictum 'panta rhei':

> [S]he minded Greek words of forgotten lessons, Παυτα ρει, *Nothing endures*. And then a queer thought came to her there in the drooked fields, that nothing endured at all, nothing but the land she passed across, tossed and turned and perpetually changed below the hands of the crofter folk since the oldest of them had set the Standing Stones by the loch of Blawearie and climbed there on their holy days and saw their terraced crops ride brave in the wind and sun.[28]

Set against the watery immediacy of the drenched fields below her feet, the rain, and the nearby echo of the sea, this realisation or revelation forms the core of the character's (and the novel's) politics of time and being, her radical affirmation of becoming, of transformation, as that which inheres in the land and its geological, anti-historical continuity. Interestingly, this notion of an affirmation of becoming, and therefore of life, is the superior value that Nietzsche also traces to Heraclitus in one of his earlier texts, *Philosophy in the*

[25] Gibbon, *A Scots Quair*, p. 41.
[26] Gibbon, *A Scots Quair*, p. 70.
[27] Gibbon, *A Scots Quair*, p. 82.
[28] Gibbon, *A Scots Quair*, pp. 122–123.

Tragic Age of the Greeks. As Deleuze comments in his study on the German philosopher, 'Heraclitus is the one for whom life is radically innocent and just ... Moreover *he made an affirmation of becoming* ... Heraclitus had taken a deep look, he had seen no chastisement of multiplicity, no expiation of becoming, no culpability of existence'.[29] The fluidity of being, its metamorphic and heterogeneous quality, is played out against and within the recursive, the returning, continuity of the land, which, as Gibbon's narrator confides, 'moved and changed below you, but was forever', dictating its cycles and punctuating the cyclicity of life itself.[30] For, as Deleuze asks apropos of Nietzsche's reading of Heraclitus, 'what is the being of becoming? What is the being inseparable from that which is becoming? *Return is the being of that which becomes*. Return is the being of becoming itself, the being which is affirmed in becoming'.[31]

It is true that this sense of unhistorical continuity is still experienced as in some ways constraining or limiting at this point – a sign that the binary oppositions of Chris's childhood universe have not been fully overcome. We read that she 'walked weeping then, stricken and frightened because of that knowledge that had come on her, she could never leave it, this life of toiling days and the needs of beasts ... she was bound and held as though they had prisoned her here'.[32] But this sense of cyclicity as entrapment will soon be replaced with a more properly Nietzschean (Heraclitean or Deleuzian) notion of return, of the 'eternal return' as the being of that which becomes and transforms itself, as the untimely temporality that proclaims, in Deleuze's words, 'the innocence of the future and the past', the present that 'coexist[s] with itself as past and yet to come'.[33] Thus, on a visit to Dunnottar Castle with her soon-to-be husband Ewan Tavendale, Chris is immediately haunted by a sense of closeness and intimacy with the oppressed of the past (from medieval prisoners to martyred Scottish Covenanters), 'sick and angry and sad for those folk she could never help now, that hatred of rulers and gentry a flame in her heart, John Guthrie's hate'.[34] For those defeated and forgotten had been '[h]er folk and his', a missing people whose predicament, and therefore existence, is not so much past – or indeed historical – as untimely in Nietzsche's sense, that is 'acting counter to our time'.[35]

---

[29] Gilles Deleuze, *Nietzsche and Philosophy*, trans. by Hugh Tomlinson (London: Bloomsbury, 2013), p. 22.

[30] Gibbon, *A Scots Quair*, p. 123.

[31] Deleuze, *Nietzsche and Philosophy*, p. 23.

[32] Gibbon, *A Scots Quair*, p. 123.

[33] Deleuze, *Nietzsche and Philosophy*, pp. 33, 45.

[34] Gibbon, *A Scots Quair*, p. 128.

[35] Friedrich Nietzsche, *Untimely Meditations*, trans. by R. J. Hollingdale (Cambridge: Cambridge University Press, 1997), p. 60.

This theme of an untimely, missing people is key. The changing reality of the peasant world of the Mearns that *Sunset Song* imagines, from the tragic loss of the desperate mother, and then of the brutal father, all the way to the collective destruction of a younger generation including Chris's husband Ewan in the First World War, revolves around this difficult perception of a historical void, of an absence of 'historical meaning' at the heart of an experience that is not only individual or private but also immediately political, even national, in an open and contingent sense.[36] The death of central characters such as Long Rob of the Mill or Chae Strachan ('killed in the first fighting of Armistice Day, an hour before the guns grew quiet') can only be described as untimely, against the sense and direction of history – not only a tragic accident but a disjunction, a dislocation emphasising the peripheral and minor status of their own position within the historical narrative.[37] This concerns the crucial relationship between art and the minorities famously described by Deleuze: 'Third world and minorities gave rise to authors who would be in a position, in relation to their nation and their personal situation in that nation, to say: the people are what is missing'.[38] Under such conditions, the resulting task 'is not that of addressing a people, which is presupposed already there, but of contributing to the invention of a people. The moment the master, or the colonizer, proclaims "There have never been a people here", the missing people are a becoming, they invent themselves'.[39] This is, of course, the task of the fabulating function to which the novel appeals directly at various points – most directly and strikingly, perhaps, in the prelude. If the epilude which closes off *Sunset Song*, and which, as we have seen, also bears the title 'The Unfurrowed Field', foregrounds this fabulating task by openly invoking the missing people, it does not do so without first inscribing a key alternative to this logic of becoming: that is, a purely messianic alternative, associated with the new minister Robert Colquohoun (who will become Chris's second husband in *Cloud Howe*). As the sermon that concludes the novel announces, what will replace this missing people, 'the Last of the Peasants, the last of the Old Scots folk', is precisely a 'new spirit' that 'shall come to the land with the greater herd and the great machines', a 'greater hope and a newer world'.[40] This is the Christian socialist vision that will be put to the test in the second novel of the trilogy.

Set in a mill town removed from the rural universe of *Sunset Song* and situated at the centre of the historical dynamics of the 1920s (most significantly,

---

[36] Deleuze, *Nietzsche and Philosophy*, p. 32.
[37] Gibbon, *A Scots Quair*, p. 247.
[38] Deleuze, *Cinema 2*, p. 217.
[39] Deleuze, *Cinema 2*, p. 217.
[40] Gibbon, *A Scots Quair*, pp. 254–255.

the industrial conflict that would climax in the General Strike of 1926), *Cloud Howe* traces an exploratory line connecting the diffusionist idea of a past Golden Age to the messianic, politico-theological notion of a redeemed future. Interestingly, these two ideological positions are fully reconciled in the characterisation of the socialist minister. For Robert, a Golden Age 'without fear or hope or hate or love' had come to an end '[*l*]*ess than four thousand years*' ago, inaugurating a properly historical age 'of kings and of Gods, all the dark, mad hopes that had haunted men since they left the caves and the hunting of deer, and the splendour of life like a song, like the wind'.[41] From the standpoint and experience of this fallen age, only a vertical redemption, a transcendence of historical time itself, can save humanity. Thus, according to Robert, 'the coming struggle in the month of May', that is, the General Strike and its revolutionary promise, may announce the 'beginning of the era of Man made free at last, Man who was God, Man splendid again'.[42] Dreaming on the Howe, on the land but also beyond the land, projecting a vision, as Chris immediately understands, is what this political theology of liberation can offer. There is a sharp contrast between these 'hunters of clouds that were such as was Robert' and the 'men of the earth that had been, that she'd known, who kept to the earth and their eyes upon it'.[43] Crucially, this makes her wonder (in a question that prefigures the failure of this transcendent, cloudy promise represented by Robert Colquohoun) 'how much was each wrong and how much each right, and was there maybe a third way to Life, unguessed, unhailed, never dreamed of yet?'[44] In other words, is there a properly fabulating alternative? If the defeat of the Strike is tangibly destructive in personal terms for these characters (it is important to note that Chris suffers a miscarriage), it also confirms the development of a more general tragedy, one that has been simmering throughout the novel: the reassertion of history, not only as a low and reactive age but as an overtly reactionary political project.

This is particularly noticeable in the scene where Mr Mowat, the mill owner, shares his vision of a fascist Scottish nation with Chris and Robert as he asks for their support in the upcoming struggle with the factory workers. Speaking in his elitist 'English bray' – as the housemaid Else describes it – he refers to the 'Rahly amazing' 'awakening' he had recently witnessed in Mussolini's Italy: 'Discipline, order, hierarchy—all that. And why only Italy; why not Scotland?'[45] The project is presented as programmatically invested

---

[41] Gibbon, *A Scots Quair*, p. 404.
[42] Gibbon, *A Scots Quair*, p. 405.
[43] Gibbon, *A Scots Quair*, p. 405.
[44] Gibbon, *A Scots Quair*, p. 405.
[45] Gibbon, *A Scots Quair*, pp. 368–369.

in a sense of historical continuity: 'Scotland a nation – that was the goal, with its old-time civilization and culture'.[46] At this point, Chris breaks her silence and retorts,

> *And what's going to happen when you and your kind rule us again, Mr Mowat? Was there ever the kind of Scotland you preach? – Happy, at ease, the folk on the land well-fed, the folk in the pulpits well-feared, the gentry doing great deeds? It's just a gab and a tale, no more, I haven't read history since I was at school, but I mind well enough what that Scotland was. I've been to Dunnottar Castle and seen there the ways that the gentry once liked to keep order. If it came to the push between you and the spinners I think I would give the spinners my vote.*[47]

We could say that this history against which Chris reacts is the fiction of power upon which its model of truth rests – that epistemic violence exerted by internal and external colonisers who declare the people missing: 'serfs and land-workers whom the Mowats rode down, whom the armies harried and kings spat on'.[48] What the novel goes on to demonstrate is that a proper strategy of resistance against 'that old darkness' threatening to return and 'torment the simple folk of her blood' cannot emerge from a traditionally messianic conception of time, from a vertical idea of redemption fixated on the clouds of an eschatological future while still secretly dreaming about a lost Golden Age.[49] Rather, its sources are – must be – telluric, geological, planted in the immanent continuities of the land and its people.

For the transcendent structure of truth embedded in religion, and institutionalised in the Kirk that Robert represents, is felt as fundamentally alien to the people – since the Scots (a minor people, a working people, removed from the authoritarian projections of a majoritarian nationalism) 'were never religious, had never BELIEVED as other folks did'.[50] Instead, there is that intimate conviction that accompanies Chris throughout her life that the earth is the sustaining basis and source, an origin that exceeds any sense of identity and closure: 'wider and stranger you knew it by far, from the earth's beginning *you yourself* had been here, a blowing of motes in the world's prime, earth, roots and the wings of an insect long syne in the days when the dragons still ranged the world'.[51] A fabulated origin, then, from which

[46] Gibbon, *A Scots Quair*, p. 369.
[47] Gibbon, *A Scots Quair*, p. 370.
[48] Gibbon, *A Scots Quair*, p. 370.
[49] Gibbon, *A Scots Quair*, p. 370.
[50] Gibbon, *A Scots Quair*, p. 317.
[51] Gibbon, *A Scots Quair*, p. 316.

the future (and the people) may (re)emerge, not as the fictional projection of power or the hopeful promise of transcendence, but as a 'hard and shining' continuity, 'unbreaking as rock'.[52]

At the heart of this vision of anti-historical time, there is the conviction that the 'life she lived now', a life still turned towards the possibilities and promises of historical redemption – 'waiting the sound of unhasting feet, waiting a Something unnamed' – 'could not go on'.[53] This is again contrasted to a diffusionist vision of a time before and against history, a nomadic and anarchic time of free men and women in which life was 'only *life*, swift, sharp, and sleepy and still, and an arm about you, life like a song, and a death at the end that was swift as well'.[54] Crucially, this evocation of an unhistorical Golden Age features, as part of its vitalist utopia, the vision of a good death (of a good feminist death, almost), ostensibly in contrast to the bad historical deaths of so many modern women: 'an hour of agony, or only a day, what woman feared death who had borne a child?'[55] But this immanent vision of death is even in sharper contrast to the great transcendent death of Robert Colquohoun that marks the ending of *Cloud Howe*. For the latter signals the sacrificial conclusion to which his religious socialism had pointed throughout the novel. Terminally ill, he rushes to the kirk and, in a final exertion, delivers his sermon, a grand theatrical reiteration of his messianic political faith in a *'sure creed that will cut like a knife'* and deliver, *'far off yet in the times to be, on an earth at peace, living and joyous, the christ come back'.*[56] He then dies spectacularly before his flock, a 'stream of blood from his lips' soaking 'all the pages of the Bible'.[57]

Interestingly, this tragic death (and the sacrificial logic it implies) is opposed, almost point by point, to Chris's vision of life as becoming. Without any explicit disavowal of Robert's mission or politics, her own trajectory and sense of life as constant transformation are reasserted emphatically: 'her last day in Segget ere she went elsewhere, to new days and ways, to changes she could not foresee or foreknow'.[58] This 'elsewhere', the setting of *Grey Granite*, will be the industrial city of Duncairn, while the 'new days and ways' will correspond to that unfolding future in which the political meaning of class conflict revolves around the historical role played by the Communist Party.

[52] Gibbon, *A Scots Quair*, p. 316.
[53] Gibbon, *A Scots Quair*, p. 448.
[54] Gibbon, *A Scots Quair*, p. 448.
[55] Gibbon, *A Scots Quair*, p. 449.
[56] Gibbon, *A Scots Quair*, p. 471.
[57] Gibbon, *A Scots Quair*, p. 472.
[58] Gibbon, *A Scots Quair*, p. 472.

The final novel in the trilogy can be read as the critical culmination of the bifurcating trajectories we observed in *Cloud Howe*. There is, on the one hand, the anti-historical cycle of continuity, the eternal return of and to the land, the earth, and the geological temporality of constant but intractable change. And on the other, the opening up of a vertical possibility of transcendence, with history as the condition of possibility and exclusive ambit of inscription of working-class experience. Chris's son Ewan will come to embody this second trajectory after initially incarnating the first (as the eponymous 'grey granite'). A worker at the local steelworks, Ewan gradually abandons his earlier diffusionist analysis of history and his youthful academic interest in geology for a socialist politics that turns openly Communist after he is arrested and tortured by the police. This is a key point in the novel – and the trilogy as a whole – for it signals the definitive reinscription of history as a specific and fully formed project of transcendence (going well beyond the failed attempts of the Christian socialist vision entertained in *Cloud Howe*). Ewan thus goes on to fully embrace the position outlined by Jim Trease, the Communist Party organiser, according to whom it is people like themselves, the class-conscious political vanguard, rather than the unreflecting, politically spontaneous workers of Duncairn, who are the working class: 'not a student, a historian, a tinkling reformer, but LIVING HISTORY ONESELF, being it, making it, eyes for the eyeless, hands for the maimed!'[59]

Shortly before breaking up with his girlfriend, Ellen Johns, due to her unwillingness to sacrifice a prospect of personal happiness with him in the name of socialism, Ewan puts it to her that joining the Party – and dissolving the ad hoc workers' league they had previously formed to support the strikers – would be '*[n]o good at all*' but rather a matter of historical necessity, not a tactical or even strategic calculation but a requisite concession to the teleology of a properly revolutionary temporality: '*we've just to go on with it, right to the end, History our master not the servant we supposed*'.[60] While Ellen becomes the target of Ewan's ire and misogynistic abuse, the real and final break in the novel is that between Ewan and Chris.[61] This is not a personal break as such, but one that goes to the heart of the trilogy's political ontology: a confrontation

---

[59] Gibbon, *A Scots Quair*, p. 620.

[60] Gibbon, *A Scots Quair*, p. 640.

[61] It is worth noting here that the 'majoritarian' version of socialism Ewan comes to embrace is violently patriarchal: 'He stood looking at [Ellen] coolly, not angered, called her a filthy name, consideringly, the name a keelie gives to a leering whore; and turned and walked down the hill from her sight', Gibbon, *A Scots Quair*, p. 664.

between two visions of time, life, and experience. In a key development, following Chris's third, brief and unsuccessful marriage, we read that

> She'd finished with men or the need for them, no more that gate might open in her heart, in her body and her soul, in welcome and gladness to any man. Quick and quick in the flying months she passed with hasting feet over ways that once had seemed everlasting: the need not only for a lover's caresses, but the need for anyone's liking, for care, kind words and safe eyes ... That dreadful storm she'd once visioned stripping her bare was all about her, and she feared it no longer, eager to be naked, alone and unfriended, facing the last realities with a cool, clear wonder, an unhasting desire.[62]

Virtually a reversal of Ewan's misogynistic rejection of Ellen, this affirmation of female autonomy as – precisely – the autonomy of becoming paves the way for the final exchange in the novel between mother and son, an exchange in which Ewan's conception of politics is explicitly assimilated to Robert Colquohoun's messianic position, to that vertical structure of belief and time of which Chris Guthrie has been sceptical from the beginning. Thinking about Robert's final sermon, Ewan asks if she remembered 'the creed he'd bade men seek out, a creed as clear and sharp as a knife? He'd never thought till this minute that that was what he himself had found'.[63] And she answers, '*The world's sought faiths for thousands of years and found only death or unease in them. Yours is just another dark cloud to me – or a great rock you're trying to push up a hill*'.[64] Crucially, he sums this up as '*the old fight that maybe will never have a finish, whatever the names we give to it ... between FREEDOM and GOD*'.[65] If this 'old fight' seems irresolvable or undecidable to Ewan, the novel is far less ambiguous in its conclusion, for it clearly accords primacy to Chris's position, reaffirming her visionary experience of freedom, once again, as one of pure becoming:

> Change who ruled the earth and the sky and the waters underneath the earth, Change whose face she'd once feared to see, whose right hand was Death and whose left hand Life, might be stayed by none of the dreams of men, love, hate, compassion, anger or pity, gods or devils or wild crying to the sky. He passed and repassed in the ways of the wind, Deliverer, Destroyer and Friend in one.[66]

[62] Gibbon, *A Scots Quair*, p. 659.
[63] Gibbon, *A Scots Quair*, p. 670.
[64] Gibbon, *A Scots Quair*, p. 670.
[65] Gibbon, *A Scots Quair*, p. 670.
[66] Gibbon, *A Scots Quair*, p. 672.

The decisive alternative, in *A Scots Quair*, is thus not between revolution or reform but between politics understood as judgement (as a theological function of historical truth) and politics understood as radical atheism and creative fabulation in the service of life.

The possibility of a life of becoming and contingency, of a true life without God, rests on the possibility of conceiving of death as a finite event in breach of the logic of infinite debt inscribed in judgement.[67] We get a significant glimpse of this in the extraordinary description of Ma Cleghorn's death in *Grey Granite*, which is worth quoting at some length:

> Ma Cleghorn was fighting her last fight with the world she had jeered at and sworn at throughout her life, gallant and vulgar, untamed to the end, her arms beating the air in this battle … And suddenly Ma's lips ceased to twist and slobber … and she stepped from the bed and out of the house and up long stairs that went wandering to Heaven … And she met at the Gates St. Peter himself … And she pushed him aside and took a keek in, and there was God with a plague in one hand and a war and a thunderbolt in the other and the Christ in glory with the angels bowing, and a scraping and banging of harps and drums, ministers thick as a swarm of blue-bottles, no sight of Jim and no sight of Jesus, only the Christ, and she wasn't impressed. And she said to St. Peter *This is no place for me*, and turned and went striding into the mists and across the fire-tipped clouds to her home.[68]

In many ways, this fabulatory account offers a direct counterpoint to the realistic description of Robert Colquohoun's sacrificial death at the end of *Cloud Howe*. The finitude and fullness of a woman's life sealed by self-affirming refusal is naturally aligned with the logic of fabulation, for it is precisely 'the power of the false of life', as Deleuze writes, that even in death can protect life from theological transcendence.[69] For what is at stake, in the face of the verticality of judgement, of History (the secular God invoked by the Communists in the novel) and the sort of redemptive necessity it entails, is the possibility of becoming – of becoming-woman, of becoming-minoritarian – without the imposition of a fixed identity or outcome. This is a radically

---

[67] 'Man does not appeal to judgement, he judges and is judgable only to the extent that his existence is subject to an infinite debt: the infinity of the debt and the immortality of existence each depend on the other, and together constitute "the doctrine of judgement"', Gilles Deleuze, *Essays Critical and Clinical*, trans. by Daniel W. Smith and Michael A. Greco (London: Verso, 1998), p. 126.

[68] Gibbon, *A Scots Quair*, pp. 585–586.

[69] Deleuze, *Cinema 2*, p. 141.

different path, of course, from the majoritarian logic of the political inscribed in the universal class subject assumed by traditional readings of socialist and proletarian literature.[70] In its refusal of the limiting truth claims of a subject of history, Gibbon's vision in *A Scots Quair* calls for a differential power of the political imagination, one whose untimeliness and 'resistance to the present' situates the people as that which is missing and therefore that which has to be invented and composed, at every turn, as a heterogeneous and contingent assemblage.[71]

2.2 Between Life and Flight: Orwell in the 1930s

I want to turn now to another prominent socialist of the 1930s whose writing similarly registers a theory of the political that is fundamentally at odds with orthodox conceptions of historical necessity: George Orwell. I will begin with a discussion of *Down and Out in Paris and London*, where we encounter Orwell's idiosyncratic engagement with poverty, before turning to his key contributions to socialist debate in the 1930s – *The Road to Wigan Pier* and *Homage to Catalonia* – and then, finally, to his crowing fictional achievement of the decade *Coming Up for Air*.

Orwell's 1933 memoir *Down and Out in Paris and London* is a gritty account of his experiences among the French and English lumpenproletariat in the 1920s. The logic of social heterogeneity on which, as we have seen, the notion of the lumpenproletariat is formally predicated is here explored through a radically empirical approach of ethnographic immersion in which the ideological or narrative coherence and signification of the resulting text is of secondary importance to the sensory and affective intensities of the experiential description.[72] The series of vignettes which make up the bulk of

---

[70] As Nick Hubble observes, there 'is a tendency among male critics of *Grey Granite* to read Gibbon's depiction of the "mobilised Left" as evidence of a failure to understand the industrial working class rather than as a trenchant critique of narrow proletarian politics'. And they add, 'Unsurprisingly, therefore, most of the best critical work on the novel has been written by feminists', *The Proletarian Answer to the Modernist Question* (Edinburgh: Edinburgh University Press, 2017), p. 114.

[71] Deleuze and Guattari, *What is Philosophy?*, p. 108. Rosi Braidotti offers a good summary of the political relevance of this concept to contemporary debates when she writes, 'The only effective materialism today being the politics of radical immanence, the task of critical theory consists in activating subjects to enter into new affective transversal assemblages, to co-create alternative ethical forces and political codes – in other words, to compose a missing people', 'A Theoretical Framework for the Critical Posthumanities', *Theory, Culture & Society* 36:6 (2019), p. 49.

[72] For a discussion of the ethnographic quality of Orwell's work, see Michael

the book resist easy generic categorisation (such is the fiction-like emphasis on characterisation in this alleged 'memoir') and offer a sharp qualitative contrast to the often awkward sociological commentary offered by the authorial voice. Through its formal unevenness and structural disorganisation, *Down and Out* seems to hint at what is arguably Orwell's principal insight at this early stage in his career: the notion – which is, as I have noted, also central to Gibbon – that class is an eminently heterogeneous and contingent entity without a necessary historical mission.

Orwell's opening description of 'a representative Paris slum' focuses on the 'eccentric characters' making up the 'floating population' of lodgers at the Hôtel des Trois Moineaux.[73] Orwell insists that the 'Paris slums are a gathering-place for eccentric people', thereby underlining the peculiar typicality of his chosen setting and its inhabitants. These, he writes, are 'people who have fallen into solitary, half-mad grooves of life and given up trying to be normal or decent', people who 'lived lives that were curious beyond words'.[74] Poverty, in this case, acts as a paradoxically liberating force, 'free[ing] them from ordinary standards of behaviour, just as money frees people from work'.[75] From the 'old ragged, dwarfish couple who plied an extraordinary trade' by selling fake pornographic postcards to the 'melancholy man' 'who worked in the sewers' and almost never spoke, down to the Englishman who 'drank four litres of wine a day, and six litres on Saturdays', these 'queer lives' form the social tapestry of Orwell's 'first contact with poverty'.[76]

For all its ethnographic intent, this is a descriptive strategy that harks back to a traditional method of novelistic characterisation associated with nineteenth-century realism. As Carolyn Lesjak has argued in an important discussion of Dickens, the Victorian writer 'drew significantly on an earlier tradition of typification and caricature' associated with eighteenth-century 'eccentric biographies' or 'character books', a genre of 'anecdotal stories about remarkable or curious characters and personalities, both historical and fantastical'.[77] By adapting this older formula in fictional universes peopled by singular

Amundsen, 'George Orwell's Ethnographies of Experience: *The Road to Wigan Pier* and *Down and Out in Paris and London*', *Anthropological Journal of European Cultures* 25:1 (2016), pp. 9–25.

[73] George Orwell, *Down and Out in Paris and London* (London: Penguin, 2001), pp. 2–3.

[74] Orwell, *Down and Out*, p. 3.

[75] Orwell, *Down and Out*, p. 3.

[76] Orwell, *Down and Out*, pp. 3–5.

[77] Carolyn Lesjak, *The Afterlife of Enclosure: British Realism, Character, and the Commons* (Stanford, CA: Stanford University Press, 2021), p. 48.

and extraordinary characters, Dickens 'refigure[s] the common by linking it to the memorable' and thereby opposes 'the forces of homogenization that increasingly define nineteenth-century commodity culture'.[78] Orwell's point of departure can be connected to Dickens's strategy (which he would go on to discuss in a famous essay), although what is arguably at stake in his case is not resistance to homogenisation in Lesjak's sense so much as a refusal to present the heterogeneity of poverty as an experiential void.[79] For Orwell, poverty is not (only) the unimaginable abyss of nineteenth-century fallen outcasts but indeed a combination – to use Lesjak's language – of the common and the memorable. The remarkable and the singular form the background to a sensory fullness that is not so much unthinkable as quietly intense and painfully ordinary. Take the following passage:

> It is altogether curious, your first contact with poverty. You have thought so much about poverty – it is the thing you have feared all your life, the thing you knew would happen to you sooner or later; and it is all so utterly and prosaically different. You thought it would be quite simple; it is extraordinarily complicated. You thought it would be terrible; it is merely squalid and boring. It is the peculiar *lowness* of poverty that you discover first; the shifts that it puts you to, the complicated meanness, the crust-wiping.[80]

The centre of this experiential description, the core from which the colourful heterogeneity of the character catalogue radiates, as it were, is precisely the affective intensity that distinguishes Orwell's empiricist method. John Michael Roberts has offered a persuasive theoretical corrective to those critics who see in Orwell a naïve empiricist crudely relying on simplistic notions of transparent experience where 'truth can simply be apprehended through our senses'.[81] According to Roberts, a more accurate and critically productive understanding of Orwell's emphasis on experience may be obtained by placing him in relation to the sophisticated version of empiricism developed by Deleuze. This is an

[78] Lesjak, *The Afterlife of Enclosure*, pp. 48, 58.

[79] To some extent, Orwell anticipates Lesjak's critical commentary when he remarks that Dickens's characters are often 'completely fantastic and incredible' 'monstrosities', and for that very reason ultimately 'more solid and infinitely more memorable' than those of 'serious novelists', 'Charles Dickens', in *The Complete Works of George Orwell: A Patriot After All, 1940–1941* (London: Secker & Warburg, 1998), p. 52.

[80] Orwell, *Down and Out*, p. 13.

[81] John Michael Roberts, 'Reading Orwell Through Deleuze', *Deleuze Studies* 4:3 (2010), p. 358.

empiricism that 'seeks to understand the forces of potential within the world, how these forces contingently assemble together during specific events, and how they impact on our sensations at a pre-subjective and pre-personal level'.[82] Orwell's purpose, then, is not so much to 'impose [his] "sensory reason" upon the world to arrive at "objective truth"' as to explore the bodily affects that unravel and transform sedimented social identities and power relations.[83] A prime example of this empiricist orientation can be found in his account of hunger in *Down and Out in Paris and London*:

> You discover what it is like to be hungry. With bread and margarine in your belly, you go out and look into the shop windows. Everywhere there is food insulting you in huge, wasteful piles [...] You discover the boredom which is inseparable from poverty; the times when you have nothing to do and, being underfed, can interest yourself in nothing. For half a day at a time you lie on your bed, feeling like the *jeune squelette* in Baudelaire's poem. Only food could rouse you. You discover that a man who has gone even a week on bread and margarine is not a man any longer, only a belly with a few accessory organs.[84]

In this passage, the linguistic and conceptual significations of hunger are secondary to the affects that define it in a particular embodiment. In true Deleuzian fashion, Orwell's hungry body ceases to operate as a 'determinate substance or subject' through 'the organs it possesses or the functions it fulfils' and becomes instead a plane of intensity defined, in this case, by affects of boredom and inertia: an immanent 'body without organs', in Deleuze and Guattari's famous formulation – that is, a body without organisation, without functional integration or subordination to the personal and the subjective.[85]

Precisely because of this refusal of subjectivation, the solipsistic privacy of destitution can be socialised and reinscribed in collective terms, for this starving body, as Orwell's second-person point of view announced earlier on, is a collective one: 'Thousands of people in Paris live it – struggling artists and students, prostitutes when their luck is out, out-of-work people of all kinds'.[86] A crucial dimension here is the specific temporality that attends upon the experience of poverty: 'For, when you are approaching poverty, you make one discovery which outweighs some of the others. You discover boredom and mean complications and the beginnings of hunger, but you also discover the

---

[82] Roberts, 'Reading Orwell Through Deleuze', p. 359.
[83] Roberts, 'Reading Orwell Through Deleuze', p. 359.
[84] Orwell, *Down and Out*, p. 15.
[85] Deleuze and Guattari, *A Thousand Plateaus*, p. 287.
[86] Orwell, *Down and Out*, p. 15.

great redeeming feature of poverty: the fact that it annihilates the future'.[87] This is different from Tressell's representational strategy, where the great fear of poverty lay in its imagined futurity: in a bottomless capacity to anticipate and announce horrors yet to come. For the Orwell of *Down and Out*, by contrast, the experiential compression of destitution removes this temporal dimension: 'When you have only three francs you are quite indifferent; for three francs will feed you till tomorrow, and you cannot think further than that'.[88] There is a reluctance here to place futurity above the immediacy of affective intensities and the distinctive versions of sociality that may be derived from them. Yet this privileging of sensation is far from necessarily affirmative. On the contrary, Orwell's invocation of an immanent experience is often rooted in gestures of repulsion. The effect, however, is one that tends to situate the body, always inescapably material because never comfortably subjectivised and 'bourgeois', at its centre.

In a similar vein, *The Road to Wigan Pier*, Orwell's 1937 account of unemployment in the North of England, begins with a notorious description of the affective traces of industrial poverty. The 'filthy' boarding house where old age pensioners and unemployed workers lie in varying states of prostration and destitution offers a catalogue of sensations accompanying and ultimately defining (non)working life in the Great Depression. An alternation between uninhabitable spaces and disabled bodies captures the essence of this socio-historical condition. The rhetorical effect is undoubtedly harsh, and the history of this book's reception is branded with accusations of middle-class prejudice and condescension, but the hammering insistence on dirty hands and vile smells, on 'stagnant meaningless decay' and 'mean grievances' is part of a deliberate process that is neither exclusively rhetorical nor expressive of a vulgar unconscious bias and whose proper political horizon is the definition of a socialism rooted in the contingency of sensation and experience.[89] That the body takes precedence through a series of inescapable sensorial effects indicates that no gesture of evasion through the affirmation of a predetermined identity can truly distort or obfuscate the immediacy of the social crisis.

I want to argue that this idea is absolutely key to Orwell's political vision in the mid-1930s, especially in *The Road to Wigan Pier*, a vision that will see him break with his middle-class identity while at the same time rejecting what he regards as its ideological colonisation of socialism. A central aspect of this rejection concerns Orwell's understanding of the reality of left-wing

---

[87] Orwell, *Down and Out*, p. 16.

[88] Orwell, *Down and Out*, p. 16.

[89] George Orwell, *The Road to Wigan Pier*, in *Orwell's England*, ed. by Peter Davison (Harmondsworth: Penguin, 2001), p. 65.

politics in the interwar period as, ultimately, little more than an extension of the exploitative dynamics of the economic system. We can usefully think about this central preoccupation in *The Road to Wigan Pier* with the help of Giorgio Agamben's theorisation of the relationship between life and politics in Western culture.

According to Agamben, our concept of the political rests on a fundamental division operating, since classical antiquity, at the heart of the notion of 'life'. The emergence of politically qualified life (*bios*), that life which is capable of participation in the public sphere of the *polis* and which is endowed with agency and identity, is only possible as the result of a process of separation and partition within the heart of natural, pre-social life (*zoè*). The qualification of life as social and political thus necessarily implies the generation of a residue which is destined to exist in a state of absolute exposure and conditionality (in a 'state of exception'), a purely biological or 'bare' life forever dependent on the sovereign will of politically qualified life. But what is the exact content of this political qualification? In other words, what is the nature of Western politics, according to Agamben? None 'other than the pure fact of the caesura as such'.[90] The included, autonomous, and identity-bound life of the political is thus nothing but the effect of a 'series of partitions that pass through the very body of *zoè*'.[91] If the systematic destruction and defilement of the excluded and exploited body of, for example, the unemployed (in the absolute reduction of their life to a state of infinite vulnerability) is the condition upon which not only a predatory system but also a supposedly enlightened politics arises, the latter cannot then be truly regarded as transformative (let alone revolutionary), at least not until its focus becomes the undoing of those partitions and the generation of an indivisible form of life – or, as Agamben puts it, '*form-of-life*'. This is a key concept for this thinker and indeed one that can help us make sense of Orwell's emphatic insistence, in the mid-1930s, on the formlessness of industrial civilization. 'With the term *form-of-life*', writes Agamben, 'we understand a life that can never be separated from its form, a life in which it is never possible to isolate and keep distinct something like a bare life'.[92] This is a way of imagining human life as never merely a series of isolable facts 'but always and above all [as] *possibilities* of life, always and above all potential'.[93] For Agamben, these possibilities and this potential are best thought of in terms of habit (or 'habitual use').

---

[90] Giorgio Agamben, *The Use of Bodies*, trans. by Adam Kotsko (Stanford, CA: Stanford University Press, 2016), p. 203.

[91] Agamben, *The Use of Bodies*, p. 203.

[92] Agamben, *The Use of Bodies*, p. 207.

[93] Agamben, *The Use of Bodies*, p. 207.

Orwell is, of course, far removed from the philosophical concerns and language that occupy Agamben, but there is nevertheless a striking air of familiarity, I would argue, in the way that the possibility of an undivided and habit-based vindication of life informs Orwell's critical engagement with industrial modernity. Indeed, Orwell's central moral indictment in *The Road to Wigan Pier* concerns the destruction of what could be described as the *form* of working-class life in the industrial districts, the ravaging of its habits and possibilities and its reduction to a series of mere facts (unemployment statistics, for example) and, ultimately, to a dehumanising experience of bare life. In this sense, the owners of the lodging house with which Orwell opens his account, the 'disgusting' Brookers, are 'one of the characteristic by-products of the modern world'.[94] This is a world defined by 'labyrinthine slums and dark back kitchens with sickly, ageing people creeping round and round them like blackbeetles', a world in which '[s]lag-heaps and chimneys seem a more normal, probable landscape than grass and trees'.[95] The first task of a socialist, then, is to confront the realities of this savage division, of this violent caesura, enabling the rise of a politically qualified, supposedly civilised, life. And it is essential to do so in a decidedly empiricist way – that is, with a focus on sensation: 'It is a kind of duty to see and smell such places again and again, especially smell them, lest you should forget that they exist'.[96]

Yet for Orwell it is important to insist that this state of being is not the native condition of the working class. Even if in a 'crowded, dirty little country like ours one takes defilement almost for granted', and although the seeds of industrial capitalism are clearly planted in this social and human devastation, there is a deep intimation of form, of habitual and undivided life, in the working class that contests the divisive socio-political logic which created it in the first place.[97] Orwell dwells on this vision of working-class life in stridently heteronormative (and not infrequently misogynistic) language, with clearly defined gender roles underpinning the 'admirable, perhaps even hopeful' continuation of 'normal life' among the unemployed workers of the industrial north.[98] The conservative quality of this form of life in Orwell's account is undeniable, but what is interesting is the fact that this ability to reclaim form from the brutal formlessness of capitalism appears to belong exclusively to the exploited, to the working class. In the best of times, that

[94] Orwell, *Wigan Pier*, p. 66.
[95] Orwell, *Wigan Pier*, pp. 66–67.
[96] Orwell, *Wigan Pier*, p. 66.
[97] Orwell, *Wigan Pier*, p. 67.
[98] Orwell, *Wigan Pier*, p. 115.

is when employment is available, working-class 'home life' is adorned with qualities of warmth, decency, and humanity that are 'not so easy to find elsewhere'.[99] These qualities are ultimately traceable to the 'sane' and 'comely shape', to the 'peculiar easy completeness' of this life, and thus to the inexhaustible potential – to adapt Agamben's terminology – that endures in its habitual uses: 'a working-class family life sitting round the coal fire after kippers and strong tea', as he puts it.[100] There is an emphatically immanent temporality to this working-class life, a sense that this fully formed experience can only belong to the immediate present and therefore that both the past and the future (but especially the future) constitute *de-forming* interferences: 'Skip forward two hundred years into the Utopian future, and the scene is completely different'.[101] The anti-utopian theme of *Nineteen Eighty-Four*, that fictional climax in Orwell's investigation of the modern demolition of forms of life, is announced here with considerable precision.

Orwell's celebratory focus on coal miners – and especially miners' bodies – in a previous section of *The Road to Wigan Pier* similarly expresses, in addition to the obvious and widely discussed androcentrism of his general approach, an obsessive search for form (indeed for 'comely shape' and 'easy completeness', in the telling phrases quoted above), at the very heart of industrial capitalism's violent formlessness.[102] Paradoxically, what is to be found on the other side of the class divide, among the middle class supposedly reaping the benefits of this mode of production under their command, is a version of the formlessness defining the system itself. For middle-class life is characterised by authoritarianism, a lack of fellowship, and ultimately by 'spiritual' fragility. Thus, for example, 'A working-class family hangs together as a middle-class one does, but the relationship is far less tyrannical'. Moreover, 'a middle-class person goes utterly to pieces under the influence of poverty; and this is generally due to the behaviour of his family – to the fact that he has scores of relations nagging and badgering him night and day for failing to "get on"'.[103] For Orwell, the political implications of this 'natural' disposition are immediately apparent: 'The fact that the working-class know

---

[99] Orwell, *Wigan Pier*, p. 135.

[100] Orwell, *Wigan Pier*, p. 136.

[101] Orwell, *Wigan Pier*, p. 136.

[102] On Orwell's androcentrism, see, for example, Daphne Patai, *The Orwell Mystique: A Study in Male Ideology* (Amherst: University of Massachusetts Press, 1984) and Beatrix Campbell, 'Orwell – Paterfamilias or Big Brother?', in *Inside the Myth. Orwell: Views from the Left*, ed. by Christopher Norris (London: Lawrence & Wishart, 1984), pp. 126–138.

[103] Orwell, *Wigan Pier*, p. 134.

how to combine and the middle class don't is probably due to their different conceptions of family loyalty'.[104]

It is evident that Orwell's analysis of working-class conditions in his earlier work, especially in the first half of *The Road to Wigan Pier*, builds up to this conclusion: that the 'road' to socialism requires a break with and a departure from his own class. But this is a departure, a flight, that does not automatically equate with an embrace of a working-class identity (or form of life) that is manifestly not his own. Rather, fleeing remains the politically – as much as artistically – creative focus of Orwell's engagement with socialism in this period. Deleuze's theorisation of flight is particularly relevant here. As he writes, for example, in an essay entitled 'On the Superiority of Anglo-American Literature', 'to flee is not to renounce action: nothing is more active than a flight'.[105] Flight is exploratory and creative, but never evasive. It is not an attempt to make 'an exit from the world' but a search for new worlds by tracing lines, by drawing 'a whole cartography', and, ultimately, by 'creat[ing] a new Earth'.[106] According to Deleuze, writing enjoys an 'intrinsic relationship with lines of flight' insofar as writing involves 'becom[ing] something else'.[107] This is why writing, 'when it is not official', is minoritarian.[108] Not in the sense that writing is the preserve of a numerical minority or elite but, on the contrary, in the sense that writing implies an encounter with 'those who do not have it', with a 'minority' (whatever its numbers) 'which does not write', and which in turn 'give writing a becoming without which it would not exist, without which it would be pure redundancy in the service of the powers that be'.[109] I think this theoretical argument is immediately applicable to Orwell's position as a writer in the 1930s. For Orwell, the act of writing is, strictly speaking, tantamount to the tracing of a line of flight from the fraudulent world of middle-class life and, in so doing, to the discovery of a working class that he will not seek to represent or speak for but rather engage with in a process of 'becoming' – an encounter, as Deleuze notes, 'in which each pushes the other, draws it on to its line of flight in a combined deterritorialization'.[110] The result of this deterritorialisation, of this writerly becoming,

---

[104] Orwell, *Wigan Pier*, pp. 134–135.

[105] Gilles Deleuze and Claire Parnet, 'On the Superiority of Anglo-American Literature', in *Dialogues II*, trans. by Hugh Tomlinson and Barbara Habberjam (New York: Columbia University Press, 2007), p. 36.

[106] Deleuze and Parnet, 'Anglo-American Literature', p. 36.

[107] Deleuze and Parnet, 'Anglo-American Literature', p. 43.

[108] Deleuze and Parnet, 'Anglo-American Literature', p. 43.

[109] Deleuze and Parnet, 'Anglo-American Literature', p. 44.

[110] Deleuze and Parnet, 'Anglo-American Literature', p. 44.

is what Orwell will refer to as socialism in *The Road to Wigan Pier*, at this point still a doctrinally rather vague label but nevertheless a precise marker of the transformation defining his political trajectory in the 1930s.[111]

Reflecting on his journey from imperial policeman in Burma (the subject of his first novel, *Burmese Days*) to 'down and out' writer in Paris and London, Orwell writes about his intense if undefined sense of injustice and his instinctive determination 'to escape not merely from imperialism but from every form of man's dominion over man', 'to get right down among the oppressed, to be one of them and on their side against their tyrants'.[112] In a rather abstract sense, the English working class 'supplied an analogy ... playing the same part in England as the Burmese played in Burma'.[113] And yet, knowing 'nothing about working-class conditions', Orwell writes, 'my mind turned immediately towards the extreme cases, the social outcasts: tramps, beggars, criminals, prostitutes ... What I profoundly wanted, at that time, was to find some way of getting out of the respectable world altogether': in other words, to trace a line of flight, to set in motion a deterritorialising process, out of which a new social reality, beyond inequality and oppression, may be created.[114] Orwell emphasises here the strategic necessity of flight, without which the transformative journey that may lead to a genuinely classless world is unthinkable. An important argument in this part of the book is that if mingling with tramps is a naïve instinctive response that does little towards solving the real structural problem, then embracing a certain image or idea of the working class, in the manner of many a middle-class socialist, is similarly ineffective and perhaps even more pernicious. The task ahead for someone like Orwell is grasping the fact 'that to abolish class-distinctions means abolishing a part of yourself':

> For to get outside the class-racket I have got to suppress not merely my private snobbishness, but most of my other tastes and prejudices as well. I have got to alter myself so completely that at the end I should hardly be recognizable as the same person. What is involved is not merely the amelioration of working-class conditions, nor an avoidance

[111] In an important book, Alex Woloch has insisted on the centrality of Orwell's formal choices as a writer to his conception of socialism: 'we need to align Orwell's politics with his expressed understanding of writing itself, his sense of its dynamics and vicissitudes, and his specific, strategic engagement with – and experiments in – writerly form', *Or Orwell: Writing and Democratic Socialism* (Cambridge, MA: Harvard University Press, 2016), p. 8.

[112] Orwell, *Wigan Pier*, p. 158.

[113] Orwell, *Wigan Pier*, p. 158.

[114] Orwell, *Wigan Pier*, p. 159.

of the more stupid forms of snobbery, but a complete abandonment of the upper-class and middle-class attitude to life.[115]

Orwell insists on the insincerity of middle-class socialists who either 'enthuse over the proletariat' in vacuous declarations of principle and occasional rituals of inter-class fellowship or who directly suggest 'level[ling] the working class "up" (up to his own standard) by means of hygiene, fruit-juice, birth-control, poetry, etc.'[116] The falsity of this stance (the 'smell of crankishness', in Orwell's notorious phrase), stems from the fact that middle-class socialism is constructed upon a fundamental refusal to break with and deterritorialise its own class bearings.[117] This is not only hypocritical but also a serious limitation in terms of the political vision on offer, for what this socialism then amounts to is 'a hypertrophied sense of order' which more than anything else betrays the overbearing middle-class prejudice of its proponents.[118] Thus, the 'present state of affairs offends them not because it causes misery, still less because it makes freedom impossible, but because it is untidy'.[119] From this standpoint, 'revolution does not mean a movement of the masses with which they hope to associate themselves; it means a set of reforms which "we", the clever ones, are going to impose upon "them", the Lower Orders'.[120] This is the crux of Orwell's critical reversal of what he regards as the dominant form of socialist discourse in *The Road to Wigan Pier*. The assumption of order, with its fully mechanised and efficient vision of the world, a vision that appeals essentially to bourgeois individuals (and whose literary model is, for Orwell, H. G. Wells), is precisely what the socialist line of flight, with its genuinely revolutionary creativity, should threaten and put at risk.[121]

The decisive step for Orwell's discovery of socialism will come, of course, at the end of 1936, with his arrival in Spain a few months after the outbreak of the Civil War. In *Homage to Catalonia*, the book that resulted from this

---

[115] Orwell, *Wigan Pier*, p. 167.

[116] Orwell, *Wigan Pier*, p. 168.

[117] As he further notes, 'our proletarian brothers – in so far as we understand them – are not asking for our greetings, they are asking us to commit suicide. When the bourgeois sees it in *that* form he takes to flight, and if his flight is rapid enough it may carry him to Fascism', Orwell, *Wigan Pier*, p. 172.

[118] Orwell, *Wigan Pier*, p. 179.

[119] Orwell, *Wigan Pier*, p. 179.

[120] Orwell, *Wigan Pier*, p. 180.

[121] Orwell, *Wigan Pier*, pp. 188–189. For Orwell's complex relationship with the Wellsian legacy, see John S. Partington, 'The Pen as Sword: George Orwell, H. G. Wells and Journalistic Parricide', *Journal of Contemporary History* 39:1 (2004), pp. 45–56.

experience and that in many ways represents the high-water mark of his political-literary development, the vague sentiments of socialist 'decency' evoked in his earlier writing become an embodied and ever intensifying affective reality.[122] Orwell's account opens with a description of the heady revolutionary 'atmosphere' (a term that, through repetition, becomes central to the description) in Barcelona, 'a town where the working class was in the saddle' and in which, at least at first sight, 'the wealthy classes had practically ceased to exist'.[123] Far from registering the experience as the practical enactment of an abstract emancipatory rationality or revolutionary programme, Orwell emphasises the affective dislocation, the deterritorialising quality of the social transformation around him: 'All this was queer and moving. There was much in it that I did not understand, in some ways I did not even like it, but I recognized it immediately as a state of affairs worth fighting for'.[124] Although initially intending to join the Communist-controlled International Brigade, Orwell finds himself in the midst of the revolutionary process led by the Anarchists and the POUM (the dissident, semi-Trotskyist Workers' Party of Marxist Unification, with whose militia he would serve in Aragón), in 'a sort of microcosm of a classless society', 'something strange and valuable' and indeed 'a community where hope was more normal than apathy or cynicism, where the word "comrade" stood for comradeship and not, as in most countries, for humbug'.[125]

For Orwell, the crucial aspect of this experience will be the full realisation, beyond his earlier intuitions in *The Road to Wigan Pier*, of the fundamental incompatibility between the two available models of socialism: on the one hand, the efficient and ordered vision represented by the Communists and, on the other, the radically democratic practice of the Anarchists. Thus, while the Anarchists' strictly doctrinal 'principles were rather vague their hatred of privilege and injustice was perfectly genuine'.[126] It is for this reason, according to Orwell, that '[p]hilosophically, Communism and Anarchism are poles apart'.[127] The vision of society, of a socialist society, embraced by each of them is contrasting in a 'quite irreconcilable' way: 'The Communist's

---

[122] According to Raymond Williams, '*Homage to Catalonia* is in some ways Orwell's most important and most moving book. It is an unforgettably vivid personal account of a revolution and a civil war', *Orwell* (London: Fontana/Collins, 1971), p. 59. See also John Newsinger, *Orwell's Politics* (Basingstoke: Palgrave, 1999).

[123] George Orwell, *Homage to Catalonia* (London: Penguin, 2000), pp. 2–3.

[124] Orwell, *Homage to Catalonia*, p. 3.

[125] Orwell, *Homage to Catalonia*, pp. 84, 83.

[126] Orwell, *Homage to Catalonia*, p. 204.

[127] Orwell, *Homage to Catalonia*, p. 204.

emphasis is always on centralism and efficiency, the Anarchist's on liberty and equality'.[128] Orwell does not conceal his sympathy for the Anarchist (and the similar POUM) position, even while he admits to his initial identification with the Communist argument of prioritising the war effort over the social revolution. But beyond the specific details of his historical chronicle, with its culminating episode in the open armed conflict between the revolutionary groups and the Communist-led Republican forces in May 1937, and in the subsequent suppression of the POUM and general persecution of revolutionary elements upon which Orwell dwells in the second half of the book, what stands out is the decisive pursuit of a politically creative line of flight, no longer just breaking with the trappings and falsehoods of bourgeois subjectivity in its colonisation of socialist discourse, but practically, experientially, and experimentally addressing the concrete stand-off between Communism as a majoritarian, regimented State form and libertarian socialism as a nomadic war machine.[129] In the final account, the difference is not one of degree or 'emphasis' (as Orwell had initially put it) but an ontological, as much as historical, split: a matter of becoming – of becoming-revolutionary – and its fundamental incompatibility with the State.

In this sense, Orwell's references to the armed conflict between the revolutionaries and the Republican forces in Barcelona are key. This is a conflict between 'splendid troops' (whom, Orwell admits, he 'could not help liking') and 'the sleek police', on the one hand, and the 'ragged soldiers' of the militias as well as local people from the 'working-class quarters' (which 'were solidly Anarchist'), on the other.[130] As a result, the 'issue was clear enough': 'On one side the C.N.T. [the Anarchist union], on the other side the police. I have no particular love for the idealized "worker" as he appears in the bourgeois

---

[128] Orwell, *Homage to Catalonia*, p. 204.

[129] This is not, of course, to suggest that the anti-Stalinist, libertarian factions Orwell associates with are in any way defined by the mechanisation (a function of the totalitarian regimentation) that in turn characterises the Communists. In the strict Deleuzo-Guattarian sense, it will be remembered, a machine 'surpass[es] any kind of mechanics', *A Thousand Plateaus*, p. 562. Moreover, the logic of the nomadic war machine, insofar as it demarcates that external limit which the State seeks to appropriate and internalise, is fundamentally averse to discipline: 'We certainly would not say that discipline is what defines a war machine: discipline is the characteristic required of armies after the State has appropriated them. The war machine answers to other rules. We are not saying that they are better, of course, only that they animate a fundamental indiscipline of the warrior, a questioning of hierarchy ... which ... impedes the formation of the State', *A Thousand Plateaus*, p. 395.

[130] Orwell, *Homage to Catalonia*, pp. 125, 112.

Communist's mind, but when I see an actual flesh-and-blood worker in conflict with his natural enemy, the policeman, I do not have to ask myself which side I am on'.[131] While the moral outrage of the ex-imperial policeman is immediately detectable in this passage, what is at stake here is much more than a simple moral choice or alternative. There is also, crucially, the unleashing of what Deleuze and Guattari call a power of exteriority, an outside in genetic contact and tension with the State, which the latter cannot fully control: 'The State is sovereignty. But sovereignty only reigns over what it is capable of internalizing, of appropriating locally'.[132] In this sense, 'bands' (of the sort that Orwell describes, with the pejorative connotation but also with the implication of their being closer to a true revolutionary logic) 'imply a form irreducible to the State' whose 'exteriority necessarily presents itself as a diffuse and polymorphous war machine'.[133] With this first-hand experience of the actual confrontation between a totalitarian State apparatus and an essentially anarchistic, decentralised, and nomadic version of socialism, Orwell's political and literary line of flight reaches a decisive stage.

The years 1938–1939 are usually regarded as a moment of simultaneous withdrawal and political radicalisation for Orwell after his Spanish experience. To offer a hasty summary, in this period he formally joined the ILP (the Independent Labour Party), developed contacts with English anarchist and pacifist milieus, and at the same time produced what is arguably his most significant fictional work up until that moment: *Coming Up for Air*.[134] This is a novel which transcribes many of Orwell's political anxieties regarding class. The narrator and protagonist, George Bowling, describes his and his lower-middle-class peers' existence as a series of reductive territorialisations around property, job, and family: 'We're all respectable householders – that's to say Tories, yes-men and bum-suckers. Daren't kill the goose that lays the gilded eggs! And the fact that actually we aren't householders, that we're all in the middle of paying for our houses and eaten up with the ghastly fear that something might happen before we've made the last payment, merely increases the effect. We're all bought, and what's more we're bought with our own

---

[131] Orwell, *Homage to Catalonia*, p. 104.

[132] Deleuze and Guattari, *A Thousand Plateaus*, p. 397.

[133] Deleuze and Guattari, *A Thousand Plateaus*, p. 397.

[134] According to Michael Levenson, what makes of *Coming Up for Air* 'Orwell's most deliberate novel of the 1930s is that it owes so much to a coherent body of thought that also informs the important essay "Inside the Whale"', his famous defence of political quietism in the manner of Henry Miller', 'The Fictional Realist: Novels of the 1930s', in *The Cambridge Companion to George Orwell*, ed. by John Rodden (Cambridge: Cambridge University Press, 2007), p. 71.

money'.[135] The ideological operation through which lower-middle-class identity is formed thus rests, crucially, on an affective undercurrent that the system mobilises efficiently: 'Fear! We swim in it. It's our element. Everyone that isn't scared stiff of losing his job is scared stiff of war, or Fascism, or Communism, or something'.[136] The pathetic class fraction of 'poor downtrodden bastards' to which Bowling belongs would naturally 'die on the field of battle to save his country from Bolshevism'.[137] But then the radical intelligentsia, the anti-fascist left (exemplified by a Left Book Club lecturer later on in the novel), is similarly articulated around fear and hate. Whether progressive or reactionary, politics emerges at this point as the logical extension of a negative apparatus of capture whose precise function is to fixate and subjectivise experience by exhausting its elusive and transformative possibilities – that is, by interrupting its lines of flight. The alternative to this oppressive experience of historical subjectivation cannot be yet another vision of historical transcendence. On the contrary, it will be the minor promise made by a fragmentary and escapist memory centred on the radical exteriority of childhood and its elusive world.

As Deleuze and Guattari point out, a fundamental tension defines the relationship between memory and becoming. Even if 'there exists a molecular memory', they write, it often operates 'as a factor of integration into a majoritarian or molar system'. In this sense, '[m]emories always have a reterritorialization function'.[138] While this reterritorialising movement is present and undoubtedly important in *Coming Up for Air*, the perceptual and affective emphasis of the various memories evoked by its protagonist – combined with the general sense of reticence about their functional integration as part of George Bowling's life story – into the present (that is to say, into the 'majoritarian or molar system of history') suggests a very different effect. For indeed, memory seems to function more as a mechanism of dispersal and dissolution of a precariously held subject position than as a factor of consolidation. Thus, prompted by a chance encounter with an advertising poster, Bowling begins to reminisce, but not without first making the following consideration about the relationship between the past and the remembering self:

> The past is a curious thing. It's with you all the time, I suppose an hour never passes without your thinking of things that happened ten or twenty years ago, and yet most of the time it's got no reality, it's just a set of facts that you've learned, like a lot of stuff in a history book.

---

[135] George Orwell, *Coming Up for Air* (London: Penguin, 2020), p. 14.
[136] Orwell, *Coming Up for Air*, p. 16.
[137] Orwell, *Coming Up for Air*, p. 14.
[138] Deleuze and Guattari, *A Thousand Plateaus*, p. 324.

Then some chance sight or sound or smell, especially smell, sets you going, and the past doesn't merely come back to you, you're actually *in* the past.[139]

This is memory as mobilisation, but not in the direction of functional closure around a present subjectivity, for both subject and present become displaced, estranged, deterritorialised towards the past. Its driving force is the sensory fragment, the affect and the percept, to use Deleuze and Guattari's terminology, rather than the transcendent historical event: the remembered smell of the local church, 'the smell of sainfoin chaff' in the kitchen, the different fruits that 'you used to find in the hedges' or the feeling of 'the grass round me', 'the heat coming out of the earth', 'the warm greeny light coming through the hazel boughs' against a backdrop of seemingly perpetual summer ('It always seems to be summer when I look back').[140]

The memory of fishing is particularly significant in this respect. In addition to working as a sort of refrain connecting various episodes and moments in Bowling's narration, the way it is referred to throughout the novel suggests a stubborn resistance, not only to the instrumental rationality governing a degraded modern world but also to the temporal and experiential structure determined by the idea of history (in this respect, the novel echoes Gibbon's *untimely* emphasis). Indeed, fishing is described as the main event in Bowling's childhood: 'when I look back the whole of my boyhood from eight to fifteen seems to have revolved round the days when we went fishing'.[141] This is an event without historical continuity or transcendence of any kind, just a series of individual fragments, molecular memories, whose significance lies exclusively in the autonomy of experience, in the 'being of sensation' that they harbour without any ulterior historical reference or motive: 'I can remember individual days and individual fish, there isn't a cow-pond or a backwater that I can't see a picture of if I shut my eyes and think'.[142] Bowling goes on to declare that '[f]ishing is the opposite of war', for it grants 'the thought of escaping, for perhaps a whole day, right out of the atmosphere of war'.[143]

Reading is the other childhood activity Bowling evokes as a withdrawal from the divisive and destructive inertia of modern history: as a form-of-life,

---

[139] Orwell, *Coming Up for Air*, p. 30.

[140] '*Affects are precisely these nonhuman becomings of man*, just as percepts ... are *nonhuman landscapes of nature*', Deleuze and Guattari, *What is Philosophy?*, p. 169; Orwell, *Coming Up for Air*, pp. 38, 40, 42.

[141] Orwell, *Coming Up for Air*, p. 76.

[142] Deleuze and Guattari, *What is Philosophy?*, p. 169; Orwell, *Coming Up for Air*, p. 76.

[143] Orwell, *Coming Up for Air*, p. 93.

to reiterate Agamben's formulation, that is, a life inseparable from its form, from its habitual uses and possibilities, and thus irreducible to a state of abject conditionality:

> I'm lying on my belly with *Chums* open in front of me. A mouse runs up the side of a sack like a clockwork toy, then suddenly stops dead and watches me with his little eyes like tiny jet beads. I'm twelve years old, but I'm Donovan the Dauntless … I'm watching the mouse and the mouse is watching me, and I can smell the dust and sainfoin and the cool plastery smell, and I'm up the Amazon, and it's bliss, pure bliss.[144]

What this memory of youthful reading invokes is an experience of life without subjective or objective content, a life of what Agamben defines as 'contemplation', in which the actuality and facticity of modern *bios*, with its assumed assimilation of subjectivity/objectivity to division and exclusion, is deactivated and rendered inoperative.[145] Like the image of fishing previously evoked, this is reading understood as flight from the debilitating constraints of personal and collective identity and experience, and therefore as deployment of a negativity that seeks to 'destitute', to 'depose' and 'revoke' those positivities, those 'factical vocations', upon which historical socio-political life is predicated.[146] Significantly, this image of reading as deactivation or destitution of the logic of history (and war, for indeed the two become synonymous in the novel) returns in Bowling's evocation of his final year of service during the First World War. This stands in marked contrast with his earlier account of the ordinary horrors of trench warfare in France. After being wounded and returning to England, Bowling is subsequently posted to a remote location on the North Cornish Coast to supervise an empty army store as part of a completely ineffectual logistics operation – an episode which highlights the irrational and entropic quality of this particular experience of history. As he acerbically says of the surreal situation, 'By 1918 one had simply got out of the habit of expecting things to happen in a reasonable manner'.[147]

The ironic outcome for Bowling is that this glitch in the system of war affords him a return to the contemplative life he had enjoyed before 1914. Forgotten by all in his remote and absurd posting, he goes on to indulge 'an appetite for books that was almost like physical thirst', his 'first real go-in at reading … since [his] Dick Donovan days'.[148] And yet the pleasure he

---

[144] Orwell, *Coming Up for Air*, p. 101.
[145] See Agamben, *The Use of Bodies*, pp. 62–64.
[146] Agamben, *The Use of Bodies*, p. 277.
[147] Orwell, *Coming Up for Air*, p. 133.
[148] Orwell, *Coming Up for Air*, p. 136.

experiences is no longer comparable to the 'pure bliss' of his youthful reading as it is overshadowed by 'the rotten meaninglessness of the life I was leading'.[149] For the brutality of history makes any partial or temporary retreat eminently precarious and experientially unsustainable – more an outlandish deviation (however actively pursued by an increasingly disaffected army, as in this case) than an effective withdrawal: 'Here I was, sitting beside the stove in an army hut, reading novels, and a few hundred miles away in France the guns were roaring and droves of wretched children, wetting their bags with fright, were being driven into the machine-gun barrage like you'd shoot small coke into a furnace'.[150] Against this background of destruction, and even in the relatively less extreme context of a post-war (actually interwar) present marked by the accumulation of divisive and deforming social dynamics, the idea of flight cannot be reduced to the assumption of a position of marginality or more or less exotic self-exclusion.

For the George Bowling of 1938, fleeing will be about attempting to experience an alternative temporality, about deactivating the functional roles and prospects of a life divided and split off from itself along the various striations of personal and collective history. The lost form from which modern life has been wrenched is thus to be intuited, and perhaps experienced, momentarily, impersonally, and utopianly, in the contemplative admiration of the natural landscape:

> Why don't people, instead of the idiocies they do spend their time on, just walk round *looking* at things? That pool, for instance – all the stuff that's in it. Newts, water-snails, water-beetles, caddis-flies, leeches, and God knows how many other things that you can only see with a microscope. The mystery of their lives, down there under water. You could spend a lifetime watching them, ten lifetimes, and still you wouldn't have got to the end even of that one pool. And all the while the sort of feeling of wonder, the peculiar flame inside you. It's the only thing worth having, and we don't want it.[151]

Contemplating nature – a pond, or a bunch of primroses – amounts to withdrawing, existentially, vitally, if also tenuously and fleetingly, from the world and its split life of victims and executioners, exploited and exploiters,

---

[149] Orwell, *Coming Up for Air*, p. 137.
[150] Orwell, *Coming Up for Air*, p. 138.
[151] Orwell, *Coming Up for Air*, pp. 188–189. As Agamben writes, 'Landscape is a dwelling in the inappropriable as form-of-life, as justice. For this reason, if in the world the human being was necessarily thrown and disoriented, in landscape he is finally at home', *The Use of Bodies*, p. 91.

and experiencing peace, not only as 'absence of war' but as 'a feeling in your guts' –in other words, as a form-of-life.[152] This is ultimately the meaning and significance of Bowling's native village and the driving force behind his decision to return in the final section of the novel: 'Peace! We had it once, in Lower Binfield. I've told you something about our old life there, before the war. I'm not pretending it was perfect. I dare say it was a dull, sluggish, vegetable kind of life. You can say we were like turnips, if you like. But turnips don't live in terror of the boss, they don't lie awake at night thinking about the next slump and the next war'.[153] Predictably, of course, this feeling of peace has definitively succumbed to the march of history, and all Bowling encounters on this final flight (for, as he himself puts it, 'Strictly speaking I was in flight') is a sense of guilt bordering on the paranoid.[154] Strikingly, this is compounded by a ghostly feeling of the 'past sticking out into the present' while exposing its real absence, its irretrievable loss.[155]

The Lower Binfield of 1938 is an urban sprawl and amalgam of '[h]ouses, shops, cinemas, chapels, football grounds – new, all new' with 'people flooding in from Lancashire and the London suburbs, planting themselves down in this beastly chaos, not even bothering to know the chief landmarks of the town by name', while the old people of the place are all gone.[156] Once again, as in *The Road to Wigan Pier*, there is the problem of an urban and social formlessness reflecting and amplifying a human one. But in this case, at the end of the road, as it were, there is no obvious strategy for restoring form to life. For, as Bowling bleakly concludes, 'The old life's finished, and to go about looking for it is just waste of time'.[157] For all its despairing pessimism – which naturally corresponds to Orwell's own moment of withdrawal in 1939 – we can read this explicit embrace of negativity as a precondition for the imminent political turn that will come with the outbreak of the Second World War and, especially, with the Blitz. If the 'old life' is missing, if form has been definitively abolished from ordinary experience, then the only hope lies in a figuration of life, both personal and social, that is necessarily indicative

---

[152] Orwell, *Coming Up for Air*, p. 190.

[153] Orwell, *Coming Up for Air*, p. 192.

[154] Orwell, *Coming Up for Air*, p. 198. 'What was more, I actually had a feeling that they were after me already. The whole lot of them! All the people who couldn't understand why a middle-aged man with false teeth should sneak away for a quiet week in the place where he spent his boyhood', Orwell, *Coming Up for Air*, pp. 198–199.

[155] Orwell, *Coming Up for Air*, p. 214.

[156] Orwell, *Coming Up for Air*, pp. 209, 218.

[157] Orwell, *Coming Up for Air*, p. 259.

of this absence – an artifice, a provisional form announcing, perhaps, a life and a people to come.

2.3 'The People are Missing': The Second World War and the Logic of Populism

The outbreak of the Second World War, and, more specifically, the signing of the Nazi-Soviet pact in 1939, marks yet another turning point in Orwell's political journey. As he writes in a 1940 article entitled 'My Country Right or Left', in what is, as John Newsinger puts it, an 'almost certainly apocryphal account',

> [T]he night before the Russo-German pact was announced I dreamed that the war had started. It was one of those dreams which, whatever Freudian inner meaning they may have, do sometimes reveal to you the real state of your feelings. It taught me two things, first, that I should be simply relieved when the long-dreaded war started, secondly, that I was patriotic at heart, would not sabotage or act against my own side, would support the war, would fight in it if possible. I came downstairs to find the newspaper announcing Ribbentrop's flight to Moscow.[158]

The fact that this is very probably a fabled account of his own conversion to a pro-war and yet, crucially, revolutionary stance offers a key insight into the nature of Orwell's socialism in the context of terminal crisis as diagnosed by *Coming Up for Air*. For, if the old life is indeed finished, if the road back to wholeness and form is cut off, then a personal and collective narrative will have to be told – a fruitful fabrication with which to interrupt the inertia of history and enable not only a radically different future but also a properly revolutionary becoming, here and now. As we have seen, for Deleuze, only 'the fabulating function [*fonction de fabulation*] of the poor' can resist 'the truth which is always that of the masters or colonizers'.[159] Fabulation in this sense concerns the invention of a people whose existence has been negated: 'The moment the master, or the colonizer, proclaims "There have never been a people here", the missing people are a becoming, they invent themselves'.[160] Orwell's thesis will be that the people is precisely what is missing in the

---

[158] John Newsinger, *Hope Lies in the Proles: George Orwell and the Left* (London: Pluto Press, 2018), pp. 74–75; George Orwell, 'My Country Right or Left', in *The Complete Works of George Orwell: A Patriot After All, 1940–1941* (London: Secker & Warburg, 1998), p. 271.

[159] Deleuze, *Cinema 2*, p. 150. See note 12 above.

[160] Deleuze, *Cinema 2*, p. 217.

so-called People's War and is therefore what is to be invented, called forth, and ultimately secured as a true becoming-revolutionary of the war.[161]

In 'My Country Right or Left', Orwell claims that something his alleged dream had taught him was that 'the long drilling in patriotism which the middle classes go through had done its work' but also argues that patriotism in fact 'has nothing to do with conservatism'. Rather, it is to be thought of as 'devotion to something that is changing but is felt to be mystically the same'.[162] That mystic continuity, an emotional fabrication, or indeed fabulation, at the heart of the nation invoked by patriotism is precisely what affirms and sustains the power of becoming that defines the people who are missing and have to be invented. In Orwell's political writings of 1940–1941, this (in principle) paradoxical identification of the English people as a missing people, as a people both negated and enabled in its revolutionary becoming by its oppression, not unlike other colonised peoples, at the hands of the ruling class of the British Imperial State, is absolutely central. It is important to observe that there is no side-stepping of the deleterious legacy of English or British colonialism in this analysis. On the contrary, as Orwell notes in an earlier article, 'Hitler is only the ghost of our own past rising against us. He stands for the extension and perpetuation of our own methods, just at the moment when we are beginning to be ashamed of them'.[163] As a socialist, he 'would sooner side with the older imperialisms – decadent, as Hitler quite rightly calls them – than with the new ones which are completely sure of themselves and therefore completely merciless'. Yet it is precisely this guilty awareness of Britain's historical continuity with the fascist regimes that secures 'the right to defend ourselves'.[164] And at the heart of this imperialist history lies racism, which 'is not merely an aberration of crazy professors' and which, crucially for Orwell's argument, 'has nothing to do with nationalism', for '[n]ationalism

---

[161] As John Newsinger pinpoints, 'his wartime writings are in fact one long protracted complaint that it was not a "People's War" and a demand that it be transformed into one', *Hope Lies in the Proles*, p. 83.

[162] Orwell, 'My Country Right or Left', p. 271.

[163] George Orwell, 'Notes on the Way', in *The Complete Works of George Orwell: A Patriot After All, 1940–1941* (London: Secker & Warburg, 1998), p. 123. There is an interesting prefiguration in Orwell's argument of the critique launched by anti-colonial thinkers such as Aimé Césaire, who was to write in 1950: 'Whether one likes it or not, at the end of the blind alley that is Europe, I mean the Europe of Adenauer, Schuman, Bidault, and a few others, there is Hitler. At the end of formal humanism and philosophic renunciation, there is Hitler', *Discourse on Colonialism*, trans. by Joan Pinkham (New York: Monthly Review Press, 2000), p. 37.

[164] Orwell, 'Notes on the Way', p. 124.

is probably desirable' insofar as it expresses a desire to resist colonisation: 'Peoples with a well-developed national culture don't like being governed by foreigners, and the history of countries like Ireland and Poland is very largely the history of this fact'.[165]

'Racialism', on the other hand, 'is something totally different. It is the invention not of conquered nations but of conquering nations'.[166] This distinction is central, for it suggests that the break with Britain's past, and therefore the successful struggle against Nazi neo-imperialism, is tantamount to the (re)invention of England as a non-conquering nation, indeed as a minor nation, we could say, joining a historical lineage of anti-colonial struggles. This reinvention necessarily entails a revolutionary becoming, not unlike that which Orwell had himself experienced in Spain. Thus, 'the feeling of all true patriots and all true Socialists is at bottom reducible to the "Trotskyist" slogan: "The war and the revolution are inseparable"', for indeed 'Hitler can only be defeated by an England which can bring to its aid the progressive forces of the world – an England, therefore, which is fighting against the sins of its own past'.[167]

The collective social subject of this nation is yet to be constructed, and this construction, for the Orwell of 1940–1941, clearly requires an articulation of heterogeneous elements (disparate and seemingly incompatible class fractions and interests) through a unifying appeal to the nation: 'Is there any chance of turning an airman, a naval officer, a railway engineer or whatnot into a convinced Socialist?' Orwell's answer is that it would be illusory to count on 'the full conversion of the entire population' as the basis for revolution, and yet it is apparent to him that the latter cannot succeed without some degree of inclusion of what he refers to as 'the indispensable middle class'. Ultimately, the 'approach to these people is through their patriotism', which, far from being a 'sham', however much '"Sophisticated" Socialists may laugh at' it, is a creative force precisely on account of its unifying capacity.[168] What is needed, then, in the critical conjuncture of 1940–1941, is a vehicle for the mobilisation of that force: 'Up to the death of George V the King probably stood for a majority of English people as the symbol of national unity. These people believed – quite mistakenly, of course – in the King as someone who was on their side against the monied class. They were patriotic, but they were not Conservative'.[169]

---

[165] Orwell, 'Notes on the Way', p. 122.

[166] Orwell, 'Notes on the Way', p. 122.

[167] George Orwell, 'Our Opportunity', in *The Complete Works of George Orwell: A Patriot After All, 1940–1941* (London: Secker & Warburg, 1998), pp. 345–346.

[168] Orwell, 'Our Opportunity', p. 347.

[169] Orwell, 'Our Opportunity', pp. 349–350.

This is particularly interesting because what seems to be at work here is the sort of ideological operation that Ernesto Laclau has theorised as populism. For Laclau, in a social field defined by antagonism, which is the very precondition of politics (and indeed the situation to which Orwell's own understanding of the political keeps returning), 'there is the experience of a *lack*, a gap which has emerged in the harmonious continuity of the social'.[170] If the 'fullness of the community ... is missing', then 'the construction of the "people" will be the attempt to give a name to that absent fullness'.[171] According to Laclau, this construction will require a process of hegemonic articulation, as that described by Orwell above, whereby a series of unmet social demands are rendered equivalent and totalised through their identification with a particular symbol that in turn acquires a universal emancipatory meaning. In the example Orwell gives, this would be the King, but in his own practical engagement, the unifying symbol (or hegemonic signifier) might as well be that People's Army in the making to which he devoted so much energy in this period – the Home Guard.[172] In any case, this presupposes the abandonment of a substantialist position where the people would be narrowly identified with a class or sectorial group. As Orwell writes in 'The Lion and the Unicorn', the 'English Revolution' which effectively began at the time of the Dunkirk evacuation is characterised by a significant blurring of traditional political identities and 'party labels' and by 'the existence of multitudes of unlabelled people who have grasped within the last year or two that something is wrong'.[173] The vagueness and imprecision surrounding this imaginary of the revolutionary people is indeed constitutive of the populist operation at work, and therefore indicative of its anti-institutionalist and radical thrust.[174] For, as Laclau notes,

---

[170] Ernesto Laclau, *On Populist Reason* (London: Verso, 2004), p. 85.

[171] Laclau, *On Populist Reason*, p. 85.

[172] In a piece for the radical newspaper *Tribune*, entitled 'The Home Guard and You', Orwell argues that 'far from being "Fascist"', the Home Guard 'is a politically neutral organization which is capable of developing in several quite different ways', with 'most of the rank and file' clearly wanting it 'to become a real People's Army', 'The Home Guard and You', in *The Complete Works of George Orwell: A Patriot After All, 1940–1941* (London: Secker & Warburg, 1998), p. 309. Orwell's description suggests the kind of discursive openness and articulatory practice at the heart of Laclau's theory of populism.

[173] George Orwell, 'The Lion and the Unicorn: Socialism and the English Genius', in *The Complete Works of George Orwell: A Patriot After All, 1940–1941* (London: Secker & Warburg, 1998), p. 418.

[174] In 'The Lion and the Unicorn', the motif of the family emerges as a problematic but potentially unifying populist symbol in its own right. As Orwell famously puts it, 'England is not the jewelled isle of Shakespeare's much-quoted passage,

'the language of a populist discourse … is always going to be imprecise and fluctuating: not because of any cognitive failure, but because it tries to operate performatively within a social reality which is to a large extent heterogeneous and fluctuating'.[175] Orwell's adoption of a populist strategy during the Blitz thus suggests a recognition, first, of the heterogeneity of the social situation – in which pre-existing social and political identities can offer no guarantees, indeed a situation in which the social is defined by its discontinuity and absent fullness (this is precisely the sense of George Bowling's declaration, in *Coming Up for Air*, that the old life is finished) – and second, the recognition of its fluctuating possibilities – an understanding that the crystallisation of a new socialist movement, fully aligned with the national interest and its radical resignification in popular terms, is finally within reach.

I want to conclude the chapter by referring to one of the key literary representatives of the sort of populism Orwell embraces around 1940: J. B. Priestley. Priestley's famous 1940 series of BBC broadcasts, entitled *Postscripts*, and the host of fictional and non-fictional writings which followed it through the remainder of the war, epitomise this shift from a class-based socialist discourse to a left-populist imaginary of radical social transformation. As Paul Addison has pointed out, '[i]f Priestley was a socialist, his socialism was of a cheerfully idiosyncratic kind, a vision of a more warm-hearted and egalitarian way of life'.[176] In his first 'Postscript', Priestley reacts to the Dunkirk evacuation, remarking on its 'typically English' quality, 'both in its beginning and its end, its folly and its grandeur'.[177] This 'queer habit … of conjuring up such transformations' whereby '[o]ut of a black gulf of humiliation and despair,

---

nor is it the inferno depicted by Dr. Goebbels. More than either it resembles a family, a rather stuffy Victorian family, with not many black sheep in it but with all its cupboards bursting with skeletons. It has rich relations who have to be kow-towed to and poor relations who are horribly sat upon, and there is a deep conspiracy of silence about the source of the family income. It is a family in which the young are generally thwarted and most of the power is in the hands of irresponsible uncles and bedridden aunts. Still, it is a family. It has its private language and its common memories, and at the approach of an enemy it closes its ranks. A family with the wrong members in control—that, perhaps, is as near as one can come to describing England in a phrase', 'The Lion and the Unicorn', p. 401.

[175] Laclau, *On Populist Reason*, p. 118.

[176] Paul Addison, *The Road to 1945: British Politics and the Second World War* (London: Pimlico, 1994), p. 119. See also John Baxendale, *Priestley's England: J. B. Priestley and English Culture* (Manchester: Manchester University Press, 2007), pp. 140–165, and Vincent Brome, *J.B. Priestley* (London: Hamish Hamilton, 1988), pp. 241–261.

[177] J. B. Priestley, *Postscripts* (London: William Heinemann, 1940), p. 1.

rises a sun of blazing glory' is 'not the German way'.[178] Introducing a theme that will become central to his wartime writing (and which resonates with Orwell's argument in *The Road to Wigan Pier*), Priestley insists that the 'vast machine' of war mobilised by the Nazis is not prone to make 'such mistakes', but neither can it 'create a glimmer of that poetry of action which distinguishes war from mass murder'.[179] The difference between the English and German approaches is symbolised by 'the little pleasure-steamers' at the centre of the evacuation. For these belong to an 'innocent foolish world' of insouciance and unpreparedness that seems to have been bypassed and effectively defeated in June 1940 by the technological superiority of the Nazis, while at the same time retaining a kernel of ordinary humanity and experiential continuity out of which an ultimately greater force – a moral force – may be unleashed. This is the 'feeling of deep continuity' and the 'rewarding sense of community' that Priestley also encounters upon joining his local branch of the Home Guard (or Local Defence Volunteers): 'There we were, ploughman and parson, shepherd and clerk, turning out at night, as our forefathers had often done before us, to keep watch and ward over the sleeping English hills and fields and homesteads'.[180]

Crucially, the continuity is historical as much as affective, an attempt to reimagine the heterogeneity of English social life, across and beyond its existential crises, as a force of ordinary creation. This is a central emphasis in Priestley's *Postscripts*, the idea of an *ordinary* impulse generated and preserved in common which may effectively resist the onslaught of fascism and subvert its corrupt logic of total power. This impulse is embodied in figures such as 'Two Ton Annie', a disabled, overweight woman Priestley had met during her evacuation to the Isle of Wight. For in spite of her state of physical prostration and her humble origins, she comes to symbolise the expansive and joyful resistance, the *conatus* (to borrow an apt term from Spinoza) of the common people:

> She was a roaring and indomitable old lioness, and wherever she was carried there was a cheerful tumult; and as she roared out repartee she saluted the grinning crowd like a raffish old empress. Yes; she was old, fat, helplessly lame and was being taken away from her familiar surroundings, a sick woman, far from home. But she gave no sign of any inward distress, but was her grand, uproarious self.[181]

---

[178] Priestley, *Postscripts*, p. 2.

[179] Priestley, *Postscripts*, p. 2.

[180] Priestley, *Postscripts*, p. 12.

[181] See Laurent Bove, *La stratégie du conatus: affirmation et résistance chez Spinoza* (Paris: Vrin, 2012); Priestley, *Postscripts*, p. 21.

This incarnation of the ordinary stands in sharp contrast to, for example, Mrs Brooker in *The Road to Wigan Pier* and the logic of formlessness and division she represents. In Orwell's book, this woman is described as a characteristic product of the Great Depression and of the derelict physical and moral landscape of the industrial districts in the mid-1930s: 'permanently ill, festooned in grimy blankets', with 'a big, pale yellow anxious face', Mrs Brooker sums up the vision of a life torn and divided, rendered abjectly impotent, by the accumulated violence of capitalist modernity.[182] Two Ton Annie, on the contrary, emerges as a prominent expression of that 'fabulating function' whereby the people – hitherto declared missing by the ordinary structures of power, and now brutally threatened with annihilation by the normalised exceptionality of triumphant fascism – 'invent themselves'.[183]

Priestley thus argues that, 'although Britannia can put up a good fight, Two Ton Annie and all her kind can put up a better one', for 'their sort of life' is whole and indivisible, a form-of-life, in Agamben's terms, which 'breeds kindness, humour and courage' and is therefore constitutively superior to the 'worried, semi-neurotic, police-ridden populations for ever raising their hands in solemnly idiotic salutes, standing to attention while the radio screams blasphemous nonsense at them'.[184] This emblem of resistant, affirmative life in common was, according to Priestley, 'a glimpse of our folk at the very beginning of the war'.[185] Yet in the far more uncertain period which ensued, during the so-called Phoney War, a 'much less heartening' cast of characters began to replace the likes of Two Ton Annie, characters who represented a stifling impulse towards the managerial and official and who 'might be described as Complacent Clarence, Hush-Hush Harold, and Dubious Departmental Desmond'.[186] Even if these 'gentlemen have their places in our wartime scheme of things', part of the effort to match the technocratic thrust of the German machine of war, for Priestley 'there was a real danger of these pundits and mandarins creating a rather thick, woolly, dreary atmosphere in which that national character of ours couldn't flourish and express itself properly'.[187] For the singularity of the moment, the transformation underway in the face of the Nazi challenge, was precisely the infusion of this national character to which he repeatedly appeals in the *Postscripts*, seemingly permanent and atemporal, with 'a unity of feeling never known

---

[182] Orwell, *Wigan Pier*, p. 58.
[183] Deleuze, *Cinema 2*, pp. 150, 217.
[184] Priestley, *Postscripts*, p. 21.
[185] Priestley, *Postscripts*, p. 21.
[186] Priestley, *Postscripts*, p. 22.
[187] Priestley, *Postscripts*, p. 22.

before in our island history' which '*we* have brought' to the war.[188] In other words, the transformation of the English national spirit or character into a radical collective affect, results from and in turn foregrounds the autonomous agency of the 'ordinary British folk'.[189] If Nazism is ultimately 'a negation of the good life', it is a mechanical negation whose reach is limited and ultimately powerless when compared with the vital affirmation of the people and their becoming.[190] A radical naturalism (truly reminiscent of Spinoza, if not Deleuze) informs Priestley's language here: 'there flows through all nature a tide of being, a creative energy that at every moment challenges and contradicts this death-worship of despairing, crazy men'.[191]

The ethical strength of the English people in 1940, their ordinary superiority, is connected, for Priestley, to their being 'deeply religious at heart', but – and this is crucial – 'not only when they're kneeling in our little grey country churches but also when they're toiling at their machines or sweating under loads in the threatened dockyards'.[192] There is a radical Christian vision in Priestley, traceable to seventeenth-century proto-socialists such as Winstanley, with his revolutionary vindication of a 'common treasury for all', through to the Christian socialist founders of the Fabian Society, who, as Mark Bevir writes, 'were looking for a new faith in tune with modern science and oriented toward humanity'.[193] It must be noted that Christian socialism was the main ideological influence upon the various political groups with which Priestley associated in this period, most notably the Common Wealth Party, which resulted from the merger of his own 1941 Committee, formed in December 1940, and Sir Richard Acland's Forward March movement. Paul Addison has described Acland as 'a quixotic Christian socialist of deep sincerity' for whom 'the war had

---

[188] Priestley, *Postscripts*, p. 22; my emphasis.

[189] Priestley, *Postscripts*, p. 22.

[190] To belabour the point in Deleuzian terms, the contrast between the 'machinic', desiring ontology of this minor (missing) people and the mechanical verticality of the Nazi State could not be starker.

[191] Priestley, *Postscripts*, p. 26.

[192] Priestley, *Postscripts*, p. 22.

[193] Gerrard Winstanley, *The Law of Freedom and Other Writings* (Harmondsworth: Penguin, 1973), p. 79; Mark Bevir, *The Making of British Socialism* (Princeton, NJ: Princeton University Press, 2011), p. 133. Not all the early members of the Fabian Society were Christian socialists, but the formative influence of figures associated with the Christian socialist 'Fellowship of the New Life' was decisive. As Bevir points out, 'The founders of the Fabian Society combined the ethical and spiritual concerns of the Fellowship with an interest in land nationalization and, in some cases, Marxism'.

to be nothing less than a crusade against selfishness, a renunciation of the economic motive in favour of truth, love, and service', as he argued in his 1940 book *Unser Kampf: Our Struggle*.[194]

Priestley's own 1941 book *Out of the People* offers a precise guide to this leftist populism with recognisable Christian socialist foundations. In this essay, Priestley begins by elaborating a distinction between the people and the masses as the ideological cornerstone of the new politics advocated by movements like his own. He insists that these are mutually exclusive conceptions, for when 'I say to myself "the people", I have a confused but lively vision of a hundred faces and hundred voices ... In short, I think of persons'.[195] On the contrary, the notion of the masses conjures up 'a grey, featureless horde': 'The masses are not real human beings. They have been de-humanised'.[196] Priestley traces the rise of this dehumanising conception of the collective to the 'decay of religious belief', which he sees as 'dangerous for democracy because it makes the individual man or woman seem less significant'.[197] He argues that if 'we have all immortal souls and are the children of God, then we are all real people', since it is 'impossible to believe that men have immortal souls and at the same time see people as masses'.[198] Consequently, any vision of the future society 'should have a religious basis' in this radical sense of affirming the individual within the collective and not in the dogmatic sense of the traditional 'creeds of the existing Churches'.[199]

Priestley's argument announces a number of themes that would soon become prominent among cultural theorists from the Frankfurt School to the British proponents of cultural studies. At the heart of the conceptual corruption induced by the idea of the masses, against this background of a decaying religious sentiment, lie the new culture industries encouraged by the 'new conservatism': 'The newspaper that tries to make its readers more intelligent is replaced by the newspaper that flatters the idiocy of its readers. The smart boys of the advertising world are kept busy. The film is used as a

---

[194] Addison, *The Road to 1945*, p. 158.

[195] J. B. Priestley, *Out of the People* (London: Collins, 1941), p. 18.

[196] Priestley, *Out of the People*, p. 18.

[197] Priestley, *Out of the People*, p. 50.

[198] Priestley, *Out of the People*, p. 50.

[199] Priestley, *Out of the People*, p. 52. Similarly, Richard Acland argues in *Unser Kampf* that what is needed, rather than a 'religious revival' that 'would seem to require of us a particular belief in God and a particular expression of our worship', 'is the adoption, in our public and political life, of those elementary ethical principles to which we have long paid lip-service in our churches', *Unser Kampf: Our Struggle* (Harmondsworth: Penguin, 1940), p. 33.

drug', and, as a result, '[a]ttention is steered away from politics'.[200] The rise to prominence of this new cultural hegemony, however, is not a product of the war or necessarily an offshoot of fascism, but an ideological trend consolidated over 'the last ten years, during which this sinister conception of the masses has captured so many shrewd, unscrupulous and melancholy minds'.[201]

Priestley's discussion prefigures here Raymond Williams's seminal analysis in *Culture and Society*. According to Williams, 'masses was a new word for mob, and the traditional characteristics of the mob were retained in its significance: gullibility, fickleness, herd-prejudice, lowness of taste and habit'.[202] A result of the 'physical massing of persons' technically required by the industrial process, the notion was assigned a moral valence, as 'a perpetual threat to culture', which would ultimately carry a political judgement against democracy itself, as 'those to whom the franchise was formerly restricted' could now express their opposition to social change 'by inventing a new category, mass-democracy'.[203] Williams directly echoes Priestley's emphasis when he writes:

> There are in fact no masses; there are only ways of seeing people as masses. In an urban industrial society there are many opportunities for such ways of seeing. The point is not to reiterate the objective conditions but to consider, personally and collectively, what these have done to our thinking. The fact is, surely, that a way of seeing other people which has become characteristic of our kind of society, has been capitalized for the purposes of political or cultural exploitation.[204]

Thus, the crucial operation, for Williams, will lie in the general social conception informing or animating our approach to the existing techniques of so-called mass communication. For indeed, the latter 'will be irrelevant to a genuine theory of communication, to the degree that we judge them to be conditioned, not by a community, but by the lack or incompleteness of a community'.[205] Priestley's critique is similarly driven by a fundamental preoccupation with this idea of community (or what he had called, in one of his *Postscripts*, 'the community view'), although his approach in *Out of the People* is also shaped by a libertarian concern about the role of the State.[206]

---

[200] Priestley, *Out of the People*, p. 21.

[201] Priestley, *Out of the People*, p. 21.

[202] Raymond Williams, *Culture and Society 1780–1950* (Harmondsworth: Penguin, 1961), p. 288.

[203] Williams, *Culture and Society*, pp. 287–288.

[204] Williams, *Culture and Society*, p. 289.

[205] Williams, *Culture and Society*, p. 301.

[206] Priestley, *Postscripts*, p. 38.

Echoing a contemporary debate about managerialism in industrial societies (whether capitalist or socialist), Priestley argues that the 'sharp division between the masters and the servants of the machines has little to do with capitalism and exploitation. If the State ran the factory, that division would still be there. It has nothing to do with the prevailing economic system'.[207] Thus, 'we must take care not to confuse the community with the state. They are not at all the same thing. The community consists of living persons' while the 'state is an organisation, an instrument, a machine, and will always have the limitations of such things. No matter how it is reformed, it will always tend to be slow, cumbersome, rigid in its workings'.[208] For this reason, 'the emphasis must always be on the living community'.[209]

The idea of an absence of community at the heart of modern industrial society (a situation exacerbated by the war) is the point of departure for Priestley's wartime fiction. His 1942 novel *Blackout in Gretley* condenses a number of themes rehearsed in *Postscripts* and *Out of the People*, but the emphasis falls on this deficit in the experience of the social, this lack of a 'living society', which the specific context of military stagnation at the beginning of 1942 (when the novel is set) throws into particularly sharp relief. The novel follows Humphrey Neyland, a Canadian engineer engaged in a counter-espionage mission in a fictional Midlands town dedicated to aircraft production. Under the cover of seeking employment in the local factory, Neyland navigates a social landscape symbolically dominated by the wartime blackout, where false identities and ambiguous loyalties prevail and displace the affirmative quality of social bonds of 1940. As the character notes about the literal blackout in Gretley ('the worst I've ever seen'), there is 'something timid, bewildered, Munich-minded about it' and thus essentially in continuity with the logic of social and national treason associated with the 'guilty men' behind the policy of appeasement and the Munich Agreement of 1938.[210] There is, according to Neyland, a moral defeat to be sensed in this defensive measure: 'We can almost hear those madmen chuckling as they think of us groping in the gloom they

---

[207] Priestley, *Out of the People*, p. 59.

[208] Priestley, *Out of the People*, pp. 91, 93.

[209] Priestley, *Out of the People*, p. 97. Writing about G. D. H. Cole, Williams restates this argument in the following terms: 'The dangers of powerful central authority, and of a general bureaucratic organization, to which the Guild Socialists drew attention, have become increasingly obvious since they were writing ... the line of thinking which is summed up in the word "community", rather than the word "state", remains an essential element of our tradition', *Culture and Society*, p. 190.

[210] J. B. Priestley, *Blackout in Gretley* (Richmond: Valancourt Books, 2021), p. 12. See 'Cato', *Guilty Men* (London: Penguin, 1998).

wished upon us. We make a darkness to fit the darkness deep in their rotten hearts'.[211] In keeping with Priestley's argument in *Out of the People*, one can also detect a more fundamental continuity between this wartime self-abasement and the sense of pervasive moral corruption inscribed in the profiteering logic of industrialism that had given rise to towns such as Gretley in the first place:

> If you ask me, these towns give the whole cynical industrial game away. They were run up as cheaply as possible as money-making machines to provide people who never came near the places, with country mansions, grouse moors, deer forests, yachts, and winters in Cannes and Monte Carlo. In most other countries, the people simply wouldn't live in a town that offered them so little of what a town can offer. But the British can take it. I hoped they'd go on taking it until the day Hitler screamed for the last time, and that then they'd pull these damned places down and throw the bricks at the greedy old fakers who'd pop up to tell them they were now all poor again.[212]

This is a succinct summary of the antagonistic logic informing Priestley's radical populist account of the war, one which makes an implicit reference to the betrayal of the people perpetrated after the First World War, with those unfulfilled promises of 'homes for heroes', as its point of departure. In the atmosphere of military and political stagnation depicted in this novel, the true antagonists, even more than the Nazis, are those individuals who, 'clinging to their privileges at the expense of the common good', had once before reneged on their pledges to the people and would willingly do so again unless they were stopped.[213] Thus, it is scarcely surprising to learn, when Neyland finally unlocks the mystery, that the ringleader behind the spying plot is none other than Colonel Tarlington, a classic Colonel Blimp figure, whose ultimate motivation – as Neyland explains – is less a lack of patriotism than a profoundly anti-democratic instinct.[214] This is the same instinct which underpins the notion of the masses and the profit motive physically etched onto the industrial landscape of Gretley:

> It isn't that you're pro-German, unpatriotic in the ordinary sense. In the last war, which seemed to you a straightforward nationalistic affair, I've

---

[211] Priestley, *Blackout in Gretley*, p. 12.

[212] Priestley, *Blackout in Gretley*, p. 22.

[213] Addison, *The Road to 1945*, p. 131.

[214] As Paul Addison notes, this was 'the creation of the New Zealand-born cartoonist David Low. Launched in the *Evening Standard* in 1943, Blimp was a rotund, bald figure with drooping walrus moustaches, a symbol of military incompetence and political reaction', *The Road to 1945*, p. 132.

no doubt you did a good job. But this war, which is quite different, was too much for you ... so you realized that to keep all you wanted to keep, it meant that the people mustn't win and that Fascism mustn't lose. So they persuaded you that a Nazi victory only meant that you'd have the sort of England you've always wanted, with yourself and a few others securely on top, and the common people kept in their place for ever.[215]

Priestley continues this fictional investigation of the anti-democratic impulse threatening the project of a People's War (and crucially, of a people's peace after the war) in his 1943 novel *Daylight on Saturday*. This is not a spy thriller like its predecessor, but rather a social realist reconstruction of working conditions – once again – in the military aircraft industry. Here, the upper-class antagonists are given a more complex treatment (even if their antagonistic profile is retained and emphasised). Thus, there is a managerial elite, represented by the senior engineer Blandford, committed to the 'true modern industrial order' and its 'reflection in politics', a hoped-for 'New Toryism' of the future.[216] While 'no potential Quisling', for he 'disliked the Nazis intensely', Blandford's 'deeply undemocratic' outlook announces a possible outcome of the Allied victory over fascism, one in which the latter's deep moral denials could remain intact, even if superficially humanised – a peace without and against the people.[217] In a discussion he has with another character about James Burnham's book *The Managerial Revolution*, where he notes how the author 'carefully left Britain out of his picture', he insists that Britain's singularity, the feature that sets it apart from the American, Russian, and German examples, is precisely the nature of its class system.[218] According to Blandford, all the 'protest and jeers' which had characterised the radical mood at the beginning of the war, were not really 'directed against the upper class simply *as* an upper class – for consider the popularity of Winston himself, and the fact that nearly all our leaders in the services, who have to be followed to hell and back, are unmistakably members of the upper class – no, they're really directed against the inefficient and old-fashioned types among the ruling class'.[219] The discredited version of the ruling class is epitomised by Blandford's own cousin, Lord Brixen, an opportunistic government official and old-style Tory without any of the meritocratic and managerial qualities Blandford invokes as part of his anti-democratic vision of a post-war modern

---

[215] Priestley, *Blackout in Gretley*, p. 182.
[216] J. B. Priestley, *Daylight on Saturday* (London: Pan Books, 1967), p. 216.
[217] Priestley, *Daylight on Saturday*, p. 58.
[218] Priestley, *Daylight on Saturday*, p. 54.
[219] Priestley, *Daylight on Saturday*, p. 55.

Britain. Thus, 'observing his cousin narrowly', he wonders 'how Brixen had contrived to get so far when he had so little to do it on ... How long would he last after the war? Not very long, Blandford told himself grimly, unless the New Toryism ... decided that it could use a few public dummies and stooges'.[220]

This is an idea to which Priestley insistently returns in the final years of the war: the fact that, however enduring in its noxious and reactionary effects, this nostalgic formulation of British Conservatism is essentially irrelevant and will necessarily be displaced by the strong anti-democratic managerialism of the future. As he writes, for example, in his 1945 pamphlet *Letter to a Returning Serviceman*, 'We are not making a mere detour but are travelling rapidly towards something quite different from anything the public man imagines. If we are not moving towards the Socialism of Morris or Robert Blatchford, it is even more certain that we shall not discover, in any possible hard Corporate-State Toryism of 1950, any way back to the sleepy Tory Britain of Lord Salisbury or Balfour'.[221] Indeed, he insists, the 'important Tories don't live in Disraeli's world, even if at times they talk in public as if they did. They are the tough fellows behind the huge monopolies and cartels, the secret emperors and warlords of finance and industry'.[222] For Priestley, this rising power of technocratic structures and vested interests cannot be arrested or counter-effected without a commensurate, and indeed *vitally* superior, imaginary of collective agency and affect. It is the split between a provisional, exceptional, but powerfully real experience of community and fellowship during the war and the attempted restoration – from above – of the old, irrelevant, but effectively estranging visions and values of a bygone Conservatism that threatens to enable, in the uncertain conjuncture of 1945, the development of that new-minted anti-democratic project.

My next chapter begins by considering a significant fictional response by the Communist writer and intellectual Jack Lindsay to the new host of political contradictions which Labour's 1945 electoral victory would lead to. Having averted the immediate danger Priestley invokes (of a strengthened Conservatism rooted in an anti-democratic managerialism), post-war British socialists would now have to contend with the mixed legacy of Labourism in power and with the specificities of a transformed ideological terrain in which 'socialism' was subject to new discursive articulations and hegemonic investments.

---

[220] Priestley, *Daylight on Saturday*, p. 216.

[221] J. B. Priestley, *Letter to a Returning Serviceman* (London: Home & Van Thal, 1945), p. 15.

[222] Priestley, *Letter*, p. 15.

Chapter Three

Realism without Guarantees

3.1 Communist Fiction and The British Road to Socialism: Jack Lindsay's *Betrayed Spring*

Jack Lindsay's 1953 novel *Betrayed Spring* is the first in a multi-volume series critically examining, as its running subtitle indicates, 'the British Way' – that is, the contemporary socio-political history of Britain since 1945. After a series of clashes with the leadership of the Communist Party of Great Britain (CPGB), fuelled by accusations of 'deviation' from the party line, Lindsay emerged in the early 1950s as 'a model of the Party writer' and as a British champion of socialist realism understood 'as the expression of unanimity between vanguard party and party intellectual'.[1] In doctrinal interventions of the period, Lindsay would insist on the impossibility of mastering the socialist realist aesthetic without first 'understand[ing] what communist leadership is' and without playing a 'part in development of that leadership, helping to change our people politically as well as culturally, seeing no division between politics and culture, and daily embodying in [one's] own experience the experience of the Party'.[2]

Despite the orthodox emphasis of this and other pronouncements, Lindsay's *practice* of socialist realism in a novel such as *Betrayed Spring* is far less linear and unproblematic than the Soviet models to which his prescriptive approach to literature in these years seemingly pledged allegiance. Thus, while the classic socialist realist novel is, as Katerina Clark notes, extremely 'formulaic' and

---

[1] John T. Connor, 'Jack Lindsay, Socialist Humanism and the Communist Historical Novel', *The Review of English Studies* 66:274 (2015), p. 350. Lindsay had joined the Communist Party during the war, following his conversion to Marxism in 1936 and a subsequent period as a fellow traveller. For a comprehensive overview of Lindsay's career, see Anne Cranny-Francis, *Jack Lindsay: Writer, Romantic, Revolutionary* (Cham: Palgrave Macmillan, 2023). For an analysis of Lindsay's novelistic output of the 1930s, see Elinor Taylor, *The Popular Front Novel in Britain, 1934–1940* (Leiden: Brill, 2017).

[2] Quoted in Connor, 'Jack Lindsay', p. 349.

'rhetorical' in its rendition of 'universal history' 'as a normative progression from dark to light' – which makes it 'structurally analogous to medieval hagiography' – Lindsay's novel is, as we will see, characterised by a sense of contingency and potentiality in its imaginative assessment of the historical conjuncture.[3] This departure from the purer models of socialist realism (including those arising from nearer contexts in the capitalist West, such as France) can be seen as mirroring Lindsay's productive response to the new strategic orientation of the party itself, as codified in the new 1951 programme *The British Road to Socialism*, which made the non-revolutionary and 'national' transition to socialism experienced by the 'People's Democracies' of Eastern Europe the new political horizon towards which British Communists now had to strive.[4] Notably, as Ben Harker observes, the 'central political agent of *The British Road* was not the proletariat or party, but an intra-class "great popular alliance", although its composition and the motivations and mechanisms that united it barely featured'.[5] The need for a new national-popular political

---

[3] Katerina Clark, 'Socialist Realism *with* Shores: The Conventions of the Positive Hero', in *Socialist Realism without Shores*, ed. by Thomas Lahusen and Evgeny Dobrenko (Durham, NC: Duke University Press, 1997), p. 28.

[4] The great exemplar of socialist realism in France in the early 50s was André Stil's *Le premier choc* (*The First Clash*), which won the Stalin Prize and was lauded, in true Zhdanovite fashion, by the orthodox British party functionary and literary editor Margot Heinemann for its 'optimism': 'Stil's book is truly optimistic because it shows ... the real, undefeatable goodness and courage of ordinary working people ... his emphasis is on the fine qualities – the toughness and devotion, the endless care and sacrifice for the children, the ability of ordinary workers to read and study and master the most complicated ideas, the unconquerable humour and initiative. And is not this essentially the *true* picture of the class that is going to change the world?', quoted by Andy Croft, 'The End of Socialist Realism: Margot Heinemann's *The Adventurers*', in *Heart of the Heartless World: Essays in Cultural Resistance in Memory of Margot Heinemann* (London: Pluto Press, 1995), p. 197. By January 1952, the Executive Committee of the CPGB had adopted a resolution on the cultural work to be developed in the context of the new strategic orientation. New tasks included a 'deeper study of the Party's programme, *The British Road to Socialism*, and continuous efforts to make it well known among their professional colleagues' as well as, crucially, '[n]ew efforts by our writers, artists and musicians to produce work relating to the British working class struggle, and based on the standpoint of Socialist Realism', John Callaghan and Ben Harker, *British Communism: A Documentary History* (Manchester: Manchester University Press, 2011), p. 182.

[5] Ben Harker, *The Chronology of Revolution: Communism, Culture, and Civil Society in Twentieth-Century Britain* (Toronto: University of Toronto Press, 2021), p. 82.

subject, as well as the inherent complexity of its 'articulatory' nature, as no essentialist working-class referent could now be assumed, inevitably imposed a logic of openness and potentiality upon the otherwise formally rigid aesthetic of the socialist realist novel.

Set in the context of the first series of crises the new Labour government had to face in late 1946 and early 1947, *Betrayed Spring* is organised around four largely separate plots offering distinct perspectives on the early promise and stagnation surrounding the Labourist project of 'democratic socialism' launched in 1945.[6] The first of these concerns a London working-class family driven by the penury of post-war conditions and the housing shortage in the capital to join a group of Communist-led squatters.[7] This plot condenses the logic of division and contradiction presiding over the entire novel, for the experience of squatting results in two very different subjective trajectories for the main characters involved – on the one hand, the father, Will Tremaine, who becomes an emblem of defeat and pessimism, and, on the other, his daughter Phyl, whose journey is one of steady growth towards militant consciousness. The latter is programmatically sketched in the opening chapter, as the group of squatters is evicted from the occupied hotel by the Communist organiser Ted King, who not only articulates a preliminary indictment of Labour's socialism that will inevitably orientate the novel's subsequent ideological progress ('We've shown the world what all the talk about caring for the people really means. We can all rot away before the sacredness of property is threatened – even when a house is lying empty and useless') but also immediately expresses the lived political *truth* of the party member – a totalising and canonically 'optimistic' integration of life and struggle: 'he was getting into his bones the realisation that the defeat was not a defeat, after all. These were the moments that made life worth living, the moments when he suddenly felt part of something vast, indomitable, endlessly struggling'.[8]

The structural opposite to this enabling optimism is then purveyed by Phyl's father who, after losing his job at the London County Council, realises the logic of political retribution at work without expressing any willingness to accept it as part of the dialectic of struggle. A defeat transformed into defeatism, rather than a moment in the logic of class conflict, is thus the impotent outcome of

---

[6] Some of the characters in the different plots are related to each other, but the plots intersect only in very limited ways.

[7] The Squatters' Movement of 1946 was one of the most visible campaigns of the CPGB in the immediate post-war period. See Noreen Branson, *History of the Communist Party of Great Britain 1941–1951* (London: Lawrence & Wishart, 1997), pp. 118–128.

[8] Jack Lindsay, *Betrayed Spring* (London: The Bodley Head, 1953), pp. 13–14.

the confused ideological standpoint with which Phyl Tremaine will ultimately break: 'She hated her father when he talked in a hopeless way ... There seemed no point of contact between those two worlds, that of helpless and recurrent misery and humiliation, and that of united song and determination to change the world'.[9] Through her ongoing involvement with the unofficial strikes of hotel workers and dockers, and through her personal attachment to the conscious workers and trade unionists at the forefront of these struggles, Phyl completes her ideological journey, which is always, crucially, an intensely *experiential* and *lived* one. As George, one of the leaders of the Savoy strike, puts it, 'That's what life is on earth, and nothing else, an awakening to the light or a falling back on deeper slumber and bad dreams. Well, we fight for the awakening, and this strike means hundreds of our brothers and sisters getting a spark in their souls'.[10] This polarised characterisation would seem to faithfully transcribe the schematic formula of high-Stalinist socialist realism, with its emphasis, as Katerina Clark points out, on a parabolic teleology of world-historical movement tropologically rendered through 'the progress of an individual character – *the* "positive hero"'.[11]

However, *Betrayed Spring*'s structural principle, with its four plots addressing the historical conjuncture of 1946–1947 in terms of its experiential heterogeneity, suggests a far less linear and rhetorical intervention. Thus, a key aspect of the novel is its presentation of the term 'socialism' as a discursive terrain of struggle rather than as a monologic and predetermined 'perspective'.[12] For if socialism is not only the social logic embodied in the working-class struggle (as imagined by the more militant sectors) but also a signifier claimed by the social democratic 'right wing' of the Labour Movement and its institutional representatives in the Attlee administration, then the field of discourse in which radical politics operates becomes open, devoid of fixity, and thus in need of hegemonic articulation – a process which is, as Laclau argues, defined by the impossibility and 'unachievable fullness' of the totality which it seeks to produce.[13] In other words, even if the commitment is ultimately

---

[9] Lindsay, *Betrayed Spring*, p. 104.

[10] Lindsay, *Betrayed Spring*, p. 83.

[11] Clark, 'Socialist Realism *with* Shores', p. 28.

[12] This notion is at work even in the more advanced, anti-Zhdanovite, definition of socialist realism offered by Georg Lukács in *The Meaning of Contemporary Realism*, where the Hungarian theorist writes that the 'perspective of socialism enables the writer to see society and history for what they are', *The Meaning of Contemporary Realism*, trans. by John and Necke Mander (London: Merlin Press, 1979), p. 96.

[13] Ernesto Laclau, *On Populist Reason* (London: Verso, 2005), p. 71.

to a programmatic perspective, to an a priori definition of the future society that the Communist Party wants to build, the historical situation, with its contradictory dynamics extending over the very meaning of 'socialism', imposes a logic of contingency rather than necessity, which only the provisionality of hegemony (the hegemony which the party has to construct, rather than assume) will manage to resolve. This, I claim, is the complexity which *Betrayed Spring*, with its three other plot lines, sets out to navigate.

The second plot follows Dick Baxter through his return from wartime service in Asia to his mining village in Lancashire, where he begins to work in the pit under the influence of his father, a veteran socialist miner and local leader. The tension between the son's admiration for the father's history and the vague resentment felt at the expectations imposed on him (for 'he, Dick, was expected to go down [the pit] to keep up his father's prestige') becomes a key aspect of this narrative.[14] In contrast to Dick's initial lack of political conviction, the father is immediately identified with the impending nation-alisation of the mines (and therefore, with the Labour government) as the culminating achievement of his and his fellow miners' struggle for socialism. Yet the purity of the older-generation politics which Daniel Baxter represents (embodied in the sense, as Dick imagines it, 'of something single-hearted, honest, magnificently four-square in the fighters of his father's generation') makes it hard to question its discursive claim over 'socialism' or to write it off as mere ideological co-optation by the system.[15] Strictly speaking, this character is, to quote Lukács, no less 'based on a concrete socialist perspective' than Communists such as Ted King.[16] However much the novel ultimately inclines itself towards the latter version of political consciousness, the indeterminacy produced by socialism's referential openness at this juncture is a reality that cannot be easily overcome. The poignancy with which nationalisation is revealed as the prominent symbol in this working-class community's horizon of social reform offers one of the defining moments in the novel:

> The pithead was illuminated with strong floodlights. Henderson and other officials were waiting on the steps of the Hall with the Union representatives. Over the door a notice read: 'This Colliery is now Managed by the National Coal Board and Belongs to the People.' [...] Suddenly the first siren cried sharply, and then sirens and whistles from all over the landscape of the night answered and mingled and rose in a wailing exultant shriek heavenwards. [...] As the bright blue flag of

---

[14] Lindsay, *Betrayed Spring*, p. 36.

[15] Lindsay, *Betrayed Spring*, p. 36.

[16] Lukács, *Contemporary Realism*, p. 93.

national ownership fluttered up the flagpole under the winding-gear, the cheers rose in ever-higher swell, and caps were flung in the air as well as waved. A bugle sounded the Last Post and then Reveille. The death of the old and the morning of the new. The silver band of the colliery, its players wearing sweaters and overcoats, broke into *Jerusalem*, and all the voices joined sweepingly in. Then as the song ended, many of the singers went straight on into *The Red Flag*, and again all the voices swung powerfully together.[17]

As one of the women observing the ceremony puts it, 'Ee, this is our Victory Night ... This is the end of our war'.[18] Once again, the sense of historical continuity and vindication is most directly associated with the older Baxter, for whom this is an occasion to recall, 'with a group of men of his own age', 'all the strikes and lock-outs and disputes of the last fifty years', how '1926 and the great hopes of the General Strike' were followed by victimisation and the horrors of the 1930s.[19] If for these older socialists the 'pattern of development' is undeniable, with nationalisation its resounding telos, for Dick what will follow is a sense of opacity and impenetrability in the experience of the social, just as the collective joy gives way to the trials of the fuel crisis during that fateful winter of 1947.

Despite the optimism in the community and the pride felt by the miners as coal production is reported to have increased even as the crisis unfolds, Dick's prevailing feeling is one of mental and physical numbness, a sense that the true pattern of personal and collective development becomes increasingly unreadable:

> His return; the break with Pat, the decision to go down the pit, Vesting Day, the fuel crisis, the mounting resolution of the men to show how Britain depended on the miners – and then a heavy check, a dullness of fatigue and confusion. Something important was summed up in the frost, the snow, the blizzard, the unending cold – the challenge and the response, the strength and the weakness, of himself and his fellows. But the more this conviction settled down on his mind, the more numbed his thoughts became.[20]

Separation and estrangement, which had been the first response offered by the character upon his return ('The rain was a mist of separation, preventing him

---

[17] Lindsay, *Betrayed Spring*, p. 238.
[18] Lindsay, *Betrayed Spring*, p. 239.
[19] Lindsay, *Betrayed Spring*, p. 239.
[20] Lindsay, *Betrayed Spring*, p. 346.

from feeling quite a part of the familiar world that he was re-entering'), are now confirmed, in the final account, not as irrevocable moments of a general disarticulation in the dynamic of social transformation but as the unavoidable features of a social experience devoid of necessity.[21]

This theme of separation and estrangement is also prominent in the Tyneside plot of the novel, where trade unionist William Emery struggles to reconcile his commitment to the new political reality with what he regards as the prejudiced and backward attitudes on both sides of the class divide: 'For the first time in his career he felt opposed both to the management with their efforts to cut rates, and to the workers with their efforts to maintain old customs'.[22] While no ready-made reality, as he acknowledges in discussions with fellow trade unionists, since the need 'to keep on fighting ... for the great day' remains, socialism from Emery's perspective is, however, no longer merely an ideological horizon but also a technical fact that has to be managed.[23] Thus, what 'was needed was a Cripps who wasn't a namby-pamby, or a Morrison who really knew something; someone who could bang sense into the heads of both sides and make them realise that a Labour government had come to stay'.[24] In other words, what is needed is not so much a strategic break from the gradualist road – for this *is* the road to socialism in Britain, one where Labour's hegemonic role is unquestionable – but a leadership capable of conveying the clarity of purpose already informing the minds and actions of veteran working-class representatives such as Emery himself. The challenge posed by resistant – and as far as he is concerned, uncomprehending – attitudes is moreover compounded by the risk of perceived compromise, by the knowledge that any failure to automatically side with the workers in their ongoing disputes with the management 'would show up badly' and allow Benson, the radical shop steward – 'the blasted red' – to 'use it against him'.[25] The sort of estrangement that results from this complex position is different from that felt by the young miner, yet both announce a breach with the political vision of class homogeneity and inexorable militancy assumed by characters such as Phyl Tremaine.

The idea of a fundamental breakdown in the class homogeneity and political teleology of the socialist project in this context is further highlighted in the Yorkshire plot, which follows the son of a Yorkshire factory owner who returns from the army to contemplate an ideologically conflicted future as an industrialist. Instinctively persuaded that 'the sane way of life lay in the army

---

[21] Lindsay, *Betrayed Spring*, p. 26.
[22] Lindsay, *Betrayed Spring*, pp. 200–201.
[23] Lindsay, *Betrayed Spring*, p. 208.
[24] Lindsay, *Betrayed Spring*, p. 201.
[25] Lindsay, *Betrayed Spring*, p. 323.

experiences' with their simplicity and wholeness of purpose, Kit's youthful reaction against paternal authority is amplified by a deeply felt moral objection to the power embodied in the capitalist's position: 'It's not right: no man should have such power ... What was driving him into his rebellion was ... the hate and fear he felt for the power expressed in his father's very voice, his walk, his eyes – the power to cross a man's name off the ledgers, off the lists of life'.[26] Kit's defiance soon takes the form of a spontaneous identification with the Labour Party as the vehicle to redress such injustice and give a discursively intelligible shape to this instinct of rebellion. This character's somewhat naïve embrace of Labourism is soon challenged by a more systematic and radical exposure to the demands and ideological offerings of the mill workers themselves. Romantically attracted to Jill, whose Communist commitment announces the possibility of a definitive break with 'his father's world' and the substitution of it with 'the new bases for which he had been confusedly questing', he ends up renouncing the more radical option represented by the Party, while trying to steer a 'middle course' between it and his father's own accommodating version of Conservatism.[27]

Even if the novel ultimately suggests that this middle course is a characteristic act of middle-class hypocrisy and betrayal (as Kit's Labourism is not averse, in the final turn of events, to a covert form of victimisation whereby the more militant workers in the mill – including his former love interest – are laid off), the sense of radical contingency and openness surrounding the political grammar of socialism in this context is not easily dispelled. For however opportunistic and misguided in this case, the prospect of a hegemonic investment in the gradualist road (a road of middle courses and managerial compromises, as symbolised by the recurring names of Labour ministers Stafford Cripps and Herbert Morrison) makes its opposite vision, that of an indomitable and essentialistic proletarian unity (as observed by Phyl among the striking dockers), increasingly elusive and marginal to the emerging social conjuncture. As in the case of William Emery, what can be felt across the gulf of personal motivations and history is not only the sense of fragility at the heart of the political in a situation defined by radical heterogeneity but also the discursive indeterminacy of all ideological struggles, and the resulting intuition that the new political subject of socialism would have to be *constructed* rather than revealed as a predetermined entity.

In a defining scene towards the end of the novel, we are given a glimpse of Phyl's confusion when attending a Communist Party meeting – also attended by Jill – as suddenly the sense of continuity between struggle

[26] Lindsay, *Betrayed Spring*, p. 107.
[27] Lindsay, *Betrayed Spring*, pp. 159, 377.

and ideology, the purity and fullness of her prior militant experience, are replaced with a discursive outpouring from this political vanguard which she is incapable of comprehending: 'She seemed to understand it all while the words were flying about, but as soon as she tried to recall what was said, she found that nothing had left a clear mark'.[28] She naturally assumes a position of inferiority, conceding that some 'key-understanding was absent', but she also develops the feeling that, 'remarkable as was the uniformity of ideas among these people, even more remarkable was the way in which they seemed to disagree all the while'.[29] Here, the principle of aesthetic subordination to the party leadership dictated by the socialist realist formula is necessarily complicated (if not effectively compromised) by a perspective which faithfully transcribes the discursive proliferation at the heart of 'socialism', even within the Party.

It is not difficult to relate this vision in *Betrayed Spring* – according to which a heterogeneity of subjects cannot be assumed to naturally cohere into an unbreakable ideological unity – to Lindsay's own heterodox positions in the immediate post-war period. For one of the latter was, as Ben Harker has noted, Lindsay's 'enthusiasm for developments in the French and Italian parties', especially 'Togliatti's innovations of a *partito nuovo*'.[30] Indeed, according to Laclau, one of the defining aspects of the Togliattian project was its determination to create 'hegemonically a unity – a homogeneity – out of an irreducible heterogeneity'. Thus, instead of exclusively becoming the representative of the industrial proletariat ('in which case it would have been an essentially workerist party, a mere enclave in the Industrial North'), it sought to present itself as the 'rallying point of a multitude of disparate struggles and demands'.[31] The Communist Party – as the party of 'real' socialism – could not assume in the highly volatile post-war context an orthodox Marxist correspondence between the universal class and its political expression. What was needed, rather, was a performative intervention: that is, to produce, out of the mass of shifting meanings and demands, a viable articulation that would situate it at the centre of national life itself. As Togliatti himself explains,

> The proletariat becomes a national class insofar as it takes on [the problems of the whole of society] as its own and thence comes to know, by the process of changing it, the whole reality of national life. In this way it produces the conditions of its own political rule, and the road

[28] Lindsay, *Betrayed Spring*, p. 399.
[29] Lindsay, *Betrayed Spring*, p. 399.
[30] Harker, *The Chronology of Revolution*, p. 83.
[31] Laclau, *On Populist Reason*, p. 182.

to becoming an effective ruling class is opened ... We have to spread the activity of an organised vanguard over the whole area of society, into all aspects of national life. This activity must not be reduced to preaching propaganda, to phrase-making or clever tactics, but must stick closely to the conditions of collective life and give, therefore, a foundation, real possibilities and prospects to the movement of the popular masses.[32]

This new *national* task for the party – 'to constitute a "people"', as Laclau puts it, even if the particular name of this 'people' was still 'the working class' – was, of course, also implicit in the new strategic orientation expressed by the CPGB in *The British Road to Socialism*.[33] Tragically for British Communists, however, '[o]n every page the document revealed the degree to which the party was ill-equipped for the national course on which it was set'.[34]

Unaccompanied by the breadth of vision displayed by the Italian Communist Party, Lindsay's inaugural novel in the 'British Way' series thus remains, when considered from a strictly political point of view, a mere testimony of foreclosed possibility. Nevertheless, its approach to realism as a specifically socialist mode of literary expression raises, as we have seen, a number of questions that are not easily answered by reference to the dogmatic pronouncements of Party theoreticians and codifiers of the Soviet-inspired aesthetic orthodoxy. If a transparent socio-political totality is absent, and what fills its void is ultimately a series of competing discourses, realism emerges as a space of negotiation between available and far more elusive contents. The common space of representation and *experience* assumed by the realist novel is reimagined in terms of its own impossibility. This, I want to argue, is the key contribution (and correction of the Marxist understanding of realism) made by Raymond Williams – both theoretically and *practically*, in his own body of fictional work.

---

[32] Quoted in Ernesto Laclau, *The Rhetorical Foundations of Society* (London: Verso, 2014), p. 98.

[33] Laclau, *On Populist Reason*, p. 182. As Laclau explains, 'To say that the Communist Party, as the party of the working class, had to concentrate its activity in the industrial North, because that is where the working class was to be found, is to say that there was a conceptual content of the category "working class" through which we recognize some objects in the world [...] To name a series of *heterogeneous* elements as "working class", instead does something different: this hegemonic operation performatively brings about the unity of those elements, whose coalescence into a single entity is nothing other than the result of the operation of naming', *On Populist Reason*, p. 183.

[34] Harker, *The Chronology of Revolution*, p. 82.

3.2 Raymond Williams: Realism and the Distance of Experience

In the years since his death in 1988, the centrality of Williams's creative writing to the totality of his oeuvre has come to be appreciated and understood with increasing clarity, to such an extent that his biographer, Dai Smith, has been able to claim that Williams's 'most abiding effort, passion, and self-directed ambition, had been for the writing of fiction throughout his working life'.[35] This creative engagement is ultimately inseparable from Williams's intervention in the cultural and literary debates of the post-war left and from the perceived need to rehabilitate, while necessarily reinventing, the critical and socially transformative agenda of realism. This need had been explicitly articulated in a number of writings throughout the 1950s, which, in turn, announced his own breakthrough realist novel of 1960, *Border Country* – a book long in the making which arguably brought to a head the main strands of his early body of thought.

Thus, in an important review of Richard Hoggart's 1957 *The Uses of Literacy*, Williams had noted: 'We are suffering, obviously from the decay and disrepute of the realistic novel, which for our purposes (since we are, and know ourselves to be, individuals *within* a society) ought clearly to be revived'.[36] In his 1959 essay 'Realism and the Contemporary Novel' (subsequently included in *The Long Revolution* from 1961), Williams went on to argue that the 'realist novel needs ... a genuine community: a community of persons linked not merely by one kind of relationship – work or friendship or family – but many, interlocking kinds'.[37] However, the difficulty of 'finding a community of this sort' in the twentieth century – since 'the characteristic experience of our century is that of asserting and preserving an individuality, (again like much eighteenth-century experience)' – was increasingly a problem that writers had to contend with.[38] The challenge of a new definition and practice of realism involved a 'struggle for relationships, of a whole kind' in a social context defined by division and the absence of an immediately accessible and transparent experience of community.[39] Thus,

> The old, naïve realism ... depended on a theory of natural seeing which is now impossible. When we thought we had only to open our eyes

---

[35] Dai Smith, *In the Frame: Memory in Society 1910 to 2010* (Cardigan: Parthian Books, 2010), p. 316.

[36] Quoted in Smith, *In the Frame*, p. 321.

[37] Raymond Williams, *The Long Revolution* (Harmondsworth: Penguin, 1971), p. 312.

[38] Williams, *The Long Revolution*, pp. 312–313.

[39] Williams, *The Long Revolution*, p. 314.

to see a common world, we could suppose that realism was a simple recording process, from which any deviation was voluntary. We know now that we literally create the world we see, and that this human creation – a discovery of how we can live in the material world we inhabit – is necessarily dynamic and active.[40]

As his early attempts at a comprehensive cultural theory – *Culture and Society* and *The Long Revolution* primarily – suggest, Williams's general formula for this 'creative discovery', which the aesthetic of realism promised to embody in its more advanced and dynamic contemporary offerings, is summed up in the notion of communication.[41] Far from exhausting itself in the techno-political denials of the discourse about 'mass communication', what was fundamentally at stake in this idea was the possibility of replacing a conception of the social founded on the inequality of pure transmission (of received meanings and values) with one guided by the logic of participation, of active reception and response.[42] Reality itself is necessarily the product of communication, for it is 'continually established, by common effort' as a dynamic, multidirectional process.[43] Crucially for Williams's definition of realism, the risks involved in this creative exploration are significant: 'the tension can be great, in the necessarily difficult struggle to establish reality, and many kinds of failure and breakdown are possible'.[44] This is the failure and breakdown that attends on the communicative process itself, that extending common effort to bridge and inhabit the fractures of a community that is no longer immediately available. Thus, ultimately, 'realism is precisely this living tension, achieved in a communicable form'.[45]

---

[40] Williams, *The Long Revolution*, p. 314.

[41] Williams, *The Long Revolution*, p. 314.

[42] Williams, *Culture and Society*, p. 301.

[43] Williams, *The Long Revolution*, p. 315.

[44] Williams, *The Long Revolution*, p. 315.

[45] Williams, *The Long Revolution*, p. 315. Williams's sustained theorisation of – and commitment to – the realist programme from a consciously socialist perspective throughout his career did not detract from his generally critical stance towards orthodox Marxist definitions such as those found in Lukács (let alone those of orthodox Soviet codifications). As Williams observes in *Politics and Letters*, 'there is a radical divergence' between his and Lukács's account of twentieth-century literature, for Lukács 'did have … the notion of a pre-existent social reality with which the literary model can be compared'. While he admits that their accounts 'could be very similar for a type of literature in which the question – how does this fiction compare with otherwise observable … social reality? – seems unproblematic', given that the 'realist novel of the 19th century does not make it *essential* to clarify the differences

What is fundamentally at stake here, as Williams argues in 'Britain in the 1960s', the essay that concludes *The Long Revolution*, is the possibility of finding an alternative method of analysis, and consequently an alternative socio-political imaginary, to 'most general descriptions' of society available in the ideological climate of the post-war consensus and the mixed economy.[46] For if an entrenched feature of dominant perceptions in the managed capitalist society of the 1950s was a tendency to 'suppress large areas of our real relationships, including our real dependences on others', while abstracting private patterns of consumption, any hope of grasping 'our true standard of living', argues Williams, must be passed through the achievement of 'some realistic sense of community'.[47] Yet, again, this is by no means a guaranteed process, and the communal and co-operative patterns historically embodied in the institutions of the Labour Movement (with their 'steady offering and discovery of ways of living that could be extended to the whole society') were now faced with a great deal of uncertainty as corporatism in practice and a high degree of semantic indeterminacy in relation to the idea of socialism embraced by the Labour Party replaced the older definitions and commitments.[48] For Williams, a particularly damaging element was that of the nationalised industries:

> [T]hey have reproduced, sometimes with appalling accuracy, the human patterns, in management and working relationships, of industries based on quite different social principles. The multiplication of such effects is indeed uninviting, and the easy identification of these institutions, as types of the supposed new society, has added to the general confusion. In being dragged back to the processes of the old system, yet at the same time offered as witnesses of the new, they have so deeply damaged any alternative principle in the economy as to have emptied British socialism of any effective meaning.[49]

between the otherwise observable and the pre-existent' (*Politics and Letters* [London: New Left Books, 1979], p. 350), the split between these aspects in the twentieth century makes, for Williams, an approach such as Lukács's wholly untenable. For, again, the growing impossibility of that full social transparency assumed by the nineteenth-century convention of the 'knowable community' imposes a necessarily tentative, and non-essentialist, interpretation of the social totality – one which posits the need to *articulate* connections (of a communicative kind, through an active sequence of offering, reception, and response) across the borders of historical experience.

[46] Williams, *The Long Revolution*, p. 320.

[47] Williams, *The Long Revolution*, p. 325. As I noted in the previous chapter, this comes very close to Priestley's argument.

[48] Williams, *The Long Revolution*, p. 328.

[49] Williams, *The Long Revolution*, p. 330.

To this general confusion – and semantic voiding of 'socialism' – must be added the complex reality of the new actual communities emerging in the context of relative affluence and the increasingly mixed composition of the labour force: a reality which, again, could not be grasped through single-pattern formulas assuming either proletarian homogeneity, or, at the other end of the sociological spectrum, 'deproletarianisation'. Thus,

> A new and uncertain factor, in those new communities where work is very mixed, is the degree of interaction between social consciousness gained at work – a classic centre of the growth of Labour consciousness – and social consciousness gained in the community. It is too early to say anything definite about this... but I am interested in some evidence of a split between trade union consciousness (the simplest thing learned at work) and Labour consciousness in the wider sense, which has to be in terms of a mixed community and a whole society.[50]

In this context, the limitations of traditional political answers and ideological formulas become dramatically apparent, since precisely what the post-1951 Labour Party seemed unable to offer was a 'different version of community, a pattern of new consciousness'.[51] Positioned as the legatee of a crucial institutional tradition for and by the working class, but currently reduced to a series of reactive and adaptative responses in the changing climate of post-war capitalism, Labourism had failed at the crucial level of intervention – that which required an exploratory search for common meanings and values, for a new sense of collective experience and indeed culture, understood as a whole way of life.[52]

The need to establish (or at least to explore and create the preconditions for) such patterns of 'new consciousness' and such novel experiential

---

[50] Williams, *The Long Revolution*, p. 360.

[51] Williams, *The Long Revolution*, p. 360.

[52] Williams's criticism here implicitly targets both the left wing of 1950s Labour (the so-called Bevanites) and the right-wing revisionists (whose key theoretical statement had been Anthony Crosland's 1956 book *The Future of Socialism*): 'Its [Labour's] compromise policies combine the two irrelevant elements of appeal to old and fading habits and memories, and of cultural adjustment to the present social confusion. Old Left and New Right in the Labour Party are unconscious allies in delaying any relevant analysis and challenge. The invocation of old habits, which to some extent people are bound to change and reject, combines with the rejection of socialism as a radically different human order, to leave the ruling interpretations and directions essentially unchallenged', *The Long Revolution*, pp. 360–361.

structures in a transitional and increasingly mixed society provides a key context for Williams's fictional intervention in *Border Country*.[53] The novel effectively begins by directly addressing its key theme: the difficulty, at the level of personal experience and intellectual 'measurement', faced by a split consciousness, by a character inhabiting the border spaces and temporalities of a life (both individual and collective) set upon heterogeneous patterns of growth and belonging while still actively shaped and informed by a far more integrated and rooted experience of change and continuity. Thus, we encounter the protagonist, Matthew Price, a university lecturer caught up in a mid-career crisis, registering what is largely a personal sense of estrangement from his immediate, yet still fundamentally foreign, social situation as a middle-class professional living in London:

> As he ran for the bus he was glad: not only because he was going home, after a difficult day, but mainly because the run in itself was pleasant, as a break from the contained indifference that was still his dominant feeling of London. The conductress, a West Indian, smiled as he jumped to the platform, and he said, 'Good evening,' and was answered, with an easiness that had almost been lost. You don't speak to people in London, he remembered; in fact you don't speak to people anywhere in England; there is plenty of time for that sort of thing on the appointed occasions – in an office, in a seminar, at a party.[54]

This is the first inscription in the novel of that dual structure of feeling that will preside over much of its narrative unfolding: the break, but also the bridge – that is, in essence, the border – defining the experience of community in a society increasingly shaped by incommensurable mobilities (the presence of the West Indian conductress is in this sense revealing) and by the abstraction, when not the outright negation, of interpersonal relations and continuities. Matthew's 'problem', both as an economic historian ('working on population movements into the Welsh mining valleys in the middle decades of the nineteenth century') and as a living product of class and geographical mobility, is thus the 'problem of measurement, of the means of measurement' – the mismatch between formal descriptions and lived patterns of experience.[55] For the question that assails him, having himself moved from

---

[53] See Laura di Michele, 'Autobiography and "Structure of Feeling" in *Border Country*', in *Views Beyond the Border Country: Raymond Williams and Cultural Politics*, ed. by Dennis L. Dworkin and Leslie G. Roman (New York and London: Routledge, 1993), pp. 21–37.

[54] Raymond Williams, *Border Country* (Cardigan: Parthian Books, 2020), p. 5.

[55] Williams, *Border Country*, p. 5.

a solidly working-class background in the Welsh border country, is 'what is it really that I must measure?':

> The techniques I have learned have the solidity and precision of ice-cubes, while a given temperature is maintained. But it is a temperature I can't really maintain; the door of the box keeps flying open. It's hardly a population movement from Glynmawr to London, but it's a change of substance, as it must also have been for them, when they left their villages. And the ways of measuring this are not only outside my discipline. They are somewhere else altogether, that I can feel but not handle, touch but not grasp. To the nearest hundred, or to any usable percentage, my single figure is indifferent, but it is not only a relevant figure: without it, the change can't be measured at all. The man on the bus, the man in the street, but I am Price from Glynmawr, and here, understandably, that means very little. You get it through Gwenton. Yes, they say the gateway to Wales. Yes, border country.[56]

What the means of measurement at the disposal of the social scientist fail to capture is precisely the lived centre of social experience. Their inadequacy lies in their need to translate this fluency of meaning – a meaning that is embodied, lived, in a complex and fundamental sense – into single patterns (as Williams had critically observed in 'Britain in the 1960s') and to render the collective logic of 'the social' itself as a disembodied abstraction. As Matthew learns in the course of the novel, the pull of his native village in the Anglo-Welsh border country is no simple sentimental attraction – the spell cast by a foreclosed past, for example – but the expression of a different sort of need: the need to rehabilitate common (that is, ordinary and shared) experience as a central, albeit increasingly opaque and mediated, place of articulation between the personal and the social. Crossing the border will thus mean confronting a dual history of individual adaptation and collective transformation, of settlement and movement, across the temporal and geographical frontiers of industrial capitalism and the labour movement in twentieth-century Britain.

Border Country's key crossing is historical: between the 1950s 'present' of Matthew's unfolding sense of crisis and decisive journey back to Glynmawr – as his father Harry suffers the stroke that will soon end his life – and the 'past' centred around the paramount event of the 1926 General Strike.[57] We are first introduced to the story of Harry and Ellen's initial arrival in Glynmawr,

[56] Williams, *Border Country*, p. 6.

[57] As John and Lizzie Eldridge have pointed out, implicit in this crucial temporal crossing is a conscious elaboration on the difficulty of 'making connections, the

to their family background in the border country, and to a vision of work intimately connected to the land, to a heightened sense of place and – through place – to a strong sense of experiential continuity. In a telling description of their early family settlement, life and work (the two elements which, according to Williams's analysis in *The Long Revolution*, post-war capitalism was splitting up along differentiated patterns of social consciousness) are virtually indistinguishable aspects of a single organic continuum:

> There was a good flower garden in front of the cottage, but the rent also included a long vegetable garden at the side of the drying green. Harry worked at this, and in the following autumn persuaded Mrs. Hybart to rent him for a pound a year a further strip adjoining it, which he put under fruit trees – apple and pear and plum. Also, that same autumn, he was able to rent two strips of garden behind the timber yard at the station, and these he put down one to gooseberries and currants, the other to potatoes. In the following spring he bought wood and made four hives, which by the end of the summer, buying swarms in the valley, he had stocked with bees ... Ellen understood the life that Harry was making, for she had known his family at home, and they had always lived like this.[58]

The central connecting dynamic, across individuals, generations, and locations in this closely knit pattern of belonging, is indeed a form of work that is inseparable from life. But, at the same time, in what is perhaps the novel's central paradox or even mystery, Harry is defined as a character by a split between forms of work that seem to belong in radically different material and symbolic contexts. After all, Harry is drawn to Glynmawr by a prospective job as a signalman at the local railway station. This job immediately opens up a wholly different reality of labour (and society) beyond the deeply organic patterns of his rural origins.

In one of the novel's main symbolic nodes, the railway – and more specifically, the work performed by the signalmen – represents a particularly telling combination of sociality and abstraction, communication and separation, border and border crossing. With this consciously contrastive gesture, two versions of community are measured against each other and ultimately explored for their mutually reinforcing possibilities. In effect, Harry's enigmatic persuasiveness as a character rests on his ability to reconcile the dissonance and even the split between forms of life that extend from radically divergent realities

problematic nature of fusing seemingly disparate elements', *Raymond Williams: Making Connections* (London: Routledge, 1994), p. 143.
[58] Williams, *Border Country*, pp. 54–55.

of work. The novel's General Strike subplot crucially offers the narrative a platform beyond the levels of family and individual for a collective articulation and interweaving of these various forms. This is introduced as a shift in the temporal frame of reference, from an organic – and almost geological – sense of continuity to a sense of history as conflict-driven and politically inflected change:

> In the spring of 1926, in Glynmawr, the green of the meadows was fresh and cool, and the blossom was white in the orchards, and on the thorns and crabs in the hedges … Here was the ordinary history of the valley, sheltered and almost isolated under its dark mountains. But now, with this May Day, a different history exerted its pressures, and reached, with the railway line, even this far. The troubled years of strike and lock-out, which had affected the village only slightly, moved now to their crisis, and touched this valley under its lonely mountains. As April ended, the Government's subsidy to the coal industry ended with it. The miners refused the owners' new terms, and lock-out notices were already posted at the pits. Up beyond the mountains, little more than ten miles from this farming valley, lay the different valleys, where the pits and the colliers' houses were crowded.[59]

Shaken out of its undisturbed and 'ordinary' natural rhythms by a contingent and indeed extraordinary history, this community is confronted with the social ordinariness of the very different communities in the adjacent industrial valleys of South Wales: 'At dusk, above Darren, the glow of the steel furnace spread up each evening into the sky, and many turned now to watch it more seriously, and to think of the black valleys that lay hidden beyond'.[60]

The effect of connection across a greater distance is new, not only at the level of space and geography but in the awakening of a more abstract sense of belonging in terms of class and labour. The experience of community is now articulated politically, through the mediation and indirectness of the strike. This higher level of class-based community soon reveals not just a promising horizon of social integration (a revolutionary promise of redemption for and by the working class) but also a sense of the precariousness of political alliances and, ultimately, of collective failure. Morgan Rosser, Harry's militant trade unionist friend, comes to embody the effects of this sense of failure in the aftermath of the General Strike. While Harry does temporarily lose his job, he is able to 'recover quickly', returning both to his post (after an unexpected gesture of solidarity by the least politically minded of his colleagues) and to

---

[59] Williams, *Border Country*, p. 81.
[60] Williams, *Border Country*, p. 81.

the organic rhythms of his ordinary life. For Morgan, on the other hand, the defeat registers as a tragic experience of loss:

> A struggle had been lost; a common effort had failed. And it was not only the failure that broke him, but the insight this gave, or seemed to give, into the real nature of society. His life had been centred on an idea of common improvement. The strike had raised this to an extraordinary practical vividness. Then, suddenly, a different reality had closed in. The brave show was displaced, in an hour, by a grey, solid world of power and compromise. It was not only that the compromise angered him: not only that he was sickened by the collapse into mutual blame. It was that suddenly the world of power and compromise seemed real, the world of hope and ideas no more than a gloss, a mark in the margin. He had lived on his ideas of the future, while these had seemed in any way probable, and they had seemed probable until now.[61]

Rendered here as a devastating insight into 'the real nature of society', the experience of failure exacerbates the logic of precariousness and contingency now defining the idea of community as a wider, more abstract, and specifically political inflection of social life. For Morgan, we learn, the only possible response is defensive, built around a 'hardening' and a 'turning away from Glynmawr' which ultimately results in his crossing the very class border upon which his political identity had been predicated.[62] Morgan eventually becomes a successful entrepreneur, selling local produce across the region. And while his professional makeover is initially tinged with doubt and hesitation on the grounds that it may be regarded as a form of class betrayal, he ends up accepting and even somewhat dogmatically promoting his new activity as the paradoxical realisation of his hopes for social transformation.

At two different points in the novel, Morgan attempts to recruit Harry and Matthew as business partners, only to be met with a calm but firm rejection. In one exchange, Morgan lays bare the full implications of his personal conversion and confirms the sense of crisis and division now surrounding the idea of work upon which the redemptive prospect of class-based community had previously been predicated: 'It's Harry I blame, and I don't mind saying it to him. There's always been this idea that business isn't good enough. And if there's one thing makes me mad, it's this looking down our noses at business. What's our politics mean if it's not good business, raising our standard of life? ... You've worked hard, Harry, admitted, but only a kind of punishing yourself. You haven't worked *for* anything,

---

[61] Williams, *Border Country*, p. 148.
[62] Williams, *Border Country*, p. 150.

not really'.[63] By condemning Harry's organic experience of working life (an experience, that is, of the *natural* interpenetration between work and life) for lacking a larger purpose, for being too immanent and self-contained, and by doing so in the context of his own ambiguous embrace of business as a higher form of socialist politics, Morgan brings to a head the logic of indeterminacy and openness introduced by the strike itself. For the experience of community inaugurated by the latter had been defined by a different sense of possibility, one without organic roots or necessary trajectories, grounded instead in the exploratory contingencies of communication (over the line, across vast distances of locality and lived experience) – in a provisional coming-together through the enactment of a political identity.

Morgan ultimately reconsiders his position and accepts, in a key exchange with Matthew, as Harry lies on his deathbed, the central lesson taught by his friend's life: 'Something that in general we all know about, but I learned it from him. He couldn't see life as chances. Everything with him was to settle. He took his own feelings and he built things from them. He lived direct, never by any other standard at all'.[64] To Matthew's remark that 'You built from your own feelings, too', Morgan replies that his were actually negative feelings: 'Just that life wasn't good enough. That others were ahead and why shouldn't I be?'[65] For Morgan, these feelings are ultimately rooted in the knowledge that 'what I wanted I couldn't have', and that was no less than 'a socialist society'.[66] When Matthew tentatively suggests that 'we're getting' such a society, 'or at least some improvement', Morgan's reply is uncompromising: 'No, Will, we're not. We're getting the result of our own denying. We're getting it all except the life'.[67] The split between trajectories and desires, between experiences and ideas, is one that Harry's life brings to a halt, offering an alternative model of profound, and yet ordinary, integration: 'What we talk about, Will, he's lived. It all depends on a mind to it, a society or anything else. And the mind we're making isn't the society we want, though we still say we want it. The mind he's got is to the things we say really matter. We say it, and run off in the opposite direction'.[68]

This clarification and restatement of the central problem in modern social experience – the split between 'mind' and feeling, between individual life and common project – does not, however, suggest an easy or straightforward

---

[63] Williams, *Border Country*, p. 245.
[64] Williams, *Border Country*, p. 280.
[65] Williams, *Border Country*, p. 281.
[66] Williams, *Border Country*, p. 281.
[67] Williams, *Border Country*, p. 281. Matthew is known in Glynmawr as Will.
[68] Williams, *Border Country*, p. 281.

resolution, a final and decisive 'crossing' to the settled and full life as a generally available possibility. For this is, strictly speaking, the ontological end of the problem, and it remains circumscribed to a peripheral location, to a singular experience. The more pressing dimension, the one from which an actual sense of the social – and therefore, perhaps, a viable politics of and for the present conjuncture – may be drawn remains, from the beginning of the novel, epistemological: a problem of measurement. As Matthew puts it upon his return to London after Harry's death, 'the end of exile' is not the result of 'going back' (for going back, across those temporal and experiential borders, to attain an unattainable, singular centre, is not an option anymore – if it ever was) but the product of measuring with the right means, in a common effort. Thus, the exile is ended because the 'distance is measured'; by 'measuring the distance, we come home'.[69] Yet crucially, this is a distance that does not disappear: on the contrary, it is the precondition for the journey, the contingency upon which the social itself is predicated, and thus the logic that will frame any political attempt to, once again, 'face the future' in the 1960s.

Published in 1964, Williams's next novel, *Second Generation*, complicates the problematic addressed in *Border Country* by removing the central reference to a life of unbroken continuity (as represented by Harry) and submitting the first novel's key formula of measuring to a new host of tensions and pressures. Set in the early 1960s, in an unnamed Oxford straddling the contradictory worlds of the university and the car industry, the novel follows two families from the same Welsh border country (Harold and Kate, with their son Peter; Gwyn – Harold's brother – and Myra, with her daughter from a previous marriage, Beth), yet whose history of migration is more traditionally proletarian: for Harold, as the novel keeps reminding us, the original break had been with the hunger-stricken Wales of the 1930s.[70] But it is in the proliferation of breaks and displacements, and in the sense of precariousness surrounding the possibility of settlement, that the novel finds its central theme. First, there is the generational break signalled by the eponymous 'second generation', as they struggle to reconcile the ambivalence of their

---

[69] Williams, *Border Country*, p. 341.

[70] In an important piece connecting Williams's fiction – including *Second Generation* – to his own experience of union struggles in Oxford, the Marxist geographer David Harvey notes that '[d]uring the 1930s and again in the 1960s and early 1970s, the car plant was the focus of some of the most virulent class struggles over the future of industrial relations in Britain. The workers' movement simultaneously created a powerful political instrument in the form of a local Labour Party that ultimately assumed continuous control of the local council after 1980', *The Ways of the World* (London: Profile Books, 2017), p. 214.

socio-symbolic position (in Peter's case, as a research student) with a desire for wholeness in a way that reiterates many of the difficulties expressed by Matthew Price in *Border Country*. This is compounded, however, by the second and more troubling break, which in turn measures the novel's distance from its predecessor and its vision of a non-generalisable but undeniably organic experience of settlement and continuity: the marital crisis between Harold and Kate, as the latter develops an affair with the radical academic Arthur Dean. Rebelling against the 'long stagnation' and 'endless series of postponements' into which her adult life has turned, for Kate the idea of socialist politics becomes indistinguishable from the vision of a 'new life', and thus from the fulfilment of a long-standing desire to break with the suffering of the past:

> She had every reason to reject the terms of the old life. She and Harold had made the break together: from the grey terraces where the men were kicking their heels month after month, in the long drizzle of poverty. And the break, too, from that stubborn scaling down of expectations which in a whole generation had been the nearest anyone got to any active virtue. Grey endurance and grey hard protest: these were the terms in which she and Harold had grown. The new life had been a phrase in the meetings up on the hill, with the wind blowing the rain like a grey sail through the huddled crowd.[71]

This desiring vision of a new life is one that clashes with the sclerotic instincts of Labourism in her and Harold's political and trade union circles: 'Talk to them about a new conception of human life and they had terrible visions of danger to their standing orders and their waistcoat buttons and their hearths and homes. Say socialism as more than a new set of committees and welfare offices and they simply didn't know what you were talking about'.[72]

A committed shop steward himself, Harold is perceived by Kate as having given in to the narrowness of the daily pressures and 'demands of the work', and thus as having become fundamentally separated from any larger and properly vital conception of politics.[73] This is, to a large extent, a result of the historical disjunction under which their earlier hopes and possibilities, as a younger generation coming into the sphere of Labour politics in the immediate post-war period, had been foreclosed. For if Harold had once been 'the convinced, experienced, determined man the party needed', '[a]ll that was a very long way back now. Men like Harold weren't asked or even

---

[71] Raymond Williams, *Second Generation* (London: The Hogarth Press, 1988), pp. 38, 37.

[72] Williams, *Second Generation*, p. 37.

[73] Williams, *Second Generation*, p. 38.

encouraged any more', and '[t]o look back over these years was to realize how swiftly and silently the idea of a new politics had been changed and dragged back. Whatever their origins, the men of the agendas and the accommodations were back in control'.[74]

The growing gulf between Kate and Harold, which culminates in her infidelity with Dean, is the symptomatic elaboration of this deeper split between two ideas – two 'minds', in the language of *Border Country* – and two structures of feeling arising from a new experience of failure, after the promise of 1945, not too dissimilar from that of 1926: on the one hand, the 'absolute' of a fresh departure from 'a system in which thinking about absolutes', as Dean puts it at one point, appears to be no longer possible, and, on the other, the increasingly precarious labour of commitment to the immediate struggle, with all its provisionality and incompleteness.[75] The former is ultimately written off, first, in the more bitter and aggressively gendered language of Harold's denunciation of Kate's 'adultery', as a sign of corruption and then, in Kate's more important retroactive assessment, as '[t]he old bourgeois fantasy. That you can do what you like'.[76]

The tension of this particular dislocation is further complicated by Peter's own series of evasions – from his relationship with Beth, from his work, and ultimately, from his parents' house – from which he is brought into a new sense and experience of maturity. But it is also Peter's journey of recovery, in search of the lost or disarticulated 'connections' between life and work, that will introduce a new possibility of settlement and continuity in the novel. In an exchange with his supervisor, Robert Lane, he contests the logic of division enshrined in the academic institution generally and the specific kind of intellectual practice, now fully detached from a whole way of life, of which Lane himself has become the model. As Peter puts it to him, 'The connections are deeper than we ever suspected: between work and living, between families, between cities. You surrendered by breaking the connections, or by letting them atrophy. We shall try not to do that, in this generation. We shall hold to the connections and ride our history'.[77] This is to be, in its unfolding and future dimensions, a history defined by convulsive change rather than the sense of stagnation so prevalent in his parents' own generation, and by a different

---

[74] Williams, *Second Generation*, p. 94.

[75] Williams, *Second Generation*, p. 101.

[76] Williams, *Second Generation*, pp. 208, 272. This is a language Kate ultimately accepts, but with an important qualification: 'Harold said I was corrupt and it's true, Peter. They say power corrupts and perhaps it does. What I know, in myself, is a quite different thing. That power corrupts the people it is exercised over', p. 338.

[77] Williams, *Second Generation*, p. 253.

kind of mobility – not necessarily upward in its social trajectory, or outward in its geographical range.

During a reception with a group of African revolutionaries, Peter is challenged by Helen, an old acquaintance from the student Labour Club, precisely on his reluctance to abandon Britain and engage with the new horizons of political transformation opening up across the Third World: 'You know perfectly well, Peter, if you stay here you'll just die by inches. I don't know how you can bear it, when in fact elsewhere there are real things happening'.[78] He replies that change, a fundamental kind of change, is also underway in Britain in the 1960s, perhaps not 'alive and exciting, as so often elsewhere', but fundamental nevertheless.[79] He mentions the example of the 'young peace marchers, the young trying to change the society' and describes them as 'a generation in mourning … The dark clothes, the set faces, the voices subdued almost to silence'.[80] The pretence of excitement, as vindicated by Helen and the sort of cosmopolitan radicalism she represents, is thus merely an obfuscation of the larger connections, of the fact that the world-making of the new nations and the 'total exposure' of the new generations are actually part of the same process: 'We're at the breaking point everywhere, and at the growing point everywhere. To move away is just shifting the burden'.[81] Peter concludes, with the African revolutionary Okoi's approval, that, while '[w]e have to pay our debt' for the colonial legacy, and 'the price will be heavy', 'what we can't do, in conscience, is start our own lives somewhere else. Using other people to live out our mistakes and frustrations. All we can honestly do is face what we are, here'.[82]

This declaration holds the key to the novel's conclusion, as Peter's decision to settle with Beth, in their city, finding work at the car factory and interrupting his academic career while pursuing a different sort of intellectual work, is announced to both families. Addressing Harold, Peter attempts to explain his final understanding of the connection between life and work, and the new sense of settlement it entails for him – one that is necessarily provisional and particular: 'Yes, Dad, I'm trying to settle. There are other places, but for me, inevitably, this is the place to begin. What I shall try to do, here, is a new kind of inquiry, with ourselves involved in it. And for our own understanding, not just for report'.[83] The experiential distance, the communicative gap, between

---

[78] Williams, *Second Generation*, p. 314.

[79] Williams, *Second Generation*, p. 316.

[80] Williams, *Second Generation*, p. 316.

[81] Williams, *Second Generation*, p. 316.

[82] Williams, *Second Generation*, p. 316.

[83] Williams, *Second Generation*, p. 344.

father and son and between generations becomes apparent here in a way that does not offer the satisfaction of closure around a common understanding. For Harold, there is a renewed sense of defeat in his son's decision to seek employment at the works – as he puts it, 'Eighteen years' education, and you want to go back where I started' – and a rejection of the terms of Peter's new intellectual project, which for Harold is just another version of the sociological survey, with its necessarily distant techniques of measurement ('Like we're the new tribe, and they hack through the jungle to find us'), indeed a reiteration of the old class divide against which his own life had been defined: 'it makes no difference, that he happened to be born here. He wants the same, just to measure and see what we're good for'.[84] Ultimately, as Kate puts it, what Peter and Beth are to find out, 'is that we're not together', that the experiential distance, in spite of the effort to draw the connections – and ride the history, as Peter had put it – remains the defining aspect of this society: 'You say what you have to, and do what you have to. We'll listen, we'll challenge it, different ways'.[85] In what amounts to an important qualification of *Border Country*'s vision, *Second Generation* thus concludes with this refusal to contain its emphasis on tension and pressure. With the absence of an organic point of reference, the only margin for composing a common life, against the uncertain experience of post-war capitalism, is to be found in the language of 'total exposure' – that is, in a social logic without guaranteed political or personal outcomes.

3.3 A Spectral Realism

Apropos of *The Fight for Manod*, the 1979 novel that completes his 'Welsh Trilogy', Williams comments that, in contrast to *Border Country* and *Second Generation*, what had shaped it was 'a specific contemporary sadness: the relation between a wholly possible future and the contradictions and blockages of the present'.[86] As Williams explains, registering his own political mood in the late 1970s, this sadness reflected a sense of separation from 'the kind of confidence in the future many of us have had', as well as the current need, in order to hope for any possible restoration of this confidence, to pass 'through the shadows of the devastating experiences of war and what happened to the best revolutionary societies and then, here, the terrible disintegration of what was once a labour movement with apparently unproblematic perspectives'.[87]

---

[84] Williams, *Second Generation*, pp. 344–345.
[85] Williams, *Second Generation*, p. 346.
[86] Williams, *Politics and Letters*, p. 294.
[87] Williams, *Politics and Letters*, pp. 294–295.

The Fight for Manod is indeed a novel in which the echoes of a Labourism in seemingly terminal crisis are clearly audible, and in which the idea of radical politics is fatefully split between a spectral longing for lost futures (including those of a utopian kind) and the disabling sense of impotence following upon the 'wearying and displacement of flesh and blood' – that is, the incorporation and neutralisation of collective agency – effected by the institutional forms of late capitalism.[88] Matthew Price, now a middle-aged and renowned academic, is invited by Robert Lane from *Second Generation* – now an official in the Labour government – to act, jointly with Peter Owen, as a special consultant on a project to develop a new kind of city in a rural valley in mid-Wales. As Lane explains, Manod was initially projected in the early 1960s as a radical experiment in town planning and regional development: 'a city of small towns, a city of villages almost' and 'one of the first human settlements, anywhere in the world, to have been conceived, from the beginning, in post-industrial terms and with a post-electronic technology'.[89] This had been a utopian vision seeking to overcome the deeply entrenched division between the country and the city which, as Williams argues in his famous book of 1973, is 'the critical culmination of the division and specialisation of labour' in advanced capitalism.[90] But what had followed the original utopian impulse, as Lane reveals in this early conversation with Matthew Price, was the logic of institutional expediency: first, a sense of deadlock compounded by the 'shortage of money' and then, suddenly, a mysterious resurgence of political interest which had now made the project 'urgently alive' again.[91]

Combining elements of speculative, detective, and Gothic fiction, this novel is, as Tony Pinkney has suggested, 'a realist "limit-text", a work where literary realism stumbles upon something which exceeds its grasp, falters badly, but is not altogether quelled'.[92] Indeed, at its centre lies a new sense of intractability for which the provisional – if ever imperfect – ideal of communication discussed above (that post-foundational substitute for the old sense of community) seems particularly ill-suited. In the late 1970s, the mystery that keeps eluding the exploratory lens of regenerative realism is revealed to be an effect of what Lane calls 'the new indifference', the 'brittleness' 'of this

---

[88] Williams, *Politics and Letters*, p. 295.

[89] Raymond Williams, *The Fight for Manod* (London: Chatto & Windus, 1979), p. 13.

[90] Raymond Williams, *The Country and the City* (London: The Hogarth Press, 1993), p. 304.

[91] Williams, *The Fight for Manod*, pp. 13, 14.

[92] Tony Pinkney, *Raymond Williams* (Bridgend: Seren Books, 1991), p. 71.

stage of capitalism', in which 'only the plan is real' and '[n]othing directly human attaches to it'.[93] In the face of such impenetrable cynicism, Matthew's commission is expected – impossibly – to be rooted in human experience. For such is the nature of the job: to conduct 'a different kind of inquiry: a lived inquiry' into the place and the people, and thus to 'live the problem' before reporting on it.[94] But this is an immediacy that is no longer available, for the logic of experience so forcefully introduced in *Border Country* as a problem of lived measurement is now fundamentally displaced in *The Fight for Manod* to a hauntological register of which loss and the (im)possibility of spectral recovery are central dimensions.

Thus, Matthew's return to Wales in this novel is less of a border-crossing *beyond* the work of mourning, ultimately leading to the definition of a liveable distance, than a form of haunting in Derrida's sense. As Mark Fisher reminds us, haunting 'can be construed as a failed mourning'.[95] With its temporal disruption, holding us in thrall to a past that refuses to make its virtual effects felt as actual, and to a future which cannot be anticipated yet confronts us, in actuality, with the sense of a radical otherness, the spectre which haunts forecloses the possibility of any simple settlement into personal and social immediacy. The real, without simply disappearing, becomes fundamentally dislocated. After accepting the job, Matthew's car journey to Manod is punctuated by this sense of spectral dislocation, a temporal rupture complicating the felt meaning of his undertaking as well as the more general understanding of the historical process of which it is a part. Getting out of the car to contemplate the surrounding landscape, Matthew observes that the simple divisions on which an earlier sense of measurement had been predicated are still visible – 'on the near side the valleys still green and wooded, on the far side blackened with collieries and slagheaps and grey huddled terraces' – but he feels that it is the 'more involving life', that which lives on after it has been, like Glynmawr station, 'not only closed but flattened, obliterated', that has 'a lasting closeness'.[96]

The lost centre of this life – his own father's experience – is now only available in spectral form as the continuous haunting of eyes 'watching', without 'focus', and, in spite of all the 'time and distance from that remembered death', transferring to his own experience an ever expanding sense of loss: 'In his own middle age, after his own first collapse, there was still a long

---

[93] Williams, *The Fight for Manod*, pp. 16, 11.

[94] Williams, *The Fight for Manod*, p. 14.

[95] Mark Fisher, *Ghosts of My Life: Writings on Depression, Hauntology and Lost Futures* (Winchester: Zero Books, 2022), p. 22.

[96] Williams, *The Fight for Manod*, p. 36.

mourning through all the reaches of his body'.[97] Yet this is a mourning which, in true spectral fashion, calls for a future that remains in excess of any modalised present – an 'instant', as Derrida puts it, 'that is not docile to time'.[98] For the difficulty of imagining just the kind of future which Manod's utopian design presupposes lies in its reductive formalism, which necessarily excludes a properly experiential dimension: 'there was no route in the senses from the thousands of details, the working papers of the city, to this green valley where they might eventually be realized'.[99] It is, Matthew doubtfully concedes, that perhaps 'any future must be like this: abstract, angular, a blank manufactured page'.[100] But the sort of temporal break, the radical futurity implied by Matthew's sense of loss and spectral experience, is one that can be neither renounced nor reduced to simple political determinations.[101]

Throughout the novel, this vision of and for the future will offer a stark contrast to the sort of revolutionary pessimism incarnated by Peter Owen. As the corrupt scheme underlying the project begins to surface, Peter sets out on an investigative mission that will ultimately lead him to uncover a web of vested corporate interests at the heart of this putatively radical State initiative. Peter's decision to expose the scandal and pursue a confrontational approach, aided by a group of Welsh militants, against the rarefied centres of late capitalist power is ultimately one that focuses on the blockage of the future defining this historical moment (the debilitating core of 'contemporary sadness' diagnosed by Williams in the 1970s) rather than on the possibilities – the 'resources of hope' – inscribed in this dislocated temporality.[102] And the latter is precisely what Matthew refuses or indeed is unable to exclude. As he admits at one point, his loyalty is primarily to the sense, which so strongly 'belongs to this country', of 'a pure idea, a pure passion, for a different world' – an inexhaustible and yet fundamentally irreducible sense of futurity which has recurrently 'moved through' the people of Wales, '[i]n their religion [and] in their politics'.[103] This is precisely the kind of future, as he says, that 'we [cannot] give up' and which Manod (however compromised its immediate realisation) may ultimately, as a local inscription of

---

[97] Williams, *The Fight for Manod*, p. 37.

[98] Derrida, *Specters of Marx* (New York: Routledge, 1994), p. xix.

[99] Williams, *The Fight for Manod*, p. 37.

[100] Williams, *The Fight for Manod*, p. 38.

[101] To quote Derrida, this is an '"[e]xperience" of the past as to come, the one and the other absolutely absolute, beyond all modification of any present whatever', *Specters of Marx*, p. xix.

[102] Raymond Williams, *Resources of Hope: Culture, Democracy, Socialism*, ed. by Robin Gable (London: Verso, 1989).

[103] Williams, *The Fight for Manod*, p. 98.

the 'leap' 'we have to make', represent.[104] A spectral future (a *to-come*), after all, in which mourning is that work which is never done and is that distance which can be experienced, but never fully grasped – or measured – in the present.

Following Matthew's second heart attack, in the middle of the ministerial meeting where his report on Manod is heard, the novel closes with his and Susan's return to Wales. The description of this final crossing captures the cautiously hopeful indeterminacy of their renewed sense of futurity:

> Where they were standing, looking out, was on a border in the earth and in history: to north and west the great expanses of a pastoral country; to south and east, where the iron and coal had been worked, the crowded valleys, the new industries, now in their turn becoming old. There had been a contrast, one, clearly seen on this border, between an old way of life and a new, as between a father living in his old and known ways and a son living differently, in a new occupation and with a new cast of mind. But what was visible now was that both were old. The pressure for renewal, inside them, had to make its way through a land and through lives that had been deeply shaped, deeply committed, by a present that was always moving, inexorably, into the past. And those moments of the present that could connect to a future were then hard to grasp, hard to hold to, hard to bring together to a rhythm, to a movement, to the necessary shape of a quite different life. What could now be heard, momentarily, as this actual movement, had conditions of time, of growth, quite different from the conditions of any single life, or of any father and son.[105]

No longer an abstract projection, the future is now, in this final vision, an undecidable movement beyond the purview of a personal experience of time, even more radically than in any utopian design. But this undecidability does not exhaust the sense of possibility. On the contrary, it exacerbates it in a general movement towards the collective sphere of history – the history of a people to be defined as much by their renewal (beyond any simple horizon of expectation) as by their past way of life.[106]

Published in 1985, Williams's last completed novel *Loyalties* offers a significant investigation of the spectral nature of the political and its irreducible

---

[104] Williams, *The Fight for Manod*, p. 99.

[105] Williams, *The Fight for Manod*, pp. 206–207.

[106] At a crucial moment in the meeting with the minister and his advisors, just before he suffers his heart attack, Matthew insists that the 'crucial factor' deciding the merit of the project, is 'who the people are to be', Williams, *The Fight for Manod*, p. 193.

role in the constitution of social bonds (or, in the novel's language, 'loyalties'). The narrative follows two families – one English and bourgeois, the other Welsh and working-class – across a series of historical and personal dislocations. It begins in 1936, as Emma Braose and her brother Norman, together with their Cambridge friends 'Monkey' Pitter, 'Georgi' Wilkes, and Mark Ryder, arrive in the South Wales Valleys to participate in a Communist Party-sponsored act of support for the Spanish Republic in the context of the incipient Civil War. In spite of the stark cultural (and even physical) contrast between the local working-class activists, who include Bert Lewis and Jim Pritchard, and their middle-class comrades from England, the political urgency of the general situation – marked by the onslaught of fascism – imposes a very specific definition of loyalty, one which basically transcends any purely sociological and pre-political notions of class identity inherited from the past. As Emma observes apropos of the obvious external differences between the classes, 'You could change your political allegiance but you still carried your appearance and manners. It was often entertaining, at either end of the spectrum, to watch people struggling with the contradictions'. But she immediately adds: 'As if any of that old stuff mattered now'.[107]

In the context of the Popular Front and its crucial mobilisation of ideological resources in the fight against fascism, the terms of definition out of which any consequential notion of loyalty may arise for socialists like these characters, whether proletarian or bourgeois, English or Welsh, rest on the possibility of articulation and the establishment of links and equivalences between struggles. The young historian Mark Ryder offers a key formulation of this expansive vision of loyalty when, in 'a strong, moving, impromptu speech', he 'relate[s] the struggle of the Spanish people to their own experiences of struggle in the valleys', adding that:

> There had never in all their lifetimes been so clear a case of the realities of proletarian internationalism. There were deep interconnections, across national boundaries, within the general class struggle. And the time was now coming close when they would have to make moves to link up these two fighting fronts. All the energies had been taken up with their own struggles, but there were moments in history when the conflict burst through into open action, with the opposing forces clearly staked out.[108]

---

[107] Raymond Williams, *Loyalties* (London: The Hogarth Press, 1989), p. 17.

[108] Williams, *Loyalties*, pp. 22–23. Yasuhiro Kondo has argued, following Bruce Robbins's reading of the novel, that this 'is a kind of Utopian moment in which an alternative form of collectivity may manifest itself beyond the divisions of classes and nationalities', '"To Feel the Connections": Collectivity and Dialectic

The 'deep interconnections' between Welsh miners and Spanish anti-fascists are not an automatic manifestation of some underlying objective reality, but rather, crucially, the outcome of a political effort to 'link up' two effectively heterogeneous struggles. This is a politics – premised on a loyalty and a socialist identity – without guarantees: that is, without narrow determinations or known outcomes and turned towards an experience of radical contingency. Laclau's claim that 'antagonism has a revelatory function, in that it shows the ultimately contingent nature of all objectivity' is directly apposite to the problematic addressed by Mark's speech.[109] As Paul Howe, the young volunteer who will soon die in Spain, tells Norman about his sense of the historical position they inhabit as committed socialists in the 1930s, 'We have to go now as strangers to fight something alien, and the outcome, either way, will be a new strangeness. If we live to see it we shall still be strangers, to each other and to ourselves'.[110] As in Mark's speech above, what is at stake here is an expansive, radically contingent, and in that sense spectral definition of political loyalty, one in which dislocation and openness to the heterogeneous remain absolutely irreducible. Thus, to engage in socialist politics, to embrace 'proletarian internationalism', in this context is not to be tied down to an objective class identity, but to welcome and to be defined by the formative 'strangeness' of the antagonisms ahead (in the connected struggle against fascists and capitalist exploiters).

It is important to insist on this opening vision of the primacy of political articulation (or loyalty) in the novel, and its implicit rejection of any sense of foundational objectivity, because this is precisely the idea whose dislocation and crisis the narrative will go on to chart in each subsequent section. The narrative immediately mobilises an imaginary of betrayal which solidifies a split between the personal and the political, ultimately reducing the latter to a logic of crude social objectivity and homogeneity from which the spectral effects of 1930s socialism are tentatively – if never definitively – excluded. This imaginary of betrayal is primarily channelled through Norman, who has a brief relationship with Nesta Pritchard, only to abandon her abruptly after the Communist Party puts pressure on him, claiming that 'sex outside the Party would be a division of loyalties'.[111] A child, Gwyn, is born from this relationship, but no contact is maintained between him and his 'natural'

---

in Raymond Williams's *Loyalties*', *Key Words: A Journal of Cultural Materialism* 9 (2011), p. 117.

[109] Ernesto Laclau, *New Reflections on the Revolution of Our Time* (London: Verso, 1990), p. 18.

[110] Williams, *Loyalties*, pp. 48–49.

[111] Williams, *Loyalties*, p. 43.

father – until a tense re-encounter takes place in his adult age. The only direct link between Gwyn's two families (and their contrasting social worlds) is provided by Norman's sister Emma, who takes an ongoing personal interest in Gwyn, Nesta, and her husband Bert Lewis. The latter, an avid working-class Communist who fights in Spain (witnessing his comrade Paul Howe's death) and then in Normandy, where he is nearly killed, sustaining injuries that will leave him deformed and chronically ill, comes to represent the fullness – one could say, the purity – of proletarian commitment and loyalty. If Norman is the treacherous absent father whose betrayal is further compounded by his role as a Soviet spy, Bert is the solid, unbreakable – yet physically broken – presence of a working-class father figure. For Bert, the Labour victory in 1945 is undoubtedly, objectively, the coming into being of working-class power. As he asserts, defiantly, in a heated exchange with his own father-in-law, 'This has been our bloody war and now it'll be our bloody peace'.[112] It is with Bert holding his hand that Gwyn will first attempt to negotiate – still in an immature, childish manner – the meaning of socialism. On Vesting Day in 1947, he observes the ceremony in which the mines are officially nationalised and listens to Bert as he explains: 'It means belonging to the people'.[113] Yet a sense of crisis, of vulnerability, besetting this experience of internal solidity and continuity associated with Bert's deeply rooted proletarian identity becomes increasingly apparent. In the extreme winter of 1947, the stalling impulse of the Labour government begins to reveal the limitations of a politics that is no longer forged in the radical contingency of antagonism: 'There was no longer an outside enemy; only a beleaguered and bewildered Labour government, its confident world suddenly frozen and chaotic, falling back desperately on slogans against a natural disaster with which a still disorganised economy was unable to deal'.[114]

On both sides of the class divide, a general political identity crisis will set in as the intractable strangeness – to reiterate Paul's point – of the post-war world begins to unfold and as the objectivism and solidified answers of a politics exclusively predicated on class seem increasingly inadequate. In 1955–1956, just as tensions begin to mount regarding the stance of international socialists towards the Soviet Union, Emma emerges as the voice of Communist orthodoxy in the novel. Following her husband Georgi's death in a motorcycle accident, Emma travels to Danycapel to visit Gwyn and his Welsh family. The conversation between her and Bert swiftly turns to the current state of the Party (of which Georgi had been a leading cadre). She

[112] Williams, *Loyalties*, p. 117.
[113] Williams, *Loyalties*, p. 119.
[114] Williams, *Loyalties*, p. 123.

says: 'There's only one worrying thing, but it's still very small. Among a few
there's a definite anti-Soviet tendency ... the thing they won't see, the Party
is still of and for the international working class. What these others represent
is something different: a sort of liberalism really, like some of it was in the
Thirties'.[115] The political loyalties of the Popular Front are thus revealed as false
loyalties in so far as their underlying class content was always suspect – or in
other words, in so far as they lacked an objective class foundation. As Emma
puts it, 'these liberals ... had nothing else [that is, apart from anti-fascism] in
common with the international working class. So now, with the Cold War,
they go back to their own colours; saying that the Soviet Union itself is a
tyranny'.[116] This is a point she will insist on as the crisis deepens in 1956
against the background of Khruschev's revelations. Speaking with Norman,
she intimates how the sense of firmness and indestructibility she perceived in
her husband, whose real source was undoubtedly his Communism, had now
passed to her: 'The Party's firmness'.[117] This is immediately equated with the
logic of objectivity inscribed in her orthodox Marxist conception of class. The
problem with the younger socialists is precisely, she claims, their 'misplaced
idea of class', the fact that they 'make it subjective, though they're supposed
to be Marxists. But class is objective: objective membership and objective
affiliation'.[118] She even goes on to describe what she refers to as the privileging
of subjectivity over class by these dissident socialists as 'this Freudian stuff ...
the whole post-war rot'.[119]

What lies at the heart of this dogmatic objectivism is, of course, a failure
to mobilise the strangeness of a world, of a social reality, defined – and
challenged – by new antagonisms. As 'Monkey' Pitter (a character whose
moral ambiguity and intractable intellectual presence provide the novel with
one of its shifting – and indeed spectral – centres) puts it at one point,
recalling Paul Howe's haunting argument, 'those of us who lived, as Paul
didn't, will be real strangers. We shall go on saying the things we learned to
say and it will be just strange talk, in a strange land'.[120] In the 'strange land'
of the 1960s and the pluralisation of struggles, Emma's (but also, to some
extent, Gwyn's) sense of objectivity meets its decisive limit.[121] The logic of

---

[115] Williams, *Loyalties*, p. 149.
[116] Williams, *Loyalties*, p. 149.
[117] Williams, *Loyalties*, p. 169.
[118] Williams, *Loyalties*, p. 168.
[119] Williams, *Loyalties*, p. 185.
[120] Williams, *Loyalties*, p. 161.
[121] Again, as Laclau puts it: 'antagonism is the *limit of all objectivity*', *New Reflections*,
     p. 17.

heterogeneity that accompanies the political discussions between Gwyn, his wife Jill, his brother Dic, and others, once again reintroduces this experience of irreducible strangeness and radical contingency. If the point of departure is the assumption that the new struggles and the emphasis 'on international events: Cuba and China and now Vietnam' 'was an extension of the old union and labour politics', and if the comparison with the 1930s becomes explicit ('Vietnam is our Spain'), the sense of rupture in the assumed objective structure of society – with class as its gravitational centre – continues to pose a challenge.[122] When Dic calls 'Maoists and Trots' (who were now doing 'much of the campaigning') 'splitters', Gwyn replies: 'No, not splitters. It isn't like that any more. There's no one big thing to split'.[123] Moreover, again in a way that makes the Popular Front context with which the novel opens directly relevant (if, at the same time, spectrally irretrievable) to this later conjuncture and its return of politics, there is the acknowledgement that the impulse for the new movements comes from 'two quite different traditions' and the 'quite different people carrying them': 'In effect – as Gwyn puts it – different classes'.[124]

If this contingent and subjectivist anchoring of the political presents something of a challenge for a young working-class socialist such as Gwyn (who is Bert's adopted son, after all), in the case of a Communist traditionalist such as Emma it leads to furious incomprehension and, ultimately, silence. A similar exchange to the one above takes place between her and Monkey, where he points out 'that a gravely weakened Party is now tagging along behind any column it sees moving: Trotskyites, Anarchists, Flower Children, New Left'.[125] While the reality of a politics without objective guarantees is confirmed by the explosions of 1968, a damning challenge to Emma's objectivist faith in class comes from the working class themselves. Repeating some of these workerist rhetorical gestures to his mother, Nesta, Gwyn suggests that London, where he now lives, is a place where a principled Communist like Bert would be thought of as 'aggressive', 'subversive', and 'greedy', yet no such mistake would be made in Danycapel, since this is after all 'the right place' with 'people … who don't need it explained'.[126] To this, Nesta replies, emphatically: 'No it isn't. You're just talking like Emma. That's all we get, whenever she comes here. How we're the real life. How we really understand things. How much stronger she feels when she's been here'.[127]

[122] Williams, *Loyalties*, pp. 221, 202.
[123] Williams, *Loyalties*, p. 221.
[124] Williams, *Loyalties*, p. 223.
[125] Williams, *Loyalties*, p. 237.
[126] Williams, *Loyalties*, p. 247.
[127] Williams, *Loyalties*, p. 247.

As the novel moves on to its concluding section and last historical conjuncture, 1984 and the Miners' Strike, we observe a further hardening in Gwyn's understanding of class loyalty. This is primarily the result of an intensified sense of personal betrayal prompted by new revelations about Norman's trajectory, but also a function of a new experience of the political in the 1980s:

> After the shattering encounter with Meele he had spent hours talking with Jill, taking it through from the beginning, admitting to emotions which for years he had only intermittently recognised and which he had always appeared to control. What had never been allowed to come through as itself was a straight anger, an aggressive anger, against what he found himself calling, to Jill, the Braoses: including Emma, as Jill was quick to point out. Over and above the personal resentments it was a straight, bitter, unreconstructed class anger.[128]

The 'shattering encounter' refers to an interview with one of the security officials vetting Gwyn for internal promotion as head of the government department that is about to develop a project on deep ocean nuclear waste disposal. In the course of the supposedly informal exchange, questions are raised about Gwyn's radical activities in his student years and then, by implication, about his current loyalty to the British State in the context of the resurgent Cold War. Meele blackmails Gwyn with insinuations about the security services' ongoing interest in Norman's post-war activities, implying that Gwyn's new role would involve having access to sensitive military information. This episode results in what could be described as a full retreat from politics understood as a contingent, articulatory practice of the sort which had defined Gwyn's own engagements in the 1960s, and those of the previous generation in the 1930s. Just as his own career takes him into the heart of the State apparatus and the specific institutional rationality governing 'public policy' (a term he emphasises, since Gwyn is, after all, a senior civil servant in Thatcher's Britain), and thus away from any direct sense of antagonism and of the articulation of oppositional political identities, class loyalty resurfaces, somewhat paradoxically, as a personal defence mechanism as well as a general symptom of withdrawal (if not defeat).[129] The language of betrayal becomes

---

[128] Williams, *Loyalties*, p. 292.

[129] Gwyn describes the background to the project thus: 'After extensive and controversial mainland testing of possible sites for the deep deposit of the more dangerous nuclear wastes, there was now an urgent and technically very difficult exploration of the possibility of drilled ocean-bed deposits: now the main work of his division. The questions of public policy did not have to be invented; they were already

all the more emphatic as the prospect of openly political confrontation within a specific horizon of achievable socialist hegemony is replaced by a moral interpretation of the class struggle itself. Thus, the treacherous actions of Pitter and Braose are recast as part of a historical sequence – guided, as it were, by the necessity of their objective class allegiance – culminating in the 'evil' of the British ruling class's concerted attack, in 1984, on the mining communities.

From this perspective, the evil is to be resisted by the opposing moral force of a solid working class enacting a sedimented and seemingly unbreakable social identity. As Phil Evans, 'who had been the youngest boy … helping to raise the flag in 1947', confirms, 'It's evil. But down here we are stronger than evil'.[130] This moral interpretation leads Gwyn (who by this point is, let us remember, a visitor, and therefore an outsider, in the embattled proletarian world of the Welsh Valleys) to vindicate an idea of socialism predicated on the objective existence of 'an actual society'.[131] As he puts it to Norman, in their final, acrimonious, encounter, 'I grew up in such a society … And then no authentic act for socialism can distance itself, let alone hide, from these ties of its own people'.[132] While the identification of loyalty with a fully-fledged metaphysics of presence based on class is certainly the position Gwyn endorses as the novel comes to an end, the dislocatory impulse governing the narrative, and the spectral effects it produces, cannot be said to disappear completely, even in this final moment of presumptive clarification (and simplification) of the struggle. In this way, an enduring sense of strangeness and contingency continues to inform the logic of politics, even if negativity is no longer explicitly connected to any new sense of possible creation or hegemonic articulation. Thus, as his brother Dic complains about the lack of active solidarity towards the miners shown by other unions and sections of the Labour Movement (he specifically mentions unionised lorry drivers), Gwyn's reply appears to momentarily suspend judgement on the emphatic class moralism he otherwise seems to have embraced, pointing precisely to the political (that is, the contingent and discursive) nature of the very idea of class loyalty. The historical problem faced by the miners in 1984 is then that 'the politics have gone wrong' and that '[w]e've taken solidarity for granted, though the whole social order has been working for years to break it up'.[133] In

being openly argued. The division's own work had been described, in the press and in pamphlets, as preparation for gross dumping in the ocean: poisoning the seas which are the common inheritance of mankind', Williams, *Loyalties*, p. 275.

[130] Williams, *Loyalties*, p. 335.
[131] Williams, *Loyalties*, p. 358.
[132] Williams, *Loyalties*, p. 358.
[133] Williams, *Loyalties*, p. 341.

other words, compared with the logic of solidarity at work in the 1930s and 40s, out of which a truly hegemonic progressive formation had emerged, by the 1980s political hegemony – and with it, as its consequence rather than precondition, a new moral economy of loyalties – lay with a new, highly active and antagonistic Conservatism.[134]

---

[134] This is confirmed in the novel by the fact that the main narrative is framed and bracketed by two separate chapters, entitled 'FIRST' and 'LAST', detailing the spectacularising approach to the novel's subject matter of an increasingly powerful media environment.

Chapter Four

The Anarchic Trace

4.1 A Politics of 'An-archy': Doris Lessing in the 1960s

I want to turn now to another distinguished offshoot of the post-war conjuncture of socialist writing discussed in the previous chapter: the work of Doris Lessing. As I intend to demonstrate in this opening section, Lessing's fiction of the 1960s (in particular, *The Golden Notebook* and *The Four-Gated City*) marks an important departure within the broadly New Leftist constellation of British literary socialism in this period, (re)introducing a key anarchic dimension into the project of a realism without guarantees.[1]

In her 1971 preface to *The Golden Notebook*, Lessing suggests that the 'central theme' of this novel, which 'nobody so much as noticed' upon its original publication in 1962, is the idea 'that sometimes when people "crack up" it is a way of self-healing, of the inner self's dismissing false dichotomies and divisions'.[2] Thus, 'the essence of the book, the organization of it, everything in it, says implicitly and explicitly, that we must not divide things off, must not compartmentalize'.[3] This theme is articulated via a concrete (and, for the Lessing of the 1950s who wrote it, biographically relevant) examination of the effects of radical political commitment (especially to the ideologically and experientially totalising project of Communism) on this social and psychological dynamic of division.[4]

---

[1] See Sandra Singer, 'Feminist Commitment to Left-Wing Realism in *The Golden Notebook*', in *Doris Lessing's* The Golden Notebook *After Fifty*, ed. by Alice Ridout et al. (New York: Palgrave Macmillan, 2015), pp. 73–95.

[2] Doris Lessing, *The Golden Notebook* (London: Fourth Estate, 2014), p. 8.

[3] Lessing, *The Golden Notebook*, p. 10.

[4] See Matthew Taunton, 'Communism by the Letter: Doris Lessing and the Politics of Writing', *ELH* 88:1 (2021), pp. 251–280. See also Matthew Taunton, *Red Britain: The Russian Revolution in Mid-Century Culture* (Oxford: Oxford University Press, 2019). For an illuminating discussion of *The Golden Notebook* as a socialist *Bildungsroman*, see Benjamin Kohlmann, 'Toward a History and Theory of the Socialist Bildungsroman', *Novel: A Forum on Fiction* 48:2 (2015), pp. 167–189.

The Golden Notebook follows Anna Wulf, a writer and increasingly reticent member of the Communist Party, through her interactions with friends, lovers, and comrades, and through the 'inner' divisions of her mental and emotional life as reflected in the four colour-coded notebooks she keeps: 'not one', Lessing observes in her preface, 'because, as she recognizes, she has to separate things off from each other, out of fear of chaos, of formlessness – of breakdown'.[5] The novel begins with the first section of 'Free Women', the recurring narrative frame through which Anna's focal story is told: in the summer of 1957, Anna and her friend, the actor Molly Jacobs, are reunited in the latter's London flat. As if offering Molly a telling report on the general state of things following her recent absence, Anna remarks, 'the point is, that as far as I can see, everything's cracking up'.[6] She goes on to share the discovery she made 'while you were away that for a lot of people you and I are practically interchangeable'.[7] This is, Molly replies, in spite of the fact that 'we're so different in every way' and 'because we both live the same kind of life' as unmarried 'free women'.[8] It immediately becomes apparent that the shared basis of this freedom goes deeper and is in fact connected to a traumatic psychoanalytic experience with the same therapist, a German woman they refer to as 'Mother Sugar':

> The reservations both had felt about the solemn and painful ritual were expressed by the pet name, 'Mother Sugar'; which, as time passed, became a name for much more than a person, and indicated a whole way of looking at life – traditional, rooted, conservative, in spite of its scandalous familiarity with everything amoral. *In spite of* – that was how Anna and Molly, discussing the ritual, had felt it; recently Anna had been feeling more and more it was *because of*[9]

While accepting the probable benefits of the actual therapy (as Anna admits, 'Oh, I'm not saying she didn't do me all the good in the world'), there is a fundamental rejection by both women of the *principle* embodied in the traditional psychoanalytic worldview in so far as it represents a discursive limiting and parcelling out of their actual experience: 'That they were both "insecure" and "unrooted", words which dated from the era of Mother Sugar, they both freely acknowledged. But Anna had recently been learning to use these words in a different way, not as something to be apologized for, but as

[5] Lessing, *The Golden Notebook*, p. 7.
[6] Lessing, *The Golden Notebook*, p. 25.
[7] Lessing, *The Golden Notebook*, p. 26.
[8] Lessing, *The Golden Notebook*, p. 26.
[9] Lessing, *The Golden Notebook*, p. 26.

flags or banners for an attitude that amounted to a different philosophy'.[10] This early intuition inscribes an alternative principle (or rather, anti-principle) that will ultimately disturb the economy of division on which social and personal, but also political, life is predicated in the novel. For, as Anna puts it, 'what is this security and balance that's supposed to be so good? What's wrong with living emotionally from hand-to-mouth in a world that's changing as fast as it is?'[11] The political reference implicit in this question in unmissable. Against the general background of the Cold War and with the 1956 crisis of Communism as one of the novel's central axes, there is an immediate sense that the world of existential security and intellectual certainty of Anna's earlier life has come to an end. If the emotional and mental fragmentation of experience is a symptom of generalised ontological crisis, it is nevertheless also the basis for another (for an *other*) possibility of ethical and political life.

When Richard, Molly's ex-husband, confronts them about their lifestyle, blaming it for his son Tommy's mental trouble (which later on results in his attempted suicide), he also offers a revealing characterisation of their politics, to the point that the lifestyle and the politics are signified as inseparable, as aspects of the same 'chaos' (a term that Anna will use to describe her notebook writing).[12] Richard says: 'It hasn't occurred to you that the real trouble with Tommy is that he's been surrounded half his life with communists or so-called communists … And now they're all leaving the Party, or have left – don't you think it might have had some effect?'[13] Anna admits that 'one of Tommy's troubles is that he was brought up a socialist and it's not an easy time to be a socialist' but says that neither she nor Molly have 'made an about-turn', as Richard puts it, since their break with the Party.[14] Rather, she suggests, it's 'a question of a way of looking at life'.[15] To this, Richard replies: 'You want me to believe that the way you look at life, which is *a sort of anarchy*, as far as I can make out, is socialist?'[16] This remark by Molly's right-wing and wealthy ex-husband captures an important aspect of what we could call the process of reversal or reinscription of division in the novel, from the psychic realm to the political and back across the eminently *anarchic* practice of writing embodied in the notebooks. Interestingly, this is a description Molly herself embraces later on in the conversation when, presumably referring to her state

---

[10] Lessing, *The Golden Notebook*, pp. 27, 31.
[11] Lessing, *The Golden Notebook*, p. 31.
[12] Lessing, *The Golden Notebook*, p. 56.
[13] Lessing, *The Golden Notebook*, p. 40.
[14] Lessing, *The Golden Notebook*, p. 40.
[15] Lessing, *The Golden Notebook*, p. 40.
[16] Lessing, *The Golden Notebook*, p. 40; my emphasis.

of mind and 'complicated living', she says: 'there's a very interesting state of anarchy up there'.[17] Indeed, the anarchy into which these 'free women' turn their lives, through their uprooting and displacement of psychological and ideological foundations and certainties, is actually the condition of possibility imagined by the novel for any completeness, for any healed life, to come.[18] Its anarchic nature actually signifies a disarticulation of the order of being and knowledge on which their adult (as in their mentally fragile *and* politically conscious) existence has so far been predicated.

I want to assimilate this notion of anarchy to Miguel Abensour's reading of the concept in the work of the philosopher Emmanuel Levinas. According to Abensour, Levinas offers a 'pluralist conception of the social' that is made possible by his assertion of the primacy of the ethical relationship (which he describes as the 'face to face relationship').[19] The preservation of a social multiplicity that cannot be reduced to the ontological 'fusion' of totality is rooted in 'the idea of a separation that resists synthesis'.[20] The notion of anarchy is introduced by Levinas precisely on the basis of this resistance to totalisation and in the name of ethical primacy. It refers to the absence of a levelling ontological principle, to the 'lack of an *arche*' that would abolish the primordial orientation of the self towards the other.[21] As Abensour points out, Levinas is logically sceptical about the political conception of anarchy (that is, anarchism) 'since such a conception amounts to imposing a principle to anarchy'.[22] As Levinas writes in *Otherwise than Being*, 'It would be self-contradictory to set it [anarchy] up as a principle (in the sense that anarchists understand it). Anarchy cannot be sovereign, like an *arche*'.[23] In this conception, 'an-archy' is proto- or metapolitical, since it 'opens the way beyond politics and ontology'.[24] Abensour, however, does not think that this conception of anarchy can be

---

[17] Lessing, *The Golden Notebook*, p. 58.

[18] Although the productivist emphasis developed by Deleuze and Guattari in their conceptualisation of schizophrenia (and the unconscious more generally) is not directly applicable to Lessing, there is nevertheless an unmissable affinity between these characters' psychic trajectory in the novel and the notion of schizophrenic deterritorialisation elaborated in *Anti-Oedipus*. See Gilles Deleuze and Félix Guattari, *Anti-Oedipus*, trans. by Robert Hurley, Mark Seem, and Helen R. Lane (London: Continuum, 2011).

[19] Miguel Abensour, 'An-archy between Metapolitics and Politics', *Parallax* 8:3 (2002), p. 8.

[20] Quoted in Abensour, 'An-archy', p. 8.

[21] Abensour, 'An-archy', p. 8.

[22] Abensour, 'An-archy', p. 9.

[23] Quoted in Abensour, 'An-archy', p. 9.

[24] Abensour, 'An-archy', p. 10.

fully detached from politics. Even if it renounces the political subordination to 'ontology, logos and *arche*', or precisely because it does so, anarchy does not abandon politics but rather operates a *'disturbance of politics'*.[25] Irreducible to the discursive closure of the political, to the affirmation of the *arche* (of the *'arche* State', as Abensour writes), anarchy leaves a trace. In Levinas's words: 'This way of passing, disturbing the present without allowing itself to be invested by the *arche* of consciousness ... is what I have called a trace'.[26]

This is a notion I want to take up and explore throughout this chapter, with the Derridean elaboration (to which I turn below) as a central point of reference. I suggest, first of all, that Lessing's *The Golden Notebook* proposes a compelling fictional investigation of the disturbance – simultaneously political, psychic, ethical, and ontological – operated by a 'way of passing' through life that renounces the dual *arche* of order and division: two principles (discursively or ideologically represented by traditional psychoanalysis and orthodox Communism in the novel) which, despite their apparent contradictoriness, are actually revealed, from the vantage point of Anna Wulf's growing 'state of anarchy', and specifically through the 'trace' of her anarchic writing, as mutually reinforcing. This is the central paradox: just as Mother Sugar had condemned Anna and Molly for the uprootedness of their lives, she had also insisted on a disabling separation between life and madness, with two levels of morality – as Anna puts it – and the idea that art can only grow from this division: 'One level for life, another for the couch. I couldn't stand it; that is, ultimately, what I couldn't stand'.[27] Communism, like psychoanalysis, represents for Anna the paradoxical turn of a promise of wholeness resulting in more division. As she writes in the red notebook, 'somewhere at the back of my mind when I joined the Party was a need for wholeness, for an end to the split, divided, unsatisfactory way we all live. Yet joining the Party intensified the split'.[28] This is not merely the effect of belonging to a semi-persecuted organisation in the increasingly hostile context of the Cold War but, more fundamentally, a result of the very principle inscribed in its politics. Reminiscing in the black notebook about her youthful engagement with Communists in Africa, she observes: 'It is now obvious that inherent in the structure of a Communist Party or group is a self-dividing principle. Any Communist Party anywhere exists and perhaps even flourishes by this process of discarding individuals or groups'.[29] Division in the name of totality:

[25] Abensour, 'An-archy', p. 15.
[26] Quoted in Abensour, 'An-archy', p. 17.
[27] Lessing, *The Golden Notebook*, p. 76.
[28] Lessing, *The Golden Notebook*, p. 157.
[29] Lessing, *The Golden Notebook*, p. 80.

such appears to be the *arche* uniting Communism and psychoanalysis against which Anna's life (Anna's 'anarchic' writing life) sets itself.

It is interesting that the first representation in the novel of this principle (fomenting splits and at the same time appealing to wholeness and rootedness) is the German refugee Willi Rodde.[30] As Anna describes him, 'He played the role of commissar, the communist intellectual leader. Yet he was the most middle-class person I have known. I mean by this that in every instinct he was for order, correctness and conservation of what existed'.[31] A political version of Mother Sugar, Willi responds to a comrade's jibe that 'if he headed a successful revolution on Wednesday, by Thursday he would have appointed a Ministry of Conventional Morality' with the remark that 'he was a socialist and not an anarchist'.[32] Fundamentally dogmatic and attached to his ideological *arche* (even if, at the same time, a willingness to 'allow freedom to others ... was his way of participating in anarchy'), this character embodies the principle on which so much of contemporary life is predicated.[33] As Anna notes, 'He despised people who allowed their lives to be disturbed by personal emotion'.[34] The organising principle, the *arche* informing Communists like Willi, is thus a rejection of emotion as the experiential basis for a description of – and intervention in – reality. As Anna complains elsewhere, in a conversation with Molly about art, this rejection now (in 1957) seems to have brought together partisans of an extremely reductive conception of realism within the Communist tradition and 'a whole lot of people, who've never had anything to do with the Party' and who are nevertheless willing to proclaim 'that little novels or plays about the emotions don't reflect reality', since reality, 'it would surprise you to hear, is economics, or machine-guns mowing people down who object to the new order'.[35] This subordination to principle in the various psychological, moral, aesthetic, and political inscriptions of modern life is thus defined by its exclusion of disturbance and disorder, or rather, by its injunction to conduct disorder through a relentless process of division and compartmentalisation. The anarchy of writing that Anna introduces into her

---

[30] 'Yes, now I remember that the quarrel [which led to the formation of Anna's Communist group] was because one half of the organization complained that certain members were not "rooted in the country". We split on these lines', Lessing, *The Golden Notebook*, p. 81. Willi Rodde is a fictionalised version of Lessing's own Communist husband in Southern Rhodesia.

[31] Lessing, *The Golden Notebook*, p. 85.

[32] Lessing, *The Golden Notebook*, p. 85.

[33] Lessing, *The Golden Notebook*, p. 86.

[34] Lessing, *The Golden Notebook*, p. 85.

[35] Lessing, *The Golden Notebook*, p. 58.

life, the sign of a life lived through but aiming beyond the divisions of reality, is the attempt to affirm a *heterogeneous* form of wholeness: the irreducible wholeness of a disturbed and disturbing experience – multiple and an-archic (as Levinas argues) in its refusal to be absorbed into a homogeneous totality of being.

The theme of madness gains increasing centrality in the novel as the oppressive principles controlling Anna's life begin to unravel and as this alternative sense of experience begins to affirm itself. Feeling the onset of her breakdown, Anna hastens to translate her psychic suffering – under Mother Sugar's guidance – into a formalistic language ('For words are form and if I am at a pitch where shape, form, expression are nothing, then I am nothing') with a characteristically psychoanalytic focus on dreams.[36] When the therapist asks her to describe, and even more importantly, to 'give a name' to her nightmare so as 'to give it a form', Anna says that 'it was the nightmare about destruction'.[37] Interestingly, 'destruction' is also the ominous and impending 'figure' which begins to overshadow Communist Party meetings at this point. As a microcosm of society, rather than its utopian supersession, the shared mental state of Communists after 1956 is described as one of 'permanent, controlled hysteria': 'they were all people on the extreme edge of themselves'.[38] This madness is, of course, the madness of a rooted and *principled* socio-political project that had promised order and wholeness in the face of anarchy: an external madness, we could say, which the internal madness of Anna's final turn – that which she narrates in the golden notebook – seeks to transcend. In this 'inner' notebook, as Lessing describes it in the 1971 preface, 'the divisions have broken down, there is formlessness with the end of fragmentation'.[39] In other words, the formal compulsion to order, homogeneity, and totality has given way to the *trace* of writing.

As Derrida says in *Of Grammatology*, in invoking the concept of 'trace' he aligns his writing with the Levinasian project of a critique of ontology that asserts the primacy of otherness. For Derrida, this notion names the 'relationship to the illeity as to the alterity of a past that never was and can never be lived in the originary or modified form of presence'.[40] At the heart of all dualisms, as well as all monisms in the history of Western thought – he argues – lies the 'subordination of the trace to the full presence summed up in

---

[36] Lessing, *The Golden Notebook*, p. 419.
[37] Lessing, *The Golden Notebook*, p. 419.
[38] Lessing, *The Golden Notebook*, pp. 428–429.
[39] Lessing, *The Golden Notebook*, p. 7.
[40] Jacques Derrida, *Of Grammatology*, trans. by Gayatri Chakravorty Spivak (Baltimore, MA: The Johns Hopkins University Press, 1997), p. 70.

the logos, the humbling of writing beneath a speech dreaming its plenitude'.[41] In Anna's golden notebook, where she records the transformative experience of madness, writing itself becomes the precise inscription of a rejection of presence. As Lessing notes in the preface, 'Anna and Saul Green the American "break down". They are crazy, lunatic, mad – what you will. They "break down" into each other [...] In the inner Golden Notebook, which is written by both of them, you can no longer distinguish between what is Saul and what is Anna, and between them and the other people in the book'.[42] A sharing of madness becomes – beyond the functional divisions of *logos*, of the word and its rationality – a sharing of writing, a joint exploration of the trace that calls forth the other.[43] Thus, Anna and Saul end up inciting each other's writing, each of them literally writing the first sentence of what is to be the other's book. Saul says: 'I'm going to give you the first sentence then. There are the two women you are, Anna. Write down: The two women were alone in the London flat'.[44] In return, Anna offers the opening sentence of what will ultimately become (as she later announces) Saul's successful short novel about an Algerian soldier. But now it is not enough for Anna to dictate it. Saul demands that she write it down for him. When she asks why, he says that she is 'part of the team' and explains: 'There are a few of us around in the world, we rely on each other even though we don't know each other's names. But we rely on each other all the time. We're a team, we're the ones who haven't given in, who'll go on fighting. I tell you, Anna, sometimes I pick up a book and I say: Well, so you've written it first, have you? Good for you. OK, then I won't have to write it'.[45] Writing is thus very precisely imagined here, through the medium of a mad unravelling that challenges the self-presence of a total and rooted life, as a modality of the radically hetero-geneous: as the trace of an otherness that would enable life as co-involvement, as a fundamentally ethical form of being – in other words, as I have begun to argue, as a form of *an-archy*.

I want to turn now to *The Four-Gated City*, the final instalment in Lessing's five-volume *roman-fleuve The Children of Violence*. In this monumental book, published in 1969, Lessing reiterates and extends many of the themes explored

[41] Derrida, *Grammatology*, p. 71.

[42] Lessing, *The Golden Notebook*, p. 8.

[43] As Anna says, 'During the last weeks of craziness and timelessness I've had these moments of "knowing" one after the other, yet there is no way of putting this sort of knowledge into words ... Anything at all, but not words', Lessing, *The Golden Notebook*, p. 549.

[44] Lessing, *The Golden Notebook*, p. 554.

[45] Lessing, *The Golden Notebook*, p. 556.

in *The Golden Notebook*, notably her exploration of psychic and political dynamics in the post-war period. After following her protagonist Martha Quest's personal and political journey in the southern African British colony of Zambesia – including, crucially, her involvement with a small Communist group, whose activities are the focus of the third novel in the series, *A Ripple from the Storm* – Lessing moves the setting to the London of 1950, which still bears the scars of the Second World War. Here, against the background of the Labour government, the still ostensibly Communist Martha will come to experience for the first time, after the projections and idealisations of her previous political engagements, the contradictory realities of British socialism. The novel begins by recording her gradual discovery of the English working class – an entity that had remained entirely foreign to her and to her colonial comrades despite its centrality to their political imaginary. But now Martha is, as it were, thrown into their midst. Leaving the room at the café where she is staying to embark on one of her exploratory walks around the city, she stops to observe a group of workmen repairing cables in a still-open crater made by a German bomb five years earlier. In what is a rather Orwellian passage, she admires their physical strength, their muscularity, while noting that there 'was no body among them that might have been chosen to represent the human form in its aspect of beauty, since all were in some way deformed; and there was no face that did not carry marks of strain, weariness, or illness'.[46] This deformity, the visible mark on the working-class physique of a history of industrialism, is mirrored by the street itself, by the earth they remove, which is entirely devoid of roots – and therefore of life: 'No trees in this street, not one tree: therefore, no roots. Martha had never before seen soil that was dead ... For two hundred years this soil had held no life at all?'[47]

This sense of estrangement provoked by the alienness of the city and its world (including its working class) is one that will pursue Martha in her further discovery of their lived experience and their politics. Decisively, it is on one of her early urban explorations of the South Bank that she comes across the internal spaces of this alien social universe. While 'wandering among the wharfs and the docks ... in a world of black greasy hulls, dark landing stages, dark warehouses, grey dirty water, gulls, and the smell of driven salt', she is approached by Stella, a native of the docklands and a pure specimen of this – for Martha – mysterious London working class.[48] The latter are also, as Martha soon finds out, not only far more beleaguered than the building

---

[46] Doris Lessing, *The Four-Gated City* (London: Flamingo, 1993), p. 16. See my discussion of *The Road to Wigan Pier* in Chapter Two.

[47] Lessing, *The Four-Gated City*, p. 16.

[48] Lessing, *The Four-Gated City*, p. 22.

of a (however reformist) socialist Britain could have made her expect but also far less amenable to an automatic alignment with Labour politics. This becomes immediately apparent with Stella's family: 'They were fiercely and bitterly working-class, class conscious, and trade union. Labour Party? That remained to be seen, they did not love the government and almost five years of a Labour Government had done nothing to win the trust of these people who trusted nothing'.[49] Their instinctive anarchism, internally constituted as a defining feature of this people's proletarian identity, prompts her to suspend her own political judgement: 'In that kitchen Martha suppressed any knowledge she might have had about politics; for she knew how amateur it would sound among these warriors for whom politics, in its defensive and bread-and-butter aspect, was breath'.[50] Confronted by this experiential truth of the class other – the idealised, but infinitely removed, proletarian other – Martha is forced to abandon the political *arche*, the ideological knowledge which had originally shaped and defined her own Communism (half-forgotten as it is by the time she gets to England), and also to accommodate the reality of a new kind of split, a new sort of division that is much harder to grasp than the brutally transparent racial divisions she had known all her life in colonial Africa: the split of an unresolved class system and the accompanying obfuscations of an ideological apparatus – the British press – which only deepened and perpetuated the estrangement and the division:

> The newspapers never stopped, not for a moment, informing the nation and the world that Britain, in the grip of red-handed socialists, was being ruined, was being turned into a place of serfs without individuality or initiative and rotted by ease … So irrelevant were these newspapers to anything she found she could not believe that anyone read them seriously, nor that anyone could be paid enough to write them.[51]

The mendacity and manipulative intent of this media environment is one of Martha's first revelations upon her arrival in England, and becomes one of the first indications of the specific failure of politics (understood as institutional, statist politics) to transform social reality on a radically ethical basis:

> For what she had found on the other side of the river, let alone in the streets around the café and around the docks, was something not far off conditions described in books about the thirties. What had changed, that the public opinion men (who presumably believed what they wrote)

---

[49] Lessing, *The Four-Gated City*, p. 22.
[50] Lessing, *The Four-Gated City*, pp. 22–23.
[51] Lessing, *The Four-Gated City*, p. 24.

could so write? Were Stella and her people poor? Very. They were better off, they said; but their demands were small and had not grown larger.[52]

The indictment here is not only of the corrupt bourgeois press but also, implicitly, of a supposedly socialist government whose failure to completely eradicate poverty attests to its inadequacy as a political instrument of radical change. For despite the government's good intentions and any real achievements it has made, the Britain Martha discovers in 1950 is still 'a country absorbed in myth, doped and dozing and dreaming'.[53] In spite of its nominal turn to socialism, this is a country in which 'a spirit of rhetoric (because of the war?) had infected everything, made it impossible for any fact to be seen straight'.[54] Paradoxically, then, the same rhetoric, the same myth forged in the war which had enabled Labour's victory in 1945, had now rendered the country impotent in radically addressing its outstanding divisions, which ominously appeared – in a way that calls to mind the perceptual economy of the Victorian social novel – as all but invisible.

When, after repeated postponements, Martha finally arranges to meet her Zambesian friend Marjorie's sister Phoebe, a government official, and is asked about her first impressions of London, Martha's thoughts immediately turn to this sense of irremediable fracture she has been developing since her arrival: 'Fragments. This was a country where people could not communicate across the dark that separated them'.[55] This experience of division is, significantly, what separates Martha from the sort of institutional politics Phoebe represents. The latter, a left-wing member of the Labour Party, is presumably 'dedicated to … the abolition' of class, thereby subsuming its reality under an ideological design which is not only felt as impractical but also as dogmatic in its condemnation of Communism: 'She was bound by her position to regard all communists with a greater hatred and suspicion than she would a Tory'.[56] Faced by this representative of official Labour politics, however avowedly left-wing and socialist, Martha retreats instinctively to her earlier Communism: 'If she were going to have to be political, communism was nearer her mark than "Labour" in its various degrees'.[57] As the conversation unfolds, Phoebe offers

---

[52] Lessing, *The Four-Gated City*, p. 24.
[53] Lessing, *The Four-Gated City*, p. 24.
[54] Lessing, *The Four-Gated City*, p. 25.
[55] Lessing, *The Four-Gated City*, p. 92.
[56] Lessing, *The Four-Gated City*, p. 93. It is important to note that, in the dystopian future narrated in the appendix, Phoebe has become a government minister implementing draconian measures against the free communes that live outside the perimeter of organised and power-sanctioned society.
[57] Lessing, *The Four-Gated City*, p. 93.

her a job as a secretary in a new government organisation for decolonisation and Martha immediately turns it down, not only expressing her reluctance to be 'in that atmosphere' but also directly questioning the necessity of such institutional forms of political intervention: 'Does one actually have to work in some organization! ... I've had enough of organized politics for the time being'.[58] This is crucial, for it provides the backdrop to Martha's subsequent development, which may be described as a politically experimental as well as a strictly metapolitical journey *beyond* organised forms of engagement and relationality.

The main plot effectively begins when Martha accepts Phoebe's second job offer, this time as a private secretary to her ex-brother-in-law, Mark Coldridge. As she is introduced to the Coldridge household, Martha is simultaneously struck by the 'sick and neurotic and hopeless' internal quality of this prime exemplar of a British ruling-class family and by its outward appearance of unbreakable 'solidity'.[59] Moreover, in representing the entire spectrum of British political options, from the matriarch's traditional Toryism to Phoebe and her ex-husband's Labour leftism to the Communism of Mark and his brother Colin (a nuclear physicist who soon defects to the Soviet Union), the Coldridges come to embody a fusion of dysfunctional principles: the compounding of class as the basic social *arche* presiding over British social experience, together with a broken Oedipalism pushed to its limits and an ineffectual adherence to organised ideologies. It is precisely in the familial underbelly, at the fraying edges of the central marital relationship between Mark and his schizophrenic wife, Lynda, 'the quintessential career madwoman' – as Kerry Myler describes her – that the possibility of an an-archic reversal, and a radical subjective transformation, beyond official truths and established principles, begins to emerge.[60] As Myler notes, the gradual rapprochement between Martha and Lynda leads the former 'to recognize the potential of schizophrenia, experimenting with madness as a means to divest her sense of self both from her female body and from her "masculine intelligence"'.[61] This is an intelligence, a knowledge of reality inherited from her own previous political commitment to official Communism, which her recent acquaintance with the divisions of English society, as much as her more extensive experience of the limits and failures of marriage, puts decisively to the test.

---

[58] Lessing, *The Four-Gated City*, pp. 94, 96.

[59] Lessing, *The Four-Gated City*, pp. 97, 106.

[60] Kerry Myler, 'Doris Lessing, Antipsychiatry, and Bodies that Matter', *Twentieth-Century Literature* 65:4 (2019), p. 448.

[61] Myler, 'Doris Lessing', p. 448.

Ultimately, for Martha (as for Anna in *The Golden Notebook*), what is at stake is a general ethical reckoning with the inscription and the effects of this dual, psycho-political *arche*, as co-ordinated under the ample discursive banner of Communism: a promise of rupture with the oppressive structures of capitalist society and the family which is soon exposed, by women like Martha (and Anna), as misleading and empty. As she puts it, 'Do you know how many people have become Communists simply because ... Communism would do away with the family. But Communism has done no such thing, it's done the opposite'.[62] Its irreducible moral conservatism similarly results in a fundamental denial of madness, in its damning characterisation of it as 'reactionary and bourgeois'.[63] Not only the Communist Party but '[s]ocialist circles' more generally, the broad camp of organised left-wing politics, 'were not admitting the possibility that mental troubles existed'.[64] The confirmation of this fact marks a key turning point in the novel. As Mark struggles unsuccessfully to reconcile his tentative commitment to Communism (which becomes more emphatic, if ultimately merely performative, after his brother's defection) with an attempt to preserve his role as Lynda's caring husband, Martha grows increasingly drawn towards the radical alternative represented by Lynda. What could be described as Martha's turn to madness – understood as an ethical rather than merely psychic process – signals a more general judgement on the world and its psycho-political order as morally compromised and pathological in a sense that also enables a radical resignification of the experience of madness.

The Four-Gated City, as *The Golden Notebook* had already begun to do in 1962, registers the direct influence of the anti-psychiatric movement and, in particular, of the radical Scottish psychiatrist R. D. Laing. By the late 1960s, as Kerry Myler points out, both Lessing and Laing shared a 'fantastical and utopian assessment' of schizophrenia, viewing the schizophrenic as a 'new voyager' 'undergoing a transformative journey and an "existential rebirth"'.[65] In Lessing's novel, the ethical and an-archic quality of this journey is of primary importance. Martha's embrace of schizophrenia is predicated on a process of learning other than that determined by established ideological or scientific knowledge, indeed, a process of subjective approximation to the other – a learning of proximity, we could say, revoking the separation and division dictated by the *arche* of normal society. As Martha reflects, 'For years, all her life, the world of mental illness ... had been alien. Not even frightening:

[62] Lessing, *The Four-Gated City*, p. 70.
[63] Lessing, *The Four-Gated City*, p. 199.
[64] Lessing, *The Four-Gated City*, p. 225.
[65] Myler, 'Doris Lessing', p. 447.

it was too distant from her'.[66] But this distance, as she admits, had at no point preserved her own world from 'strain, stress, [and] neurosis'.[67] Crucially, 'between this climate, the ordinary air in which one had always lived, and that other, where people were under psychiatrists, had been an absolute separation'.[68] It is this separation – formal, violent, *archic* – that Martha's turn to madness (through Lynda and *with* Lynda) sets out to undo, with a radically utopian and an-archic exercise of proximity in the Levinasian sense. For, as Miguel Abensour reminds us: 'Emmanuel Levinas invites us to think utopia under the aegis of the encounter, of the relation to the other as such ... he removes utopia from the order of knowing, and its effects from the order of power, so as to assign it to the order ... of proximity'.[69]

In contrast to the desperate and 'bitter nihilism' of a quite common turn to 'anarchy' among 'the extreme left' after the debacle of 1956, Martha's own utopian and anarchic journey beyond the political and moral ruins of this period remains untouched by opportunism or flippancy.[70] It is, on the contrary, a fundamental questioning of those orders of knowing through which her own lifelong apprenticeship in division (across the boundaries of gender, race, class, politics, and mental health) had been forged. Her proximity to Lynda, and the education that it entails – a proper 'education of desire', in Abensour's famous phrase – amounts to an opening and transformation, as Levinas suggests, without the mediation of established rules (of thought, expression, or feeling): 'Martha could easily hear what Lynda was thinking ... now it was not far off being inside Lynda's head, for the jumble of connected words and phrases linked together by past experiences ... this stream ran through her mind beside her own stream, or sometimes displaced it'.[71] Nor is this simply an absorption into the solipsistic world of the other imagined as just another self, for 'it is not a question of "Lynda's mind", or "Martha's mind"; it is the human mind, or part of it, and Lynda, Martha, can choose to plug in or not'.[72]

[66] Lessing, *The Four-Gated City*, p. 240.
[67] Lessing, *The Four-Gated City*, p. 240.
[68] Lessing, *The Four-Gated City*, p. 240.
[69] Miguel Abensour, *Utopia from Thomas More to Walter Benjamin*, trans. by Raymond N. MacKenzie (Minneapolis: Univocal, 2017), p. 11. In Levinas's own words: 'anarchically, proximity is a relationship with a singularity without the mediation of any principle, of any ideality', *Autrement qu'être ou au-delà de l'essence* (Paris: Le Livre de Poche, 2019), p. 158–159; my translation.
[70] Lessing, *The Four-Gated City*, p. 311.
[71] Lessing, *The Four-Gated City*, p. 519.
[72] Lessing, *The Four-Gated City*, p. 520.

Following a lengthy exploration of Martha's turn to madness, which gradually but decisively results in an abandonment of realism as the narrative's predominant mode, the novel operates an even more radical formal turn by concluding with an 'appendix' made up of a variety of textual fragments composed in an increasingly dystopian – and, after a certain point, post-apocalyptic – future. As we read, these include '*Various Documents, Private and Official, Dated between 1995 and 2000, in the Possession of Amanda, Francis Coldridge's stepdaughter, destroyed by her before the Northern National Area (formerly North China) was overrun by the Mongolian National Area*'.[73] The most substantial of these documents is a letter addressed by Francis, Lynda and Mark's son, to Amanda, in which he offers, from his post-apocalyptic standpoint, a 'future' history of the social and political events leading up to and following the nuclear 'Catastrophe' which was to ensue. An outstanding characteristic of this *other* history, of this history to-come, is the intensification and acceleration of that normal and normalising madness which had already defined, in the 1950s present in which the bulk of the novel is set, society and politics (as much as their personal or private ramifications). Francis records in his letter how, as the 1960s unfolded, 'the general madness deepened' and alternative social arrangements, such as the openly anarchistic commune with which he had become involved, were a pole of attraction for a steadily growing number of people deemed by 'authority' to be 'eccentric', 'damaged', or 'ill'.[74] These are people either 'unwilling or unable to live according to the norms of the time – which were the more savagely defended as norms, as society got crazier and crazier'.[75] Significantly, this community is defined by the proximity of its members, by a willingness 'to live together' that necessarily excludes the unifying *arche* of any specific ideological orientation. As Francis notes, 'perhaps because so many of us had had contact with psychiatry' and 'with politics', the 'chief characteristic' of the group was that 'we had no ideology, plan, constitution, or philosophy', only 'a feeling of community'.[76] As the various technical and institutional dimensions of society begin to collapse in the 1970s, inaugurating 'an age of anarchy', the relative success of properly anarchic and utopian communities such as this one becomes all the more inassimilable by organised society, for 'by then no one was able to believe in the possibility of something unorganized, unregimented, undoctrinaire'.[77] The anarchic emphasis of Francis's letter is insistent. Connecting this future

---

[73] Lessing, *The Four-Gated City*, p. 619.
[74] Lessing, *The Four-Gated City*, p. 619.
[75] Lessing, *The Four-Gated City*, p. 619.
[76] Lessing, *The Four-Gated City*, p. 620.
[77] Lessing, *The Four-Gated City*, pp. 623, 625.

dystopia with the anti-psychiatric theme of schizophrenia, he observes that people like Martha and her mother Lynda, now considered as being endowed with 'telepathic powers', pose a fundamental threat, perhaps even a greater one than that represented by the utopian communities, to the State. For at this point what madness signifies is a complete ontological overhaul of the human itself and thus the possibility of an alternative foundation for a humanity yet to come. Thus, Francis describes the euphoria produced by his conversations with Martha and Lynda soon before the catastrophe:

> I remember the evening ended on the thought that all existing forms of government were as irrelevant as dinosaurs: government by concealment, lies, trickery, even stupidity was – dead. The old right of the individual human conscience which must know better than any authority, secular or religious, had been restored, but on a higher level, and in a new form which was untouchable by any legal formulas. We quoted to each other, Blake's 'What now exists was once only imagined' – and did not, for once, choose to remember the dark side of the human imagination.[78]

4.2 On E. P. Thompson's 'Antinomian' Socialism

I would like to suggest at this point that there is a striking similarity between Lessing's vision of *an-archy* in this novel (and more generally, in her writing of the 1960s) and the libertarian socialism of her old friend and early New Left comrade E. P. Thompson, whose historical and political work from the mid-1950s (as a dissident member of the Communist Party of Great Britain (CPGB)) until his death in 1993 is marked by an emphatic commitment to the renewal of radical humanism as an ethico-political project. The reference to Blake in the passage quoted above, and the generally antinomian emphasis of Lessing's novel as a whole, are particularly close to Thompson's own ideological itinerary – an itinerary whose literary roots were always prominent and which notably commenced in 1955 with the publication of his seminal study of William Morris and concluded with a posthumously published book on William Blake himself and the antinomian Protestant tradition of seventeenth-century English Dissent.

Thompson came to prominence in 1956 as a leading dissident intellectual in the CPGB, initially attempting to push the Party towards de-Stalinisation with the publication of a journal meant for internal discussion and ideological clarification entitled *The Reasoner*, but soon afterwards breaking

---

[78] Lessing, *The Four-Gated City*, p. 640.

with the Party altogether as a reaction to the official Communist response to the Soviet crushing of the Hungarian Revolution. Thompson's impatience with the Executive Committee's dogmatic and uncritical approach to developments in Eastern Europe had been growing in the months after the Twentieth Congress in the Soviet Union. At one point he was to remark in a letter to a Party official: 'All I can say is, thank God there is no chance of the EC ever having power in Britain; it would destroy in a month every liberty of thought, concern and expression, which it has taken the British people over 300 odd years to win'.[79] Aligned with the group of dissident intellectuals behind *The Reasoner*, Lessing herself would contribute a letter on 'The Cult of the Individual' to the final number of the journal (before it became *The New Reasoner*, after Thompson and his co-editor John Saville left the Party in November 1956). This letter emphasises the idea that, following the exposure of Stalinism, only the vindication of individuality (the 'old right of the individual human conscience', as Francis puts it in *The Four-Gated City*) could provide a foundation for the reformation of Communism. Lessing argues that the mistake in official reactions to Khrushchev's revelations had been to insist on the notion of 'the cult of the individual' under Stalin, implying that 'what caused the breakdown of inner-party democracy was an excess of individualism'.[80] In fact, writes Lessing, the 'opposite is the truth': 'What was bad is not that one man was a tyrant, but that hundreds and thousands of party members, inside and outside the Soviet Union, let go their individual consciences and allowed him to become a tyrant'.[81]

Thompson was to famously translate this complaint theoretically as a call for 'socialist humanism' in the face of the mechanical rigidities of Stalinism and its ultimate negation of human agency. Thus, in the lead article of *The New Reasoner*'s inaugural issue, entitled 'Socialist Humanism: An Epistle to the Philistines', Thompson explained this vindication of humanism in the socialist movement in the following terms: 'It is humanist because it places once again real men and women at the centre of socialist theory and aspiration, instead of the resounding abstractions – the Party, Marxism-Leninism-Stalinism, the Two Camps, the Vanguard of the Working Class – so dear to Stalinism'.[82]

---

[79] Letter to Bert Ramelson, quoted in Keith Laybourn and Dylan Murphy, *Under the Red Flag: A History of Communism in Britain* (Stroud: Sutton Publishing, 1999), p. 145.

[80] Quoted in Doris Lessing, *Walking in the Shade: Volume Two of My Autobiography, 1949–1962* (London: HarperCollins, 1997), p. 191.

[81] Quoted in Lessing, *Walking in the Shade*, p. 191.

[82] E. P. Thompson, 'Socialist Humanism: An Epistle to the Philistines', in

Here, as in Thompson's more famous historical work, the central emphasis falls on the notion of agency and self-activity of real people, for 'it is precisely the element of agency which distinguishes them from the beasts, which is the *human* part of man, and which it is the business of our consciousness to increase'.[83] For Thompson, this was not only a necessary political corrective to the ideological automatisms of Communist orthodoxy but also a key dimension of the historical identity and experience of the British labour movement (which he would go on to study in his 1963 magnum opus *The Making of the English Working Class*). At the heart of this experience, Thompson singles out an *antinomian* theme to which he will return emphatically at the end of his life: 'The most striking thing about the British labour movement is that it cannot be said to have either a false consciousness or a true one: it has a hotch-potch, of capitalist ideas, humanitarian aspirations, working-class attitudes. We are a protestant people, distrustful of system-building: we have not suffered under an ideological orthodoxy, backed by the power of the state, for several hundred years'.[84]

Thompson's last book, *Witness Against the Beast: William Blake and the Moral Law* (published shortly after his death in 1993) is a detailed restatement of the libertarian impulse which had driven his earlier political and scholarly work. In this final study, Thompson connects Blake to a lineage of radical theological and political oppositionality arising from the revolutionary maelstrom of the English Civil War in the seventeenth century. Thompson traces the antinomian impetus to radical sects emerging in the 1650s such as the Ranters and the Muggletonians, who opposed the idea of an internal and autonomous 'Gospel of Love', sustained and justified by faith alone, to the external impositions of the 'Mosaic' or 'Moral Law'. Thus, 'the antinomian position was consciously anti-hegemonic':

> For what the antinomian or Muggletonian declaimed against as 'Reason' we might today prefer to define as 'Ideology', or as the compulsive constraints of the ruling 'discourse'. Antinomian doctrine was expressive of a profound distrust of the 'reasons' of the genteel and comfortable, and of ecclesiastical and academic institutions, not so much because they produced false knowledges but because they offered specious apologetics ('serpent reasonings') for a rotten social order based, in the last resort, on violence and material self-interest. In short, the antinomian stance

---

E.P. Thompson and the Making of the New Left: Essays and Polemics, ed. by Cal Winslow (New York: Monthly Review Press, 2014), p. 53.

[83] Thompson, 'Socialist Humanism', p. 66.

[84] Thompson, 'Socialist Humanism', p. 84.

was not against knowledge but against the ideological assumptions which pretended to be knowledge and the ideological contamination of the rest.[85]

This comes notably close to Lessing's repudiation of psychiatric knowledge and power, with its 'serpent reasonings' and refusal to acknowledge and engage a radical dimension of the human – together with those analogous ideological orders, from Labourism to official Communism, let alone Cold War capitalism – in her fiction of the 1960s. Thompson's own fictional elaboration on these themes, a novel entitled *The Sykaos Papers* and published in 1988, could be read as an extension and reinscription of Lessing's project in specifically antinomian terms.[86]

The Sykaos Papers tells the story of Oi Paz, an extra-terrestrial 'poet-astronaut' from the planet Oitar on a mission to explore Sykaos (Earth) in preparation for its forthcoming Oitarian colonisation. The rumbunctious narrative follows Oi Paz's adventures and experiences, from his comic introduction to 'Sykotic' codes and customs at a time of Cold War intensification all the way to his period of 'captivity' in a government facility (Martagon Hall) under the observation of anthropologist Helena Sage. Most of the narrative is made up of fragments from Oi Paz's and Helena's journals, diaries, notebooks, and 'field notes' – the main device through which the comic clash of mutually alien perspectives on the human is rendered in the novel (for Oitarians regard themselves as human, while referring to earthlings as 'beastly'). Thus, the Oitarian visitor struggles to comprehend the logic (or lack thereof) of life on Sykaos, and especially the Sykaans' seeming irreducibility to the rational 'Rule' of 'the Wheel' – the *arche* governing Oitar. For example, at one point he observes that 'the entire society of Sykaans is controlled within a code whose name is "property"', and even if property is 'a no-thing', for it 'cannot be touched or smelled or weighed', it nevertheless 'governs all their intercourse from birth to dead-line, and, were property to be removed, no one would know how to come or how to go'.[87] Property is thus 'for Sykaans, an equivalent to the Rule', while money 'is its Messenger', for it is 'money which commands obedience'.[88] Oi Paz goes on to record numerous other irrationalities in the functioning of beastly society, from the recent 'enclosure' of the previously 'nationalised' 'social stock' (a reference,

[85] E. P. Thompson, *Witness Against the Beast: William Blake and the Moral Law* (Cambridge: Cambridge University Press, 1993), pp. 108–109.

[86] Bryan Palmer has described this novel as 'perhaps the single richest elaboration of E.P. Thompson's refusals', *E.P. Thompson: Objections and Oppositions* (London: Verso, 1994), p. 155.

[87] E. P. Thompson, *The Sykaos Papers* (London: Bloomsbury, 1988), p. 92.

[88] Thompson, *The Sykaos Papers*, pp. 92–93.

of course, to Thatcher's Britain) to the various magical properties of money, such as credit.[89] But the pinnacle of 'Sykotic abominations', a development in keeping with 'the beastly propensity of mortals to do their own dead-line', corresponds to their recent discovery of nuclear fission: 'Nothing better has come into their beastly minds than to compact this force into "bombs" (or "nukes") which burn out cities like the eye in its socket and which leave the impacted region for the half-life-of-ever in a radiation-stew'.[90] This self-destructive earthly propensity is thus the main obstacle to Oitarian colonisation, for it not only threatens the species but also the planet and all of its life forms.[91] As Oi Paz concludes, 'The species is not accessible to reason' and, knowing 'no awe of the Rule', it 'can be regulated only by fear, greed or lust'.[92]

The novel fully embraces its antinomian argument through Helena and Oi Paz's exchanges, initially of a strictly scientific nature but then increasingly close and personal, during their residence in Martagon Hall. The Oitarian submission to reason is thus first cast in a critical (humanist, antinomian) light as Helena and her colleague David begin to make observations about Oi Paz's cognitive skills: his language does not appear to be 'so much a language as a reason-code that has been cured or disinfected of all affective context'.[93] Moreover, his reasoning does not contain any 'concepts of *chance*' or 'choice' and his 'numeracy has atrophied' to the point that Oi Paz cannot count beyond ten.[94] As David and Helena hypothesise, this suggests 'a culture in an advanced state of computer-dependency' where decision-making and freewill have been replaced by artificial intelligence.[95] The very notion of 'event' is similarly absent from Oitarian culture: 'What happens is happened, by the Rule. Hence scarcely any concept of "history" in our sense'.[96] As she develops her investigations, Helena advances a detailed description of Oitar as 'a rigid caste society' at whose bottom may lie, she hypothesises, 'a pool of discards', 'a sort of Oitarian proletariat?'[97] The trans-human surpassing of earthly madness (or 'Sykosis') embodied in Oitarian rationality is thus exposed, at the same time, as a radical denial of agency and freedom, as well as a paradoxical continuation of

[89] Thompson, *The Sykaos Papers*, p. 93.

[90] Thompson, *The Sykaos Papers*, p. 121.

[91] There is a substantial ecological theme in the novel that goes beyond the anti-nuclear argument.

[92] Thompson, *The Sykaos Papers*, p. 200.

[93] Thompson, *The Sykaos Papers*, p. 183.

[94] Thompson, *The Sykaos Papers*, p. 181.

[95] Thompson, *The Sykaos Papers*, p. 181.

[96] Thompson, *The Sykaos Papers*, p. 228.

[97] Thompson, *The Sykaos Papers*, p. 236.

all-too-human patterns of inequality. As the 'exterminist' machine of the Cold War engulfs the scientific project under which Oi Paz is held in Martagon Hall, and the premises are taken over by NATO, the protagonists are relocated to an internal zone of exclusion referred to as the 'Zone of Eden'.[98] In this neo-Biblical setting, the antinomian opposition between the Gospel of Love and the Mosaic Law of both Oitarian and Sykotic 'Rules' becomes central. Interestingly, as the Oitarian editor of Oi Paz's manuscripts observes in the note opening this section: 'Oi Paz neglected scientific researches and commenced a "Diary" which has on its cover the single letter "I"', thus suggesting a gradual slippage towards the irrational and subjectivist realm of human feeling.[99]

There is a distinct resonance here with the argument Thompson puts forward in *Witness Against the Beast*, for what will gradually flourish in this withdrawn Zone of Eden is nothing less than the old antinomian (and 'socialist humanist') doctrine of justification by faith: faith, that is, in the human and its mortal divinity (as proclaimed by radical dissenting sects such as the Ranters) and thus in stark opposition to the *external* sanction given by a superior Moral Law or Reason.[100] As Oi Paz puts it at one point, 'To be free is to lie under law'.[101] His blockage of feelings is also revealingly described in terms that suggest Oitar's alignment with the moral and legalistic conception rejected by the antinomians. Thus, controlled by a centralised and impersonal artificial intelligence, affect is regularly blocked and inhibited and only allowed to be 'switched on' as a 'we-feeling' by 'a moral organ'.[102] Yet now, secluded from the external threat of nuclear destruction and interplanetary war and cloistered in this utopian space of evidently antinomian Christian resonances (complete with a Tree of Knowledge and a serpent presiding over their fall), Oi Paz and Helena Sage become a sort of post-historical version of Adam and Eve, choosing 'knowledge and free will' in lieu of their respective programmes.[103] The product of their transgression is a son, aptly named Adam and later re-named Ho Mo on Oitar. The seed of this intergalactic union thus matches the old antinomian notion of Christ 'risen within' as an immanent rebirth of Man.[104]

---

[98] See Edward Thompson, 'Notes on Exterminism, the Last Stage of Civilization', *New Left Review* I:121 (1980).

[99] Thompson, *The Sykaos Papers*, p. 301.

[100] See, especially, chapter 3 of Thompson, *Witness Against the Beast*.

[101] Thompson, *The Sykaos Papers*, p. 358.

[102] Thompson, *The Sykaos Papers*, p. 183.

[103] Thompson, *The Sykaos Papers*, p. 378.

[104] This is a key idea that runs through the antinomian tradition. Thus, for the Ranters, 'the essential presence of God is to be found only in men and women ... hence these *are* God', Thompson, *Witness Against the Beast*, p. 26. Similarly, for Gerrard

The novel's conclusion brings this antinomian emphasis to a head. As Earth plunges into a nuclear holocaust, unable to agree on a common plan against Oitar's invasion, Helena, Oi Paz, and Adam find themselves in the Oitarian colony on the moon. Faced with the realities of this alien civilisation, and ultimately singled out for elimination by the Oitarian authorities, Helena makes a final vindication of her freewill and human autonomy, taking her own life.[105] Her writing ends with an overtly antinomian reference to Blake that connects the various strands of Thompson's oppositional argument in *Witness Against the Beast*: 'Blake thought it was the Wheel of Religion but it is also Ideology and Rule'.[106] This is followed, as the order for her execution arrives, by a 'Last Will and Testament', written upside down on the back of the notebook. Offering a final rationale and ethico-political manifesto of her own, the text concludes with the following lines:

> I go out, leaving Curses upon Power and Abstract Enmities and Public Lies.
>   I go out through the gate of my flesh, carrying with me, like a basket of flowers, my memories of love and of friendship and natural joys
>   Accepting the Knowledge of Good and Evil
>   Sorry that the Good lost out (it was a near thing)
>   RENOUNCING MY CONSCIOUSNESS NOT AT ALL
>   REFUSING THE LEAST TRIBUTE TO THE RULE OF NIHIL
>   I leave life of my own free will[107]

Yet, in a way that reproduces Lessing's formal strategy in *The Four-Gated City*, this an-archic declaration is not the end of the novel. The final section is made up of a number of 'appendices' reconstructing what could be described as the *trace* left by the human in a post-human, Oitarian, universe. The bulk of these documents centres on the disruptive development of Ho Mo, Oi Paz and Helena's 'feral child' (as he is described by the 'Sublime Couch' of Oitar): a half-mortal who will carry forward the anarchic and antinomian faith of the species. Breaking with his 'programme' and 'roll', Ho Mo, now

---

Winstanley and the Diggers, 'God dwells and rules in man, and man lives in God', Christopher Hill, *The Religion of Gerrard Winstanley* (Oxford: Past and Present Publications, 1978), p. 3.

[105] Helena's depiction of Oitarian civilisation includes a brutal class stratification: 'Clearly the butlers are the proles or the blacks, and so deeply assumed – like the plumbing and wiring – that they don't get mentioned much', Thompson, *The Sykaos Papers*, p. 436.

[106] Thompson, *The Sykaos Papers*, p. 459.

[107] Thompson, *The Sykaos Papers*, p. 460.

become the first Man of this post-human future, challenges Oitar's circular and self-perpetuating *arche*, announcing to his stunned audience: 'We must break the Wheel to be born, and if we break the Wheel, then we must die'.[108] Furthermore, contesting the Oitarian pretence of immortality on the basis that eternity is nothing but 'a flash of consciousness, set like a glittering diamond in the clasp of dying flesh', he also challenges an idea of rationality that denies the possibility of a search without guarantees, intimating that this was, ultimately, the destructive principle common to both Oitarians and humans:

> Our ratios must always be in flux. We must search always for the perfect ratio: but even as we reach out to grasp it, we have become changed through searching, and the ratio is no longer ours but it has become our own alienation, and we must begin the search again. My species destroyed itself in the search, but they might have reached out to new ratios far beyond your circinate programmes. They failed because they became too much like you. They fell into your binary logic-paths and feedback loops. They feared their identity, and hung themselves round with the dead.[109]

Adam/Ho Mo's antinomian proclamation thus suggests that an alternative rationality, an *other* future, had always been inscribed in the unprogrammed fate of humanity: no law or rule, no *arche*, but only a horizon of possibility defined by otherness as the basis of their existence. Both Thompson and Lessing identify writing as a subversive act that fundamentally disturbs the *archic* suppression of this otherness at the centre of the human. In a post-human world marked by devastation and the madness of a self-destructive order of power and knowledge, only writing – the fragmentary inscription of lives that are no longer, in anticipation of futures that are not-yet – carries forward the promise of a redemptive heterogeneity.

4.3 The 'Ranting Impulse': On James Kelman

I want to bring this argument about 'antinomianism' (and what Thompson refers to as the 'ranting impulse') in British literary socialism up to date by considering it in relation to one of the foremost libertarian socialist writers in contemporary Britain: James Kelman.[110] Kelman's oeuvre can be regarded as

---

[108] Thompson, *The Sykaos Papers*, p. 476.

[109] Thompson, *The Sykaos Papers*, pp. 476–477.

[110] For an overview of Kelman's libertarian-socialist commitments, see his recent collection *The State Is the Enemy: Essays on Liberation and Racial Justice* (Oakland, CA: PM Press, 2023).

an extended meditation on the anarchic trace of writing as well as a writerly intervention in public debates geared towards the radical disturbance of the order of the State (to reiterate Abensour's formulation). I will begin by considering Kelman's 2004 novel *You Have to Be Careful in the Land of the Free*, which offers one of the most explicit engagements with antinomian and anarchic ideas in his fiction.

This novel follows Jeremiah Brown, a Glaswegian man about to return home from the US after an absence of eight years, as he reflects on his life as an 'unassimilatit furnir' in the increasingly threatening atmosphere of post-9/11 America. The novel consists of Jeremiah's jagged internal monologue, written in Kelman's characteristic Scottish (or 'Skarrish') vernacular – with only occasional moments of (typically awkward) dialogue – as he spends his last night in the country visiting local bars in the unidentified town from which his flight will depart the following day. The general mood of estrangement and suspicion which surrounds Jeremiah's musings on his failed relationship with Yasmin, the mother of his four-year-old 'wean', as well as on his edgy experiences working as a security operative, is compounded by the fact that the novel ends without any certainty that Jeremiah will ultimately manage to make his flight. Virtually delusional and lost in the snow somewhere outside the bar where he spends most of the evening, Jeremiah is stopped by a police patrol as he offers what reads like a final apophatic disclaimer of liability for his entire monologue: 'This is no polemical diatribe against the evils of imperialism, colonialism, capitalism and all the rest of it. No sir, being a guest in the place I shall not abuse ma hosts, nor query the criteria relating to'.[111] For a 'polemical diatribe' against the legacies of American-led capitalist globalisation at its most oppressive is precisely what the novel as a whole amounts to. The holder – as we are informed – of a Class III Red Card, Jeremiah has been legally branded as 'an unassimilatit unintegratit alien socialist', and thus confined to one of the lowest strata in its dystopian order of State surveillance.[112] Yet, in spite of the oppressive quality of power in this version of America, Jeremiah remains stubbornly defiant, insisting throughout the novel on his class-conscious anarchism (which strongly resembles Kelman's own).

[111] James Kelman, *You Have to Be Careful in the Land of the Free* (London: Penguin, 2005), p. 437. See Vincent Dussol, 'James Kelman's Confrontational Ethics in *You Have to Be Careful in the Land of the Free*', in *Ethics of Alterity, Confrontation and Responsibility in 19th- to 21st-Century British Literature*, ed. by Jean-Michel Ganteau and Christine Reynier (Montpellier: Presses universitaires de la Méditerranée, 2013), pp. 181–192.

[112] Kelman, *You Have to Be Careful*, p. 379.

The novel can thus be properly read as an anarchic diatribe: both as an objective indictment of 'the evils of imperialism, colonialism, capitalism and all the rest of it' and as a subjective (and linguistic) revolt against their effects – a libertarian declaration of non-compliance. For as Vincent Dussol points out: 'Jeremiah is an angry man. How could a Jeremiah not complain! A man conscious of the Biblical legacy of his first name, he vehemently rails against the state of things as they are'.[113] In this sense, *You Have to Be Careful* can be said to pertain to the seminal American genre of the jeremiad. This is a point briefly mentioned by Dussol which I would like to clarify here as it can help us understand the precise remit of the novel's anarchic engagement (and more generally, of Kelman's politics). Dussol references Sacvan Bercovitch's classic study, *The American Jeremiad*, where he offers a substantial correction of Perry Miller's thesis that the New England jeremiad developed by the Puritan settlers of the seventeenth century focused on 'the long list of afflictions an angry God had rained upon them ... to prove how abysmally they had deserted the covenant'.[114] According to Bercovitch, however, what is truly distinctive about the American iteration of this old European genre is 'its unshakeable optimism'.[115] Jeramiah Brown's complaint is thus arguably closer to the 'traditional mode', and thus a 'lament over the ways of the world'.[116] But his jeremiad is also marked off by a subversive virulence that dispels any simple suggestion of resigned theological quietism (not least since Jeremiah's atheism is a constituent aspect of his ideological outsiderness). More often a verbal act of insurgency than a weary cry of despair (although it is the latter too), I would argue that Jeremiah's 'Skarrish' jeremiad approximates a different seventeenth-century Puritan subgenre emerging from the revolutionary cauldron of the English Civil Wars: the Ranter pamphlet.[117]

Commonly regarded as the most radical faction of the various sects and groups making up the 'left wing' of the parliamentary side fighting Charles

---

[113] Dussol, 'Confrontational Ethics', p. 182.
[114] Perry Miller, *Errand into the Wilderness* (Cambridge, MA: The Belknap Press of Harvard University Press, 1956), p. 6.
[115] Sacvan Bercovitch, *The American Jeremiad* (Madison: The University of Wisconsin Press, 1978), p. 7.
[116] Bercovitch, *The American Jeremiad*, p. 7.
[117] This historical context is central to Miller's seminal argument about the American jeremiad: 'in the 1640s, during the Civil Wars, the colonies, so to speak, lost their audience ... the Independents, who in polity were carrying New England's banner and were supposed, in the schedule of history, to lead England into imitation of the colonial order, betrayed the sacred cause by yielding to the heresy of toleration', Miller, *Errand into the Wilderness*, p. 13.

I during the 1640s, the Ranters are considered to have come to prominence at the turn of the decade as a dual symptom of revolutionary effervescence and incipient retreat from the democratic aspirations associated with the Levellers. Politically (and militarily) defeated by the Cromwellian 'right wing' of the movement, many plebeian Puritans, radicalised by the revolutionary experience of the wars and their logical conclusion (the regicide of 1649), seem to have turned to an extreme form of antinomianism that in many ways (both theologically and politically) prefigured modern anarchism. As Thompson notes in *Witness Against the Beast*,

> The defeat of the Leveller soldiers at Burford in 1649 served as a sharp check to the temporal political hopes of the more advanced democrats. Like a gymnast on a trampoline, the democratic faith which met its check at Burford, soared back into the air once more in 1649–51, somersaulting and displaying itself in the brief Ranter climax. For a moment the revolutionary spirit, which had met a set-back in realistic political objectives, leapt to even more outrageous heights of utopian ideals and visionary teachings.[118]

In his classic study of 1970, A. L. Morton similarly observes that Ranterism was to attract 'a number of embittered and disappointed former Levellers', suggesting that '[w]here Levelling by sword and by spade had both failed what seemed called for was Levelling by miracle, in which God himself would confound the mighty by means of the poorest, lowest and most despised of the earth'.[119]

The extraordinary theo-political writing that emerged from this movement was to push the discursive matrix out of which the New England jeremiad had also arisen to its logical and expressive limits. As Nigel Smith points out, for the Ranters, 'It is not so much a question of flying a colour of political or religious identity, as might a polemicist, but a strategy of driving home the locus and consequence of the Antinomian experience'.[120] Thus, the 'essence of Ranter experience is beyond language' as well as 'anti-rational and non-aesthetic'.[121] A central aspect of this discursive strategy, of course, has to do with the 'Ranter writers' propensity for cursing and swearing', from which their collective moniker was derived.[122] For these anarchic Puritans, swearing is

---

[118] Thompson, *Witness Against the Beast*, p. 23.

[119] A. L. Morton, *The World of the Ranters: Religious Radicalism in the English Revolution* (London: Lawrence & Wishart, 1970), p. 71.

[120] Nigel Smith, 'Introduction', in *A Collection of Ranter Writings: Spiritual Liberty and Sexual Freedom in the English Revolution* (London: Pluto Press, 2014), p. 24.

[121] Smith, 'Introduction', pp. 24, 26.

[122] Smith, 'Introduction', p. 25.

ultimately the 'manifestation of a privileged knowledge', since 'in their view it is God who is swearing in the individual' and thus intimating an 'angelic knowledge' which promises to transcend not only established morality (the hated Mosaic Law) but also a regime of truth which is perceived as obnoxious and fundamentally oppressive.[123] As the leading Ranter Abiezer Coppe declares in his scandalous pamphlet 'A Fiery Flying Roll', 'God hath so cleared cursing, swearing, in some, that that which goes for swearing and cursing in them, is more glorious then [*sic*] praying and preaching in others'.[124] Thus, ranting in the strict sense becomes a new and (from Coppe's perspective) definitive form of 'levelling', a performative commentary on the betrayed promise of equality as well as a high-pitched injunction to the powerful: 'The very shadow of levelling, sword-levelling, man-levelling, frighted you (and who, like yourselves, can blame you, because it shook your Kingdome?) but now the substantiality of levelling is coming'.[125]

Similarly, I would argue, Jeremiah's monologic tirade against the 'land of the free', characteristically formulated in a Glaswegian vernacular that is, as one of his American interlocutors puts it, 'a little hard on the ears', ultimately amounts to a *divinely inspired* rant against the ungodly inequality of the American way.[126] A preoccupation with social inequality, and its central expression in terms of class, is the key dimension of Jeremiah's postmodern jeremiad. As a precarious migrant worker in the hyper-mobile yet post-liberal regime of globalised capitalism, his sense of class is defined by an acute awareness of new forms of super-exploitation and extreme social exclusion as well as of the historical recurrence of inequality and the struggle against it. Thus, his ancestor and namesake Jeremiah Brown, a politically conscious working-class Scot who came to America during the nineteenth-century gold rush, is invoked throughout the novel. According to Jeremiah's colourful account, this ancestor 'grew tired of men's avarice', thereby forsaking the road to the Colorado gold mines and instead heading 'south on the Santa Fe trail and maybe onwards to find farm work in the vineyards of California'.[127] Yet, in a turn of events that prefigures his own confused and contradictory nomadism

---

[123] Smith, 'Introduction', p. 25.

[124] Abiezer Coppe, 'A Fiery Flying Roll', in *A Collection of Ranter Writings: Spiritual Liberty and Sexual Freedom in the English Revolution*, ed. by Nigel Smith (London: Pluto Press, 2014), p. 84.

[125] Coppe, 'A Fiery Flying Roll', p. 82.

[126] Kelman, *You Have to Be Careful*, p. 389. See Aaron Kelly's discussion of Kelman's 'democracy of voice', *James Kelman: Politics and Aesthetics* (Oxford: Peter Lang, 2013).

[127] Kelman, *You Have to Be Careful*, p. 155.

in twenty-first-century America, 'auld Jeremiah blundered and found himself heading west on the Oregon Trail', only to become 'a devout christian and a god-fearing body' while working for the Pinkerton Detective Agency as 'the custodian of pioneering business interests'.[128] Despite this obviously reactionary turn in his later life, the old Jeremiah had started out as a Chartist and a socialist, which persuades his descendant that he never actually 'renege[d] on his principles' and that deep down he 'never fell for that fucking christian patter'.[129] Finding himself at a similar crossroads, between the original impulse of solid radical principle (in his case, of an openly anarchist kind) and a 'blundering' drift through jobs at the heart – indeed at the repressive forefront – of the system, Jeremiah carries forward this contradiction in a globalised but similarly greedy, oppressive, and unequal modern America.

Working as an airport security operative, he becomes complicit with and even directly functional to the dystopian order of State power inaugurated by the Patriot Act (the Patriot Holding Centers where Jermiah and his colleagues work are a clear reference to this order of juridical exceptionality in the novel). Yet, significantly, this complicity only reinforces the expository edge of Jeremiah's narration, rendering his portrait of inequality and State repression all the more savage. Thus, through his detailed description of recent developments in the American airline industry, we learn that masses of 'poverty-stricken folks' were now 'booking flights on these cheapo airlines' and developing their own brutal, lumpenproletarian version of the flourishing casino economy of globalisation by taking – as the novel's running pun has it – 'persian bets': that is, by gambling on the chances of 'perishing' in a plane crash.[130] As a result, airports themselves were turning into complex border zones in which the ordinary regime of exceptionality imposed upon aliens by the American State was now extended to a 'true-born' 'Uhmerkin' underclass of 'ragged persons bearing blankets or pushing grocery carts' while participating in this suicidal and socially threatening parody of financialised capitalism.[131] These native outcasts are spontaneous antinomians, refusing to do 'what the authorities telt them to do and … ignoring all the rules and regulations'.[132] In a characteristically parodic reversal of his own radical

---

[128] Kelman, *You Have to Be Careful*, p. 155.

[129] Kelman, *You Have to Be Careful*, p. 60.

[130] Kelman, *You Have to Be Careful*, p. 128. As Simon Kővesi notes, 'The "security" that airports and flying attempt to embody, is undermined by a complex parodic interplay between gambling, flying and insurance', *James Kelman* (Manchester: Manchester University Press, 2007), p. 181.

[131] Kelman, *You Have to Be Careful*, p. 128.

[132] Kelman, *You Have to Be Careful*, p. 135.

feelings, Jeremiah ventriloquises the logic of power, suggesting at one point that a 'correct procedure had to be resolved' 'to deal with these unusual true-borns' who, reaching the peak of their natural lack of respect for authority and class differences, 'were not even content with the ordinary public areas [of the airport] but were continually discovered in the plush leather lounges of the VIP executive suites'. As a result,

> The legal team entered discussions with the politicians to discover or create a ruling based on the nature of patriotism, whether it might be deemed unlawful to bring shame on the Uhmerkin people. Surely the 'flaunting of one's poverty in public' by tiny minorities caused undue suffering and stress to the vast majority of folks who didnay *have* poverty, and was not only socially unacceptable but a breach of their civil rights?[133]

The intensity of the parody is heightened by Jeremiah's contrarian awareness of his own paradoxical location as simultaneously inside and outside of the socio-political pale. As a 'furnir' and 'member of the alienigenae', an immigrant whose own lineage 'got stuck in class relations at the time of William the Conqueror', and as an 'unashamed Class III Red neck Card carrier in this land of give and take, this land of hurry home', Jeremiah knows himself to be a sociologically, juridically, and ideologically marked outsider.[134] But he also acknowledges that he is on the inside of the decisive racial border underpinning the American social and political order, and that in that sense – despite the general precariousness of his situation – he is relatively privileged.

Yet subjectively, Jeremiah insistently and emphatically inhabits a position of exteriority that refuses to become 'integratit' or 'assimilatit'. Thus, commenting on the fact that he 'was the only pink furnir in the section', and that in order to find 'another ye had to go to management level or take a walk inside the terminal buildings', since there were 'thousands of the fuckers in there, either true-borns or with an appropriate status', he remarks that he did not want 'to be one of these cunts anyway, even if they offered me', before launching into one of his characteristically hyperpoliticised and both linguistically and ideologically anarchic rants:

> Imagine being related to der pinker WASP königin ingilander and her barrel-load of kowtowing arselicking subject cunts. No sir. Ah am a republican, vive la république! Ah am a socialiste, vive le socialiste! Ah am a Worker of the World; vive le internationale; vive vive vive, emancipation, egalité and the rights of man, and woman and humanity,

[133] Kelman, *You Have to Be Careful*, p. 197.
[134] Kelman, *You Have to Be Careful*, pp. 86, 151, 224.

all humankind, which includes children. And also the cratur kingdom in its entirety; animal, insect and fish, whose existence forever should be treasured.[135]

With soaring vernacular impetus, Jeremiah's antinomian jeremiad becomes in this passage a heterogenous compound of revolutionary motifs, tracing a path from his 'Skarrish' indictment of the British monarchy and its implicit association with white supremacy (and, ultimately, with Nazism) to a playful amalgam of radical possibilities, from Jacobinism to syndicalist internationalism, notably culminating in a vision of universal liberation that includes the natural world in all its pantheistic glory. As Jeremiah insists, 'Craturs also have rights and then too we have the sanctity of plant life, every wee leaf that flutters has a name and a wee soul and benefits from the guid lord's acquaintance; take away the heavenly breath and that wee leaf goes fluttering to the ground, deid as a fucking dodo man bring on the bulldozers, let us lay the concrete'.[136] More than a mere atheistic coda to the unrestrained irony of his discourse, Jeremiah's final turn in this passage to a near-Spinozian notion of God-as-nature is fully consistent with the 'ranting' vocation of his anarchic jeremiad. By including the natural world in his idea of emancipation, and by associating it with a certain, potentially revolutionary, conception of the divine, Jeremiah once again comes closer to the seventeenth-century Ranters than to the New England Puritans evoked by his name. Thus, Jacob Bauthumley's famous statement on the nature of God in one of the most famous Ranter pamphlets, 'The Light and Dark Sides of God', resonates strongly with Jeremiah's pantheistic imaginary:

> I see that God is in all Creatures, Man and Beast, Fish and Fowle, and every green thing, from the highest Cedar to the Ivey on the wall; and that God is the life and being of them, and that God doth really dwell, and if you will personally; if he may admit so low an expression in them all, and hath his Being no where else out of the Creatures.[137]

At the end of Jeremiah's detailed, circular, and sometimes contradictory account of his time as a security operative, what we encounter is a frontal attack on the Protestant work ethic and its genetic embeddedness in the ideology of the American Way. Even before going into the intricacies of his employment history,

---

[135] Kelman, *You Have to Be Careful*, pp. 209–210.

[136] Kelman, *You Have to Be Careful*, p. 210.

[137] Jacob Bauthumley, 'The Light and Dark Sides of God', in *A Collection of Ranter Writings: Spiritual Liberty and Sexual Freedom in the English Revolution*, ed. by Nigel Smith (London: Pluto Press, 2014), p. 227.

he announces – in a display of divine swearing that Abiezer Coppe would have recognised as directly involved in 'the substantiality of levelling' – that his 'job was lousy fucking boring fucking shit fucking crap'.[138] More transcendentally, Jeremiah recognises that the general obsession with 'work work work' is a symptom that 'the world was gripped by a psychotic masochism' – namely that of capitalism.[139] After momentarily contemplating the idea of 'forming a branch of the Wobblies', and inviting his globally mobile and precariously employed 'compañeros' to join in 'the fight for worker dignity and the politicization of wur common struggle', Jeremiah turns to a more messianic vision of class struggle (a reorientation that almost parallels the Ranters' own turn from 'Levelling by sword and by spade' to 'Levelling by miracle'), ultimately announcing: 'I was in favour of a universal strike, an eternal strike'.[140]

I would argue that this embrace of messianism (of a messianism 'without messianism', in Derrida's sense), which becomes increasingly apparent towards the end of the novel, leads Jeremiah both to a spectral communion – of sorts – with his ancestor and namesake and to an implicit measuring of his experiential sense of (in)justice against 'auld' Jeremiah's, across a historical distance beyond measure.[141] In a final transposition of the recurring motif of 'blundering' (since that inaugural moment when the nineteenth-century ancestor had 'blunder[ed] off the Santa Fe trail'), Jeremiah gets lost in the bar where he has been drinking, reminiscing, and talking with an elderly American couple for most of the evening, just as he tries to find the toilet.[142] Disoriented and seemingly delusional, he apostrophises the old Jeremiah in language that explicitly mixes the theological with the political:

> Because I ignored the path of righteousness I was being pushed, pulled and harried to my doom. At times like these I needed my guardian angel, my good auld great-great. Jeremiah! Jeremiah! Wherefore art thou! Arise and walk ye spirit of the mighty!
>
> Seriously but. Heh! I need rescuing here, us International Workers of the World need reuniting. Heh Jeremiah![143]

In the spectral intimacy of this absence, in the transcendent hope Jeremiah inscribes in the name of his long-gone ancestor, there is the promise – however

---

[138] Kelman, *You Have to Be Careful*, p. 139.

[139] Kelman, *You Have to Be Careful*, p. 316.

[140] Kelman, *You Have to Be Careful*, pp. 220, 316; Morton, *World of the Ranters*, p. 71.

[141] Derrida, *Specters of Marx* (New York: Routledge, 1994), p. 74.

[142] Kelman, *You Have to Be Careful*, p. 339.

[143] Kelman, *You Have to Be Careful*, p. 401.

desperate and rooted in an experience of solitude and loss – of a future beyond measure and of a justice, beyond law and authority, of a truly divine nature (not unlike that imagined by the Ranters and other antinomian Christian radicals), projecting itself above historical time in the mystical image of an 'eternal' – and indeed holy – strike.[144] Suddenly finding himself outside of the building, and lost in the snow, Jeremiah concludes that the guardian angel whose benign presence he has been sensing all along is not his ancestor but his estranged partner Yasmin, whose haunting absence nevertheless makes his sense of abandonment, in this 'town with no name' from which everybody – including 'the folk in the bar' – seems to have 'vanished', all the more oppressive.[145]

For, in contrast to the radical alterity suggested by the memory of the old Jeremiah (an impossibly distant, yet spectrally relatable and hopeful other), the fading spectrality of his ex dawns upon him with a revelation about the general ghostliness of human relationships (in this kind of society).[146] Other people are 'ghostly personages' like '[s]hips that pass in the night', while it remains incumbent upon the lonely individual 'to make them comfortable … in the off chance they might want to hang around and fucking haunt ye'. The individual is thus no more than 'a fucking salesperson, offering yer present and future to a bunch of ephemeral strangers'.[147] Throughout the novel, the idea of contact and community with other people is marked off by this split sense of haunting, by a division in the experience of alterity between an intractable but *just* (and thus welcoming, redeeming) sense of otherness and a sense of radical estrangement and inhospitability, even in the closest forms of contact.[148] The latter is invariably associated with the dystopian version of America against which the novel's postmodern jeremiad is launched – a most unwelcoming society for others of all kinds. Haunted by this lack of hospitality, by this systematic and brutal reduction of human beings to the status of commodities (and worse still, to chances, to bets, as in the case of

---

[144] Derrida's concept of justice, via his elaboration on the idea of 'divine violence' proposed by Walter Benjamin in *Zur Kritik der Gewalt*, is apposite. See Jacques Derrida, 'Force of Law: The "Mystical Foundations of Authority"', in *Deconstruction and the Possibility of Justice*, ed. by D. Cornell et al., trans. by Mary Quaintance (New York: Routledge, 1992), pp. 3–67.

[145] Kelman, *You Have to Be Careful*, p. 422.

[146] The echoes of a distinctively nineteenth-century discourse on the spectrality of ethical relations, which I addressed in Chapter One in my discussion of *Mary Barton*, are particularly strong here.

[147] Kelman, *You Have to Be Careful*, p. 422.

[148] Derrida, *Specters of Marx*, pp. 32–33.

the 'persian bets'), Jeremiah tends to turn, without any degree of conviction or faith in the traditional sense, yet animated by a radicalised sense of spectrality, to the divine and the messianic. Thus, as a true Ranter, oscillating between Puritanism and atheism, his final thoughts are directed towards the received (and in the American context, hegemonic) idea of God as vindictive and omnipotent: 'Gods are no so much good, no so much merciful as all-powerful'.[149] Suffering the effect of the freezing temperatures on his body, Jeremiah is momentarily tempted by the idea that God may actually be merciful and willing to save an atheistic sinner like himself from hypothermia 'without the barter of thrice three prayers five times daily'.[150] But Jeremiah is also, like so many Ranters before him, willing to offer a recantation – in this case, from his militant atheism.[151] While he imagines an American-style angry God saying, 'The mystery about us gods is how we offer nothing and receive everything; that is the measure of wur unfathomability to all you atheists, and until ye accept it ye remain doomed to a life of bodily discomfort', he also concedes that, in the throes of his present torment, 'I could see me converting' – not unlike 'Poor auld Jeremiah' who 'must have been at his wits' end' when he 'laps[ed] into christianity'.[152]

The novel ends in the same atmosphere of oppressive and threatening loneliness that punctuates it throughout, with the added menace of the arrival (which upturns the hopeful expectation of a redemptive other, just when it is most needed) of a police patrol. It is unclear what the outcome of this final encounter will be and whether or not it will result in Jeremiah's loss of the chance to fly home the following day (which at this point emerges as the only viable prospect of salvation for him, the only horizon of an intangible justice to-come), but it is interesting to note that, in this final extremity of his American nightmare, and after having put theology – in however atheistic a version – at the heart of his ranting, Jeremiah briefly returns in the final pages to a radically anti-authoritarian and even utopian vision of religion and the divine. Drawn by his habitual pattern of free association from the

---

[149] Kelman, *You Have to Be Careful*, p. 422. The title of a famous jeremiad by Jonathan Edwards, 'Sinners in the Hands of an Angry God', is called to mind here.

[150] Kelman, *You Have to Be Careful*, p. 428.

[151] As Christopher Hill observes, 'the Ranters were not by nature martyrs. Like Lollards and Familists before them, they usually recanted when called upon to do so ... Indeed, if there is no immortality, the satisfactions of martyrdom are less obvious: resistance to the death would call for a deeper and more consistently worked out ideology than most Ranters had', *The World Turned Upside Down* (London: Penguin, 1991), p. 209.

[152] Kelman, *You Have to Be Careful*, pp. 428–429.

physical pain he feels in his feet to a thought about ancient monastic life, he ends up expressing his amazed admiration for these early Christians devoted to 'the Glory of the Lord' – a trace of that 'brave but foolhardy attempt at unity with God' which, regardless of the more intractable (or, as he says, 'unfathomable') theological dimension, continuously attests to the fact that 'people are amazing [and that] they have been getting up to such mischief for 5 hundred thousand years'.[153] This celebration of the human amounts – in true Ranter fashion – to a proclamation of the sanctity of humanity. And it is precisely the latter that a society such as America denies with its pervasive authoritarianism and xenophobia, with its exclusion and negation of the other and thus of the possibility of democracy itself understood, as Derrida does, as hospitality, that is, as a democracy-for-the-other, as a *democracy to come.*

As I pointed out at the beginning of this discussion, *You Have to Be Careful in the Land of the Free* concludes with Jeremiah's apophatic claim – presumably addressed to the police officer he runs into – that his meandering jeremiad is 'no polemical diatribe against the evils of imperialism, colonialism, capitalism and all the rest of it'.[154] Crucially, returning to a central theme in his lengthy indictment of those evils and their American incarnation, he adds that his status as a guest in a foreign nation does not allow him to 'abuse ma hosts'. His truncated remark (for the sentence is left unfinished), which again brings to the fore the defining problematic of hospitality as limited and conditional, is preceded by a vision of hostility towards the other that only confirms the contradictory and self-cancelling nature of its logic in this society. Thus, Jeremiah imagines what might happen if he decided to start running down the streets of this brutally impersonal and impenetrable American town 'without no fucking sidewalks, having to step on people's lawns': 'In some states the lieges have the right to gun ye down for that transgression. All ye do is place a foot on their grass and bang. If they discover ye are a Red Card carrier then fine, nay cunt gets done for killing ye'.[155] The feudal language and vision of sovereign exceptionality – with the Red Card-carrying foreigner as a sort of *homo sacer* whose killing would go unpunished – offers a sharp contrast to the invoked imaginary of relations between a host and a guest.[156] But it also emphasises the irreducible connection between hospitality and hostility upon which Derrida has commented at length. For the ambiguity that inheres in the *law* of hospitality (understood precisely as such, in juridico-political terms)

[153] Kelman, *You Have to Be Careful*, p. 434.
[154] Kelman, *You Have to Be Careful*, p. 437.
[155] Kelman, *You Have to Be Careful*, p. 437.
[156] See Giorgio Agamben, *Homo Sacer: Sovereign Power and Bare Life*, trans. by Daniel Heller-Roazen (Stanford, CA: Stanford University Press, 1998).

concerns the fact that it 'violently imposes a contradiction on the very concept of hospitality in fixing a limit to it, in de-termining it'.[157] For, in being formulated as a law, the hospitable gift of *'greeting ... the foreign other'* is premised 'on the condition that the host ... remains the master of the household', 'thus limiting the gift proffered and making of this limitation, namely, the *being-oneself in one's own home*, the condition of the gift and of hospitality'.[158] This makes of hospitality, then, insofar as it is construed and put to work in the context of a juridico-political and sovereign order, a fundamentally 'self-contradictory concept and experience which can only self-destruct'.[159]

We could argue that Kelman pushes this self-cancelling logic to its limit in this novel, which, after all, begins with and then develops the idea of failed social interaction through its protagonist's realisation that the principle of hospitality in 'the land of the free' is not only predicated on a stringent conditionality but is also defined by a sense of radical opacity. Thus, for example, the atmosphere of suspicion and threat which accompanies Jeremiah's interactions in the first bar he visits is amplified by the impossibility of both offering and acknowledging hospitality among strangers. As he prepares to leave the premises, he announces his intention of returning the courtesy and buying the man he has been talking to a drink: 'It was hospitable you buying me one and I'd just like to return it'.[160] The response he obtains is not merely one of vaguely hostile suspicion; it is effectively one of seeming incomprehension, as if this formal language, indeed this social formalisation of the law of hospitality, had become internally colonised and dismantled by a now-dominant law of hostility (the setting is, after all, a dystopian version of post-9/11 America).[161]

4.4 'Society Does Not Exist': Kelman and the Politics of Lack

This idea of a general voiding of the language and experience of hospitality is one to which Kelman returns in his more recent novel *God's Teeth and Other Phenomena*, where Kelman's fictional alter ego Jack Proctor, a 66-year-old Glaswegian author and winner of the 'Banker Prize', is invited

---

[157] Jacques Derrida, 'Hostipitality', trans. by Barry Stocker with Forbes Morlock, *Angelaki* 5:3 (2000), p. 4.

[158] Derrida, 'Hostipitality', p. 4.

[159] Derrida, 'Hostipitality', p. 5.

[160] Kelman, *You Have to Be Careful*, p. 27.

[161] Later on, while reminiscing about his ex-partner's musical tours across the country, Jeremiah is struck by 'the lack of hospitality' displayed by the organisers: 'They didnay even offer us a coffee never mind a sandwich', Kelman, *You Have to Be Careful*, p. 309.

to take up a writer's residency abroad under the auspices of a presumably prestigious cultural institution. Snubbed and humiliated by his hosts through a combination of mismanagement and disinterest, Jack becomes increasingly confused and embittered by a role he did not want in the first place yet was forced to accept ('I was skint and that was that') and one where its ruling principle or law of hospitality seems to have been completely distorted.[162] The confusion he experiences upon arriving at one of the first events organised by the hosting 'House of Art and Aesthetics' is a good summary of his plight throughout the novel:

> This reminded me that nobody had said hullo. Right from when I entered the building the first time. If it wasnay deliberate it was weird. Here I was on the very first night of my residency, my first public event. Maybe it was me. Maybe I was to say hello to them. Maybe I was representing the House of Art. So I was expected to circulate and welcome folk. I trust you are enjoying the show: I trust you are enjoying the show. My name is Jack Proctor and I am the conduit and creative literary developer, I trust you're enjoying the show, young Mark there, the boy genius.
>
> I thought I was the damn guest maybe it was them.[163]

The seething hostility which characterises the law of hospitality in *You Have to Be Careful in the Land of the Free* is replaced here with a powerful sense of indifference, a refusal to understand or acknowledge the guest as other (as a true ethical Other, in Levinas's and Derrida's sense).[164] In both cases, the self-limiting and ultimately self-cancelling logic of a hospitality that does not respect the fundamental alterity – the fundamental deference towards the other – implicit in its offering results in the affirmation of a political principle defined by violence and oppression. In the earlier novel, this principle, this

---

[162] James Kelman, *God's Teeth and Other Phenomena* (Oakland, CA: PM Press, 2022), p. 3.

[163] Kelman, *God's Teeth*, p. 41.

[164] 'Hospitality assumes "radical separation" as experience of the alterity of the other, as relation to the other, in the sense that Levinas emphasizes and works with the word "relation," that is, in its ferential, referential or, as he sometimes notes, deferential *bearing* [*portée*]. The relation to the other is deference', Jacques Derrida, *Adieu to Emmanuel Levinas*, trans. by Pascale-Anne Brault and Michael Naas (Stanford, CA: Stanford University Press, 1999), p. 46. As Jack Proctor puts it at one point, 'In order to "understand" one must firstly recognize the other, I said, the validity of the other, fellow sufferer in this vale of nincompoop misery', Kelman, *God's Teeth*, p. 55.

political *arche*, is of course embodied in the figure of a near-totalitarian society penetrated by a generalised impulse of sovereign hostility towards the other as both poor and foreign. Without abandoning his fundamentally anarchic critique, Kelman's later book connects this problematic to the specific set of conditionalities attending on – and hindering – the practice of writing in the power-sanctioned regimes of the contemporary literary world. For the basic hospitality that a non-conforming writer such as Jack Proctor (or James Kelman) is denied by the cultural establishment is the respect for his need to write without subordination to any regulative or institutional principle – that is, to write anarchically, beyond and against any law of calculation or measurement. As he puts it in the final report he submits (which the novel presents under the heading 'Author's Afterword'), 'I knew nothing about it when they offered the residency. Predictably, the elemental dynamic is governed by the drive towards the standardization of language, thought and being. In this the centralization of the Creative Writing industry is crucial'.[165] And yet, he adds, '[w]hether the authorities like it or not Creative Writing is art and art is the beating heart of liberty'.[166] In other words, behind the principles of standardisation and central-isation governing the institutional – and indeed, economico-political – regime of creative writing, there lies a radical and indomitable, as well as traumatic, impulse that cannot be assimilated by the system.

This impulse to write beyond the standardising and centralising law of the creative writing industry defines the antagonistic nature of the subject in this novel. Borrowing from Lacan, we could say that, failing to answer the injunction of the big Other (that impenetrable mandate inscribed in the 'invitation' extended by the House of Art and Aesthetics), Proctor's position as subject is revealed precisely through his self-presentation as a writer whose writing cannot be assimilated by the symbolic law of official literary culture. In effect, writing emerges in the novel as that object which eludes symbolisation, which cannot be properly signified or explained, and which nevertheless provides the subject with its most irreducible – and real – anchoring point.[167] This is the object Lacan names *objet a* or *objet petit a* and whose status as 'Real' (in terms of the famous Lacanian triad of Real, Symbolic, and Imaginary) concerns its resistance to symbolisation as a trace and impossible – because effectively irretrievable – rem(a)inder of a fullness that is forever lost.[168] The *objet a* thus

---

[165] Kelman, *God's Teeth*, p. 343.

[166] Kelman, *God's Teeth*, p. 343.

[167] The repeated failure of Proctor's writing seminars with students is a prime example of this.

[168] According to Bruce Fink, this object is '*the scrap that evades the grasp of symbolization. It is a reminder that there is something else, something perhaps lost, perhaps yet*

designates the necessary support through which the subject is constituted but also the trace of the limit that prevents its symbolic integration.[169] It fills out the subject with a 'bit' of that Real which cannot be accessed (except indirectly, fantasmatically), while indicating that the true nature of the subject is that of a failure, of a gap in the symbolic order. This is accurately rendered in the novel when Proctor declares that '[t]he writing is the thing. It keeps us sane', for writing simultaneously reveals the failure in the structure of institution-alised Creative Writing, Proctor's status as subject (as the unsymbolisable gap or dislocation that prevents the structure from achieving closure, filling it with antagonism and contingency), and, finally, its own imaginary function as the object that provisionally and precariously 'sutures' the gap, 'keep[ing] us sane'.[170]

In *You Have to Be Careful in the Land of the Free*, writing performs a similar structural function as both the trace of a real lack and the imaginary support for a subjective identification without possible integration into the symbolic – or socio-political – order. At various points in the novel, Jeremiah turns to his fantasy of becoming a novelist, even elaborating on details of plot and characterisation: 'Occasionally I got into the fantasy and did do that, they all had their stories and I had made a start on one myself, it was gauny be a novel about a scabrous private eye'.[171] He even says, anticipating Proctor's claim, that the 'writing itself becomes the thing'.[172] We could add here that 'the Thing' is precisely, as Lacan argues in his translation and discussion of Freud's *das Ding*, that which remains lost and unattainable, and, only in that sense, also intimately connected to the subject. What stands in for the Thing is the object 'as a point of imaginary fixation', that is, as the trace of a lack that is called upon to support and thus complete the fantasy, giving the subject its place and role.[173] Jeremiah's

to be found', *The Lacanian Subject: Between Language and Jouissance* (Princeton, NJ: Princeton University Press, 1995), p. 94.

[169] As Slavoj Žižek puts it, 'there is a certain left-over which cannot be integrated into the symbolic universe, an object which resists subjectivation, and the subject is precisely correlative to this object', 'Beyond Discourse-Analysis', in Ernesto Laclau, *New Reflections on the Revolution of Our Time* (London: Verso, 1990), p. 254.

[170] Kelman, *God's Teeth*, p. 63. As Laclau writes, 'Subject equals the pure form of the structure's dislocation, of its ineradicable distance from itself. An examination of the subject's forms of presence in the structure must therefore be an exploration of contingency's discursive forms of presence in the field of objectivity – or more precisely, the ways in which objectivity is subverted by contingency', *New Reflections*, pp. 60–61.

[171] Kelman, *You Have to Be Careful*, p. 41.

[172] Kelman, *You Have to Be Careful*, p. 43.

[173] Jacques Lacan, *The Ethics of Psychoanalysis*, trans. by Dennis Porter (London: Routledge, 2008), p. 140.

writing project remains a fantasy in this precise sense. Punctuated by all sorts of deferrals and postponements, the writing is, in effect, nothing but the absence (for it never really materialises in any textual product) that allows Jeremiah to constitute himself as a subject – and more specifically, as an antagonistic subject. Through the invocation of this object-lack, of this 'yarn', this 'private-eye ditty' he is going to write, Jeremiah constructs an ideal I (his imagined protagonist) in open confrontation with the order of power:

> My hero wasnay the usual apolitical right-wing hollywood prick, his sympathies went to the underdog, he was anti-cops and anti-robbers, anti-authoritarian, he was also a good anarchist; anti-sexist, anti-homophobic, anti-racist, pro-justice, pro-truth, pro-asylum seeker, pro-immigration, pro-equality – christ I could go on forever. And the place to do it was the book. And I was gauny.[174]

This connection between lack and antagonism in Kelman's construction of subjectivity throughout his oeuvre is central as it puts the focus on a conception of the social defined by negativity. It could be said that the key point in Kelman's fiction (as in Laclau and Mouffe's theorisation of the political) is that 'society does not exist' as an immediately accessible and objective reality. The imaginary production of an object that is nothing but the trace of a lack and the place where the subject is constituted is also what prevents the social (the symbolic order from which the subject receives its mandates and ideological interpellations) from achieving fullness and objectivity, and, consequently, what makes the antagonism constitutive.[175] The subjective lack that defines a character such as Jeremiah Brown is correlative to the objective lack in a society that, having disavowed hospitality in all its forms, knows only hostility towards the other – that is, a society that is nothing but the affirmation of power and political decision, and, in that sense, the affirmation of its own incompleteness.

This logic of impossible social objectivity and irreducible antagonism between the opacity of a totalitarian State apparatus and a bare subject defined by lack and exclusion is also at the heart of Kelman's best-known work, his

---

[174] Kelman, *You Have to Be Careful*, pp. 48, 59, 67.

[175] As Jacques Lacan writes about the paradoxical nature of the *objet a*, 'designating this little *a* with the term object is merely a metaphorical use of this word, since it's borrowed from the subject-object relation, from which the term *object* is constituted. It's no doubt suitable for designating the general function of objectivity, but the object we have to speak about under the term *a* is precisely an object that is external to any possible definition of objectivity', *Anxiety*, trans. by A. R. Price (Cambridge: Polity Press, 2014), p. 86.

Booker Prize-winning novel *How Late It Was, How Late*.[176] This book begins with its lumpenproletarian Glaswegian protagonist, Sammy Samuels, waking up in a street corner, sore and in a state of drunken amnesia. As he recovers consciousness, the first thing Sammy notices is that he is wearing 'an auld pair of trainer shoes' while his 'new pair of leathers' are missing.[177] Sammy first imagines that 'somebody must have blagged them ... [a]nd then left him with these' but then considers the possibility that the thief may have thought 'he was dead' ('ye could see that, some poor cunt scratching himself and thinking, Naybody's there, naybody's there') and just taken them from him.[178] The missing shoes are the first of a series of lost objects that constitute the relationship between Sammy and his surroundings in the novel, defining the objective impossibility of the socio-symbolic order itself. The latter is immediately introduced as an irrepressibly hostile Other in the form of a group of 'sodjers', as Sammy idiosyncratically refers to the police officers who arrest him. When he is taken into custody, Sammy is beaten up by these 'sodjers' and becomes blind. Sammy's lost eyesight is the central object around which the character is constructed, as well as the foundation on which the irreducible antagonism defining his development throughout the novel rests. There is a strictly fantasmatic dimension to this development: as Sammy considers the effects of his lack, he conjures up imaginary scenarios of entrapment in the nightmarish web of the big Other. Thus, for example, he fantasises about the monstrous 'Blind Asylum' which, he imagines, is awaiting him at the other end of his impending transactions with doctors (or 'quacks') and the ominous 'DSS':

> The Blind Asylum but what a hell-hole that sounded, straight out some victorian fucking nightmare in the name of christ ye could picture them all, the poor bastards, moping and groping their way about these whitewashed stone rooms; men, women and children; all sharing these pits, wearing these long droopy nightshirts summer and winter, feeling their way around, groaning and moaning; the gentry coming in to check out the shareholdings, the black silk top hats and white scarves, the ballgowns, on their way to the fucking ballet or something[179]

What lies at the centre of this fantasy is the traumatic kernel of the Other's enjoyment – an imaginary rendition of that impossible satisfaction of desire

---

[176] I have offered a rather different theoretical approach to this novel in my book *British Working-Class Fiction: Narratives of Refusal and the Struggle Against Work* (London: Bloomsbury Academic, 2016).

[177] James Kelman, *How Late It Was, How Late* (London: Vintage, 1998), p. 1.

[178] Kelman, *How Late It Was*, pp. 1–2.

[179] Kelman, *How Late It Was*, p. 67.

of which his lost object is the trace and support. This is the irreducible *arche* of the socio-symbolic universe Sammy has to confront: a two-faced State apparatus (repressive, on the one hand, and impenetrably bureaucratic, on the other) whose *jouissance* is symmetrical to the lack constituting the embattled subject himself.

The various scenes where the 'sodjers' openly taunt Sammy about his blindness ('Anybody find an eyesight! There's a guy here looking for an eyesight!') are compounded by his encounters with the traumatic 'Real' of a Welfare State bureaucratic machinery now reduced to pure linguistic excess.[180] Take the following example from one of the DSS employees with whom Sammy tries to register his claim for compensation:

> Ye must understand also Mister Samuels that if as you suggest the alleged dysfunction is an effect of physical restraints and is established as such then the secondary factor arises in respect of those restraints, and this secondary factor may become primary, why were those restraints being exercised ... it would tend to cast doubt on the question of causation; you could find yerself in the invidious situation where it is argued, on the balance of probability, that it was you yerself that cause the alleged dysfunction, that you were the primary cause.[181]

The Kafkaesque quality of this passage – and of this novel as a whole – is of course unmissable.[182] It is useful, in this regard, to think about the role that the logic of pure, impossible, and traumatic enjoyment – or *jouissance* – plays in Kafka's own imagination of the bureaucratic Other. As Slavoj Žižek notes about the representation of the Law and the judicial apparatus of the State in *The Trial*, 'the court is above all *lawless* in a formal sense: as if the chain of "normal" connections between causes and effects is suspended'.[183] Thus 'the fatal error' Kafka's protagonist makes, in 'address[ing] the court, the Other of the Law, as a homogeneous entity, attainable by means of consistent argument', is to ignore the proximity of the traumatic obscenity of *jouissance* (represented in *The Trial* through the sexual act that interrupts the proceedings) to the opacity of a symbolic order that has become colonised and subverted by this 'real' excess.[184]

---

[180] Kelman, *How Late It Was*, p. 13.

[181] Kelman, *How Late It Was*, p. 106.

[182] Kelman's interest in Kafka is well known and has been widely discussed. See, for example, Michael Gardiner, *From Trocchi to Trainspotting: Scottish Critical Theory Since 1960* (Edinburgh: Edinburgh University Press, 2006), pp. 159–164.

[183] Žižek, 'Beyond Discourse-Analysis', p. 257.

[184] Žižek, 'Beyond Discourse-Analysis', p. 258.

In Kelman's novel, as in Kafka's, the State apparatus is 'flooded with enjoyment' and thus firmly anchored in a failure of calculable or rational objectivity.[185] Its *truth* is one which only an antagonistic relation, founded on lack and traumatic displacement, can capture and resist. It could be argued that, through his constant negotiation of the lost object (from his eyesight to his various dysfunctional or lost relationships, including that with his girlfriend Helen, who has disappeared), Sammy manages to avoid Joseph K.'s error in *The Trial*. For what underpins his fantasmatic elaborations is often a stance of what could be described as alert – and therefore, in a sense, resistant – anxiety: an anxiety punctuated by his awareness of that object-trace of lack that founds his antagonistic position vis-à-vis the oppressive Other. Thus, for example, he meets the linguistic outburst of bureaucratic enjoyment in the passage I have quoted above with a characteristic reaction of anxious, yet in a sense also lucid, anticipation: 'Sammy knew what was coming. He fucking knew it'.[186] Or, later on, when he fears – and correctly anticipates – the presence of intruders (who will turn out to be the police) in his own home: 'Alright man alright; he took off his jacket and hung it on the peg; it was just how folk could be in the house and how would ye know, ye wouldnay, ye would have to wander about listening for sounds ... Every wee detail, ye wind up making a mountain out a molehill. A raving fucking Loonie man that's what ye end up'.[187]

It is worth noting that Sammy's anxious 'hallucinating', as he calls it at one point, together with his other references to madness in the novel, are fundamentally different from the 'madness' Lessing explores in *The Golden Notebook* and *The Four-Gated City*.[188] If an *an-archic* dimension is common to both psychic strategies of resistance against the socio-political *arche*, in Kelman we find no proto-utopian opening towards otherness (a Levinasian theme we encounter in Lessing), but rather the confirmation that hetero-geneity can only shed light on the crisis of social objectivity, substituting antagonism and contingency for society's incompleteness and impossibility. This is the precise sense of the class struggle as a recurring but radically subjective imaginary in Kelman. Jeremiah Brown's ranting, for example, has

---

[185] Žižek, 'Beyond Discourse-Analysis', p. 258.

[186] Kelman, *How Late It Was*, p. 106.

[187] The police even go on to offer a mock diagnosis as part of their psychological torture: 'You're a kind of anxious guy arent ye? ... you do find that with people suffering sensory dysfunctions. Quite often when they're examined by the medical authorities they're found to have a history of anxiety', Kelman, *How Late It Was*, p. 203.

[188] Kelman, *How Late It Was*, p. 51.

an undeniable class dimension that underpins his declared socialism, but this is a political identity without positivity, indeed an act of fantasmatic identification with that impossible object, that residue of otherness that cannot be symbolised (or, as Jeremiah puts it, 'integratit') and is also the locus where the lacking subject himself comes into being.[189] In fact, this is also the class meaning of Sammy Samuels's antagonistic anxiety. For if anxiety is, as Lacan points out, that which 'introduces us' to 'the function of lack', that which exposes the real kernel that certifies the impossibility of symbolic closure, it is also the mechanism that signals the presence of an irreducible antagonism.[190] Sammy's class identity lacks positivity: in a sense, it is only accessible through this anxious structure and its oppositional effects, and this is precisely the logic of political irreducibility on which Kelman's literary anarcho-socialism is predicated.[191] It is not surprising that characters such as Jeremiah Brown and Sammy Samuels inevitably gravitate towards the horizon of social heterogeneity associated with the lumpenproletariat, a notion that brings us back to the discussion of nineteenth and early twentieth-century imaginaries of exclusion from the order of 'society'. The lumpenproletariat is that 'real' excess which destabilises the imagination of the social as a saturated and positive totality. It is also, in that sense, a class non-identity – or, to say it with Deleuze, a missing people – interrupting the symbolic homogeneity of the working class as an agent of history and pre-empting the possibility of a socialism *with* guarantees.

---

[189] As Lacan writes, 'This remainder, this ultimate Other, this irrational entity, this proof and sole guarantee, when all is said and done, of the Other's otherness, is the *a*', *Anxiety*, p. 27.

[190] Lacan, *Anxiety*, p. 132.

[191] Slavoj Žižek's discussion of 'class struggle' in terms of the unsymbolisable logic of antagonism is entirely applicable to Kelman: 'antagonism is precisely such an impossible kernel, a certain limit which is in itself nothing; it is only to be constructed retroactively, from a series of its effects, as the traumatic point which escapes them; it prevents a closure of the social field. In this way we might reread even the classic notion of the "class struggle": it is not the last signifier giving meaning to all social phenomena ... but – quite the contrary – a certain limit, a pure negativity, a traumatic limit which prevents the final totalization of the social-ideological field. The "class struggle" is present only in its effects, in the fact that every attempt to totalize the social field, to assign to social phenomena a definite place in the social structure, is always doomed to failure', *The Sublime of Object of Ideology* (London: Verso, 2008), p. 184.

Coda

A Politics of Heterogeneity

I want to conclude by insisting on the centrality of the notion of heterogeneity with which I ended the previous chapter and on its status as the conceptual linchpin of my investigation of literary socialism in this book. In order to do that, let me return to the nineteenth-century context with which I began.

In *The Country and the City*, Raymond Williams notes the contrast between Dickens's treatment of the new kind of northern industrial city to which he devotes his Condition-of-England novel *Hard Times* and the very different representation of London for which the novelist is better known. Thus, Coketown is described as 'severely workful' and a 'triumph of fact', a pure specimen of social homogeneity as imagined in the most dogmatic pronouncements of utilitarian ideology: 'It contained several large streets all very like one another, and many small streets still more like one another, inhabited by people equally like one another, who all went in and out at the same hours, with the same sound upon the same pavements, to do the same work, and to whom every day was the same as yesterday and tomorrow, and every year the counterpart of the last and the next'.[1] As Williams observes, this is a simple rhetorical denunciation that falls short of Dickens's more profound understanding of city experience 'in the full sense': 'For a city like London ... could not easily be described in a rhetorical gesture of repressive uniformity. On the contrary, its miscellaneity, its crowded variety, its randomness of movement, were the most apparent things about it, especially when seen from inside'.[2] In other words, what Dickens's characteristic imagination of urban dynamics registers is, precisely, the irreducibility of that heterogeneous experience which tended to escape the homogenising totalisations of various nineteenth-century ideological designs.

In a famous passage from *Dombey and Son*, for example, we encounter the shock of that traumatic otherness at the heart of modern society that would

[1] Charles Dickens, *Hard Times: A Norton Critical Edition*, ed. by Fred Kaplan, 4th edn (New York: W. W. Norton & Company, 2017), p. 23.
[2] Raymond Williams, *The Country and the City* (London: Hogarth Press, 1993), pp. 153–154.

ultimately render its idea (the idea of society as an objective symbolic order) impossible. The narrator evokes a 'dense black cloud' made of 'the noxious particles that rise from vitiated air' in the horrid slums 'rolling slowly on to corrupt the better portions of a town'.[3] The moral translation of this physical squalor is then imagined, with far more damning effects:

> But if the moral pestilence that rises with them, and, in the eternal laws of outraged Nature, is inseparable from them, could be made discernible too, how terrible the revelation! Then should we see depravity, impiety, drunkenness, theft, murder, and a long train of nameless sins against the natural affections and repulsions of mankind, overhanging the devoted spots, and creeping on, to blight the innocent and spread contagion among the pure. Then should we see how the same poisoned fountains that flow into our hospitals and lazar-houses, inundate the jails, and make the convict-ships swim deep, and roll across the seas, and over-run vast continents with crime.[4]

Dickens's catalogue here rehearses the breakdown of homogeneous society in Bataille's sense, precisely through the identification of that 'force or shock' that turns 'productive' or 'useful society' (in this case, the society imagined by Liberal ideology in the 1830s–40s), into 'a precarious form'.[5] The morally coded excess that characterises modern urban experience in Dickens – beyond the simplifications of the industrial formula – is an index of that untotalisable quality, that impossible objectivity of social reality with which socialist politics had to contend throughout the long twentieth century. Slums and their lumpenproletarian denizens are, as we know, at the centre of nineteenth-century controversies and tensions in the socialist imagination. It would suffice to recall Engels's dismissive remarks about London's East Enders in his famous letter to Margaret Harkness (which I mentioned in the Introduction). If the naturalist rendition of the London poor flouted the principle of typicality, thus contradicting the aesthetic vocation of a recognisably socialist realism, this could be explained and excused – according to Engels – on account of the inassimilable heterogeneity that characterised these inadequately proletarianised masses.

I think that Engels's treatment of the East End and its lumpen population remains a revealing index of the contradictory status assigned to

---

[3] Charles Dickens, *Dombey and Son*, ed. by Alan Horsman (Oxford: Oxford University Press, 2001), p. 684.

[4] Dickens, *Dombey and Son*, pp. 684–685.

[5] Bataille, 'Psychological Structure', pp. 137, 142, 139; see again my references to Bataille in the Introduction to this book. In *Hard Times*, Dickens satirises the liberal vision of 'useful society' through the figure of Mr Gradgrind.

the heterogeneous in class-reductionist accounts of socialism, and also, by implication, an index of the sort of discursive leap, beyond totalisation and homogenisation, that the literary imagination mobilises against such accounts. Thus, for example, in his 1892 preface to the English translation of *The Condition of the Working Class in England* (originally published in German in 1845), Engels offers a contradictory reading of the transformations affecting this notorious section of the English proletariat since the time of his initial observations in the early 1840s. On the one hand, he suggests, for 'the great mass of the working people, the state of misery and insecurity in which they live now is as low as ever, if not lower. The East End of London is an everspreading pool of stagnant misery and desolation, of starvation when out of work, and degradation, physical and moral, when in work'.[6] But then, a few pages later, Engels contradicts this diagnosis, linking instead the revitalisation of English socialism since the 1880s to what he now sees as the radically modified reality of the East End: 'That immense haunt of misery is no longer the stagnant pool it was six years ago. It has shaken off its torpid despair, has returned to life, and has become the home of what is called the "New Unionism", that is to say, of the organization of the great mass of "unskilled" workers'.[7] Thus, socialism, and in particular its most undeniably objective expression, that which has its roots in the organised labour movement, can only be imagined on the basis of a homogenised class landscape now (almost magically) shorn of its unproductive excess.

Interestingly, this is not a confusion we encounter in Engels's literary interlocutor Margaret Harkness. As we can observe, for example, in her 1889 novel *In Darkest London* – where, to some extent, she responds to Engels's 1888 critique of *A City Girl* – the unsymbolisable 'Real' of the lumpenproletariat remains an undiminished, festering wound of heterogeneity in the side of productive society and its progressive and homogenising class dynamics. The passage from abject poverty to socialist politics is not a guaranteed one (for despair and Christian Salvationism are also distinct alternatives in this novel), but it remains a compelling option in its own right, without requiring any magical (or, for that matter, dialectical) transformation within a homogeneous social logic. At one point, we read about a socialist doctor who, quoting from Engels's own book, responds to the immoral (and stupid) cant of the bourgeois West Enders affecting ignorance about the condition of the East End. When asked by Captain Lobe (the Salvation Army protagonist of the novel), 'What do you think can be done?', his answer is unambiguous:

---

[6] Friedrich Engels, *The Condition of the Working Class in England*, ed. by David McLellan (Oxford: Oxford University Press, 2009), pp. 321–322.
[7] Engels, *The Condition of the Working Class*, p. 324.

If I were a younger man I would give up medicine and go into politics. I would teach the people to use their votes, to send their own men into Parliament; and I would agitate myself in St. Stephen's for measures that would make the proletariat master of the situation. In fact, I would be a constitutional socialist, using all lawful means to improve the condition of the working man. God knows that it wants improving![8]

Socialism, in this novel, as in the literary genealogy I have been considering throughout this book, remains a promise, a spectre turned towards and inventing its own heterogeneous future. As one of the characters points out, 'Socialism is in the air, it is touching every one, and tingeing everything'.[9] However impractical (and even inept) the leaders of the various factions and organisations, and however contradictory the various political programmes, the transforming impulse of socialism – its announced break with the present state of affairs and its reimagination of the old radical promise of democratic transformation – seems unstoppable: 'Socialism is growing every day, both the sentiment *and* the economic theory. What it will become in time no one can tell. At present its most hopeful sign is an embryonic labour-party. This party is spreading all over the United Kingdom. It is a new Chartist movement, with twice as many points as were contained in the old Charter'.[10] Socialism is thus explicitly compared to the great radical-popular movement of the mid-nineteenth century, while its political task is identified, by implication, as no less than the construction of a people out of the radical heterogeneity, out of the vast expanse of social exclusion and disorganisation that characterises *fin-de-siècle* Britain.

This tension between an irreducible social heterogeneity and the political impulse to invent a collective subject-to-come has been at the heart of this book's investigation. Emerging out of the traumatic core of an insurmountable impossibility in the experience of the social and projecting itself towards the radical strangeness of a future beyond measure, the literary socialism imagined by British writers from the nineteenth to the twenty-first century remains an invitation to rethink the Left as a radical political project without guarantees.

---

[8] Margaret Harkness, *In Darkest London* (Cambridge: Black Apollo Press, 2003), p. 77.

[9] Harkness, *In Darkest London*, p. 131.

[10] Harkness, *In Darkest London*, p. 132.

Bibliography

Abensour, Miguel, 'An-archy between Metapolitics and Politics', *Parallax* 8:3 (2002), pp. 5–18

Abensour, Miguel, *Utopia from Thomas More to Walter Benjamin*, trans. by Raymond N. MacKenzie (Minneapolis: Univocal, 2017)

Abensour, Miguel, *Utopiques IV: L'histoire de l'utopie et le destin de sa critique* (Paris: Sens & Tonka, 2016)

Abensour, Miguel, 'William Morris: The Politics of Romance', in *Revolutionary Romanticism*, ed. by Max Blechman (San Francisco: City Lights Books, 1999), pp. 125–162

Acland, Richard, *Unser Kampf: Our Struggle* (Harmondsworth: Penguin, 1940)

Addison, Paul, *The Road to 1945: British Politics and the Second World War* (London: Pimlico, 1994)

Agamben, Giorgio, *Homo Sacer: Sovereign Power and Bare Life*, trans. by Daniel Heller-Roazen (Stanford, CA: Stanford University Press, 1998)

Agamben, Giorgio, *The Use of Bodies*, trans. by Adam Kotsko (Stanford, CA: Stanford University Press, 2016)

Allison, Mark A., *Imagining Socialism: Aesthetics, Anti-Politics, and Literature in Britain, 1817–1918* (Oxford: Oxford University Press, 2021)

Amundsen, Michael, 'George Orwell's Ethnographies of Experience: *The Road to Wigan Pier* and *Down and Out in Paris and London*', *Anthropological Journal of European Cultures* 25:1 (2016), pp. 9–25

Baker, Timothy C., '*A Scots Quair* and History', in *International Companion to Lewis Grassic Gibbon*, ed. by Scott Lyall (Glasgow: Scottish Literature International, 2015), pp. 47–59

Baldick, Chris, *In Frankenstein's Shadow: Myth, Monstrosity, and Nineteenth-Century Writing* (Oxford: Clarendon Press, 1987)

Barrow, Clyde W., *The Dangerous Class: The Concept of the Lumpenproletariat* (Ann Arbor: University of Michigan Press, 2020)

Bartley, Paula, *Ellen Wilkinson: From Red Suffragist to Government Minister* (London: Pluto Press, 2014)

Bataille, Georges, 'The Psychological Structure of Fascism', in *Visions of Excess: Selected Writings, 1927–1939*, ed. by Allan Stoekl, trans. by Allan Stoekl, with Carl R. Lovitt and Donald M. Leslie, Jr. (Minneapolis: University of Minnesota Press), pp. 137–160

Bauthumley, Jacob, 'The Light and Dark Sides of God', in *A Collection of Ranter Writings: Spiritual Liberty and Sexual Freedom in the English Revolution*, ed. by Nigel Smith (London: Pluto Press, 2014), pp. 222–256

Baxendale, John, *Priestley's England: J. B. Priestley and English Culture* (Manchester: Manchester University Press, 2007)

Beers, Laura, 'Feminism and Sexuality in Ellen Wilkinson's Fiction', *Parliamentary Affairs* 64:2 (2011), pp. 248–262

Bercovitch, Sacvan, *The American Jeremiad* (Madison: The University of Wisconsin Press, 1978)

Bevir, Mark, *The Making of British Socialism* (Princeton, NJ: Princeton University Press, 2011)

Bogue, Ronald, *Deleuzian Fabulation and the Scars of History* (Edinburgh: Edinburgh University Press, 2010)

Bove, Laurent, *La stratégie du conatus: affirmation et résistance chez Spinoza* (Paris: Vrin, 2012)

Braidotti, Rosi, 'A Theoretical Framework for the Critical Posthumanities', *Theory, Culture & Society* 36:6 (2019), pp. 31–61

Branson, Noreen, *History of the Communist Party of Great Britain 1941–1951* (London: Lawrence & Wishart, 1997)

Brantlinger, Patrick, *The Reading Lesson: The Threat of Mass Literacy in Nineteenth-Century British Fiction* (Bloomington: Indiana University Press, 1998)

Brome, Vincent, *J.B. Priestley* (London: Hamish Hamilton, 1988)

Cairnie, Julie, 'Imperial Poverty in Robert Tressell's *The Ragged Trousered Philanthropists*', *Journal of Commonwealth Literature* 37:2 (2002), pp. 175–194

Callaghan, John and Ben Harker, *British Communism: A Documentary History* (Manchester: Manchester University Press, 2011)

Campbell, Beatrix, 'Orwell – Paterfamilias or Big Brother?', in *Inside the Myth. Orwell: Views from the Left*, ed. by Christopher Norris (London: Lawrence & Wishart, 1984), pp. 126–138

'Cato', *Guilty Men* (London: Penguin, 1998)

Césaire, Aimé, *Discourse on Colonialism*, trans. by Joan Pinkham (New York: Monthly Review Press, 2000)

Claeys, Gregory, *Citizens and Saints: Politics and Anti-Politics in Early British Socialism* (Cambridge: Cambridge University Press, 2002)

Clark, Katerina, 'Socialist Realism *with* Shores: The Conventions of the Positive Hero', in *Socialist Realism without Shores*, ed. by Thomas Lahusen and Evgeny Dobrenko (Durham, NC: Duke University Press, 1997), pp. 27–50

Clark, Katerina, *The Soviet Novel: History as Ritual* (Bloomington: Indiana University Press, 2000)

Connor, John T., 'Jack Lindsay, Socialist Humanism and the Communist Historical Novel', *The Review of English Studies* 66:274 (2015), pp. 342–363

Coppe, Abiezer, 'A Fiery Flying Roll', in *A Collection of Ranter Writings: Spiritual Liberty and Sexual Freedom in the English Revolution*, ed. by Nigel Smith (London: Pluto Press, 2014), pp. 72–89

Cranny-Francis, Anne, *Jack Lindsay: Writer, Romantic, Revolutionary* (Cham: Palgrave Macmillan, 2023)

Crockett, Clayton, *Deleuze Beyond Badiou: Ontology, Multiplicity, and Event* (New York: Columbia University Press, 2013)

Croft, Andy, 'The End of Socialist Realism: Margot Heinemann's *The Adventurers*', in *Heart of the Heartless World: Essays in Cultural Resistance in Memory of Margot Heinemann*, ed. by David Margolies and Maroula Joannou (London: Pluto Press, 1995), pp. 195–215

D'Albertis, Deirdre, 'The Streetwalker and Urban Observations in *Mary Barton*', in Elizabeth Gaskell, *Mary Barton: A Norton Critical Edition*, ed. by Thomas Recchio (New York: W. W. Norton & Company, 2008), pp. 583–593

Del Valle Alcalá, Roberto, *British Working-Class Fiction: Narratives of Refusal and the Struggle Against Work* (London: Bloomsbury Academic, 2016)

Deleuze, Gilles, *Cinema 2: The Time-Image*, trans. by Hugh Tomlinson and Robert Galeta (Minneapolis: University of Minnesota Press, 1997)

Deleuze, Gilles, *Essays Critical and Clinical*, trans. by Daniel W. Smith and Michael A. Greco (London: Verso, 1998)

Deleuze, Gilles, *Nietzsche and Philosophy*, trans. by Hugh Tomlinson (London: Bloomsbury, 2013)

Deleuze, Gilles and Félix Guattari, *Anti-Oedipus*, trans. by Robert Hurley, Mark Seem, and Helen R. Lane (London: Continuum, 2011)

Deleuze, Gilles and Félix Guattari, *A Thousand Plateaus*, trans. by Brian Massumi (London: Continuum, 2011)

Deleuze, Gilles and Félix Guattari, *What is Philosophy?*, trans. by Hugh Tomlinson and Graham Burchill (London: Verso, 1994)

Deleuze, Gilles and Claire Parnet, 'On the Superiority of Anglo-American Literature', in *Dialogues II*, trans. by Hugh Tomlinson and Barbara Habberjam (New York: Columbia University Press, 2007), pp. 36–76

Derrida, Jacques, *Adieu to Emmanuel Levinas*, trans. by Pascale-Anne Brault and Michael Naas (Stanford, CA: Stanford University Press, 1999)

Derrida, Jacques, 'Force of Law: The "Mystical Foundations of Authority"', in *Deconstruction and the Possibility of Justice*, ed. by D. Cornell et al., trans. by Mary Quaintance (New York: Routledge, 1992), pp. 3–67

Derrida, Jacques, *Of Grammatology*, trans. by Gayatri Chakravorty Spivak (Baltimore, MA: The Johns Hopkins University Press, 1997)

Derrida, Jacques, 'Hostipitality', trans. by Barry Stocker with Forbes Morlock, *Angelaki* 5:3 (2000), pp. 3–18

Derrida, Jacques, *Rogues: Two Essays on Reason*, trans. by Pascale-Anne Brault and Michael Naas (Stanford, CA: Stanford University Press, 2005)

Derrida, Jacques, *Specters of Marx*, trans. by Peggy Kamuf (New York: Routledge, 1994)

Derrida, Jacques and Bernard Stiegler, 'Spectrographies', in *The Spectralities Reader: Ghosts and Haunting in Contemporary Cultural Theory*, ed. by María del Pilar Blanco and Esther Peeren, trans. by Jennifer Bajorek (London: Bloomsbury Academic, 2013), pp. 37–52

Dickens, Charles, *Dombey and Son*, ed. by Alan Horsman (Oxford: Oxford University Press, 2001)

Dickens, Charles, *Hard Times: A Norton Critical Edition*, ed. by Fred Kaplan, 4th edn (New York: W. W. Norton & Company, 2017)

Di Michele, Laura, 'Autobiography and "Structure of Feeling" in *Border Country*', in *Views Beyond the Border Country: Raymond Williams and Cultural Politics,* ed. by Dennis L. Dworkin and Leslie G. Roman (New York and London: Routledge, 1993), pp. 21–37

Disraeli, Benjamin, *Sybil; or The Two Nations*, ed. by Nicholas Shrimpton (Oxford: Oxford University Press, 2017)

Dussol, Vincent, 'James Kelman's Confrontational Ethics in *You Have to Be Careful in the Land of the Free*', in *Ethics of Alterity, Confrontation and Responsibility in 19th- to 21st-Century British Literature*, ed. by Jean-Michel Ganteau and Christine Reynier (Montpellier: Presses universitaires de la Méditerranée, 2013), pp. 181–192

Eldridge, John and Lizzie Eldridge, *Raymond Williams: Making Connections* (London: Routledge, 1994)

Engels, Friedrich, *The Condition of the Working Class in England*, ed. by David McLellan (Oxford: Oxford University Press, 2009)

Engels, Frederick, 'Engels to Margaret Harkness', in Karl Marx and Frederick Engels, *Marx and Engels Collected Works, Vol. 48* (London: Lawrence & Wishart/Electric Book, 2010), pp. 166–169

Fink, Bruce, *The Lacanian Subject: Between Language and Jouissance* (Princeton, NJ: Princeton University Press, 1995)

Fisher, Mark, *Ghosts of My Life: Writings on Depression, Hauntology and Lost Futures* (Winchester: Zero Books, 2022)

Foucault, Michel, *The Punitive Society: Lectures at the Collège de France 1972–1973*, trans. by Graham Burchell (Basingstoke: Palgrave Macmillan, 2015)

Fox, Pamela, *Class Fictions: Shame and Resistance in the British Working-Class Novel, 1890–1945* (Durham, NC: Duke University Press, 1994)

Gardiner, Michael, *From Trocchi to Trainspotting: Scottish Critical Theory Since 1960* (Edinburgh: Edinburgh University Press, 2006)

Gaskell, Elizabeth, *Mary Barton*, ed. by Shirley Foster (Oxford: Oxford University Press, 2008)

Gaskell, Elizabeth, *Mary Barton: A Norton Critical Edition*, ed. by Thomas Recchio (New York: W. W. Norton & Company, 2008)

Gibbon, Lewis Grassic, *A Scots Quair*, ed. by Ian Campbell (Edinburgh: Polygon, 2006)

Hall, Stuart, *The Hard Road to Renewal: Thatcherism and the Crisis of the Left* (London: Verso, 2021)

Hall, Stuart and Bill Schwarz, 'State and Society, 1880–1930', in Stuart Hall, *The Hard Road to Renewal: Thatcherism and the Crisis of the Left* (London: Verso, 2021), pp. 95–122

Hardt, Michael and Antonio Negri, *Commonwealth* (Cambridge, MA: The Belknap Press of Harvard University Press, 2009)

Harker, Ben, *The Chronology of Revolution: Communism, Culture, and Civil Society in Twentieth-Century Britain* (Toronto: University of Toronto Press, 2021)

Harker, Dave, *Tressell: The Real Story of* The Ragged Trousered Philanthropists (London: Zed Books, 2003)

Harkness, Margaret, *In Darkest London* (Cambridge: Black Apollo Press, 2003)

Harvey, David, *The Ways of the World* (London: Profile Books, 2017)

Haywood, Ian and Maroula Joannou, 'Introduction', in Ellen Wilkinson, *Clash* (Nottingham: Trent Editions, 2004), pp. vii–xxv

Hill, Christopher, *The Religion of Gerrard Winstanley* (Oxford: Past and Present Publications, 1978)

Hill, Christopher, *The World Turned Upside Down* (London: Penguin, 1991)

Hubble, Nick, *The Proletarian Answer to the Modernist Question* (Edinburgh: Edinburgh University Press, 2017)

Idle, Jeremy, 'Lewis Grassic Gibbon and the Urgency of the Modern', *Studies in Scottish Literature* 31:1 (1999), pp. 258–268

Jameson, Fredric, *Archaeologies of the Future: The Desire Called Utopia and Other Science Fictions* (London: Verso, 2005)

Jameson, Fredric, *The Political Unconscious* (London: Methuen, 1981)

Jones, Gareth Stedman, *Languages of Class: Studies in English Working Class History* (Cambridge: Cambridge University Press, 1983)

Joyce, Patrick, *Democratic Subjects: The Self and the Social in Nineteenth-Century England* (Cambridge: Cambridge University Press, 1994)

Kelly, Aaron, *James Kelman: Politics and Aesthetics* (Oxford: Peter Lang, 2013)

Kelman, James, *God's Teeth and Other Phenomena* (Oakland, CA: PM Press, 2022)

Kelman, James, *How Late It Was, How Late* (London: Vintage, 1998)

Kelman, James, *The State Is the Enemy: Essays on Liberation and Racial Justice* (Oakland, CA: PM Press, 2023)

Kelman, James, *You Have to Be Careful in the Land of the Free* (London: Penguin, 2005)

King, Amy Mae, 'Taxonomical Cures: The Politics of Natural History and Herbalist Medicine in Elizabeth Gaskell's *Mary Barton*', in Elizabeth Gaskell, *Mary Barton: A Norton Critical Edition*, ed. by Thomas Recchio (New York: W. W. Norton & Company, 2008), pp. 615–631

Klaus, H. Gustav, 'Introduction', in *The Socialist Novel in Britain: Towards the Recovery of a Tradition* (Brighton: Edward Everett, 2018), pp. 1–6

Kohlmann, Benjamin, 'Toward a History and Theory of the Socialist Bildungsroman', *Novel: A Forum on Fiction* 48:2 (2015), pp. 167–189

Kondo, Yasuhiro, '"To Feel the Connections": Collectivity and Dialectic in Raymond Williams's *Loyalties*', *Key Words: A Journal of Cultural Materialism* 9 (2011), pp. 112–123

Kornbluh, Anna, *The Order of Forms: Realism, Formalism, and Social Space* (Chicago, IL: The University of Chicago Press, 2019)

Kővesi, Simon, *James Kelman* (Manchester: Manchester University Press, 2007)

Lacan, Jacques, *Anxiety*, trans. by A. R. Price (Cambridge: Polity Press, 2014)

Lacan, Jacques, *The Ethics of Psychoanalysis*, trans. by Dennis Porter (London: Routledge, 2008)

Laclau, Ernesto, *New Reflections on the Revolution of Our Time* (London: Verso, 1990)

Laclau, Ernesto, *On Populist Reason* (London: Verso, 2005)

Laclau, Ernesto, *The Rhetorical Foundations of Society* (London: Verso, 2014)

Laclau, Ernesto and Chantal Mouffe, *Hegemony and Socialist Strategy: Towards a Radical Democratic Politics* (London: Verso, 2001)

Laybourn, Keith and Dylan Murphy, *Under the Red Flag: A History of Communism in Britain* (Stroud: Sutton Publishing, 1999)

Ledger, Sally, *Dickens and the Popular Radical Imagination* (Cambridge: Cambridge University Press, 2007)

Lesjak, Carolyn, *The Afterlife of Enclosure: British Realism, Character, and the Commons* (Stanford, CA: Stanford University Press, 2021)

Lesjak, Carolyn, *Working Fictions: A Genealogy of the Victorian Novel* (Durham, NC: Duke University Press, 2006)

Lessing, Doris, *The Four-Gated City* (London: Flamingo, 1993)

Lessing, Doris, *The Golden Notebook* (London: Fourth Estate, 2014)

Lessing, Doris, *Walking in the Shade: Volume Two of My Autobiography, 1949–1962* (London: HarperCollins, 1997)

Levenson, Michael, 'The Fictional Realist: Novels of the 1930s', in *The Cambridge Companion to George Orwell*, ed. by John Rodden (Cambridge: Cambridge University Press, 2007), pp. 59–75

Levinas, Emmanuel, *Autrement qu'être ou au-delà de l'essence* (Paris: Le Livre de Poche, 2019)

Lindsay, Jack, *Betrayed Spring* (London: The Bodley Head, 1953)

Lucas, John, 'Carson's Murder and the Inadequacy of Hope in *Mary Barton*', in Elizabeth Gaskell, *Mary Barton: A Norton Critical Edition*, ed. by Thomas Recchio (New York: W. W. Norton & Company, 2008), pp. 501–504

Lukács, Georg, *The Meaning of Contemporary Realism*, trans. by John and Necke Mander (London: Merlin Press, 1979)

Lukács, Georg, 'Realism in the Balance', in Theodor Adorno et al., *Aesthetics and Politics*, trans. by Rodney Livingstone (London: Verso, 1980), pp. 28–59

Malcolm, William K., 'Art for Politics' Sake: The Sardonic Principle of James Leslie Mitchell (Lewis Grassic Gibbon)', in *'To Hell with Culture': Anarchism and Twentieth-Century British Literature*, ed. by H. Gustav Klaus and Stephen Knight (Cardiff: University of Wales Press, 2005), pp. 35–50

Marx, Karl, 'The Eighteenth Brumaire of Louis Bonaparte', in *The Political Writings* (London: Verso, 2019), pp. 477–583

Miles, Peter, 'Introduction', in Robert Tressell, *The Ragged Trousered Philanthropists* (Oxford: Oxford University Press, 2005), pp. ix–xxxvii

Miller, Perry, *Errand into the Wilderness* (Cambridge, MA: The Belknap Press of Harvard University Press, 1956)

Morton, A. L., *The World of the Ranters: Religious Radicalism in the English Revolution* (London: Lawrence & Wishart, 1970)

Mouffe, Chantal, *For a Left Populism* (London: Verso, 2018)

Myler, Kerry, 'Doris Lessing, Antipsychiatry, and Bodies that Matter', *Twentieth-Century Literature* 65:4 (2019), pp. 437–460

Newsinger, John, *Hope Lies in the Proles: George Orwell and the Left* (London: Pluto Press, 2018)

Newsinger, John, *Orwell's Politics* (Basingstoke: Palgrave, 1999)

Nietzsche, Friedrich, *Untimely Meditations*, trans. by R. J. Hollingdale (Cambridge: Cambridge University Press, 1997)

Ó Donghaile, Deaglán, 'Modernism, Class and Colonialism in Robert Noonan's *The Ragged Trousered Philanthropists*', *Irish Studies Review* 26:3 (2018), pp. 374–389

Orwell, George, 'Charles Dickens', in *The Complete Works of George Orwell: A Patriot After All, 1940–1941* (London: Secker & Warburg, 1998), pp. 20–57

Orwell, George, *Coming Up for Air* (London: Penguin, 2020)

Orwell, George, *Down and Out in Paris and London* (London: Penguin, 2001)

Orwell, George, *Homage to Catalonia* (London: Penguin, 2000)

Orwell, George, 'The Home Guard and You', in *The Complete Works of George Orwell: A Patriot After All, 1940–1941* (London: Secker & Warburg, 1998), pp. 309–312

Orwell, George, 'The Lion and the Unicorn: Socialism and the English Genius', in *The Complete Works of George Orwell: A Patriot After All, 1940–1941* (London: Secker & Warburg, 1998), pp. 391–434

Orwell, George, 'My Country Right or Left', in *The Complete Works of George Orwell: A Patriot After All, 1940–1941* (London: Secker & Warburg, 1998), pp. 269–272

Orwell, George, 'Notes on the Way', in *The Complete Works of George Orwell: A Patriot After All, 1940–1941* (London: Secker & Warburg, 1998), pp. 121–127

Orwell, George, 'Our Opportunity', in *The Complete Works of George Orwell: A Patriot After All, 1940–1941* (London: Secker & Warburg, 1998), pp. 343–350

Orwell, George, *The Road to Wigan Pier*, in *Orwell's England*, ed. by Peter Davison (Harmondsworth: Penguin, 2001)

Owen, Robert, *A New View of Society and Other Writings* (London: Penguin, 2001)

Palmer, Bryan, *E.P. Thompson: Objections and Oppositions* (London: Verso, 1994)

Partington, John S., 'The Pen as Sword: George Orwell, H. G. Wells and Journalistic Parricide', *Journal of Contemporary History* 39:1 (2004), pp. 45–56

Patai, Daphne, *The Orwell Mystique: A Study in Male Ideology* (Amherst: University of Massachusetts Press, 1984)

Perry, Matt, *'Red Ellen' Wilkinson: Her Ideas, Movements and World* (Manchester: Manchester University Press, 2014)

Pinkney, Tony, *Raymond Williams* (Bridgend: Seren Books, 1991)

Priestley, J. B., *Blackout in Gretley* (Richmond: Valancourt Books, 2021)

Priestley, J. B., *Daylight on Saturday* (London: Pan Books, 1967)

Priestley, J. B., *Letter to a Returning Serviceman* (London: Home & Van Thal, 1945)

Priestley, J. B., *Out of the People* (London: Collins, 1941)

Priestley, J. B., *Postscripts* (London: William Heinemann, 1940)

Rancière, Jacques, *The Philosopher and His Poor*, trans. by John Drury, Corinne Oster, and Andrew Parker (Durham, NC: Duke University Press, 2003)

Roberts, John Michael, 'Reading Orwell Through Deleuze', *Deleuze Studies* 4:3 (2010), pp. 356–380

Salton-Cox, Glyn, 'Uncivil Society: Margaret Harkness, Engels and the Lumpenproletariat', *Key Words: A Journal of Cultural Materialism* 16 (2018), pp. 23–40

Schaffer, Talia, *Communities of Care: The Social Ethics of Victorian Fiction* (Princeton, NJ: Princeton University Press, 2021)

Shelley, Mary, *Frankenstein: A Norton Critical Edition*, ed. by J. Paul Hunter, 2nd edn (New York: W. W. Norton & Company, 2012)

Shiach, Morag, 'Lewis Grassic Gibbon and Modernism', in *The International Companion to Lewis Grassic Gibbon*, ed. by Scott Lyall (Glasgow: Scottish Literature International, 2015), pp. 9–21

Siméon, Ophélie, *Robert Owen's Experiment at New Lanark: From Paternalism to Socialism* (Cham: Palgrave Macmillan, 2017)

Singer, Sandra, 'Feminist Commitment to Left-Wing Realism in *The Golden Notebook*', in *Doris Lessing's* The Golden Notebook *After Fifty*, ed. by Alice Ridout et al. (New York: Palgrave Macmillan, 2015), pp. 73–95

Smith, Dai, *In the Frame: Memory in Society 1910 to 2010* (Cardigan: Parthian Books, 2010)

Smith, Nigel, 'Introduction', in *A Collection of Ranter Writings: Spiritual Liberty and Sexual Freedom in the English Revolution* (London: Pluto Press, 2014), pp. 1–33

Stallybrass, Peter, 'Marx and Heterogeneity: Thinking the Lumpenproletariat', *Representations* 31 (1990), pp. 69–95

Stoneman, Patsy, *Elizabeth Gaskell* (Bloomington: Indiana University Press, 1987)

Surridge, Lisa, 'Working-Class Masculinities in *Mary Barton*', *Victorian Literature and Culture* 28:2 (2000), pp. 331–343

Taunton, Matthew, 'Communism by the Letter: Doris Lessing and the Politics of Writing', *ELH* 88:1 (2021), pp. 251–280

Taunton, Matthew, *Red Britain: The Russian Revolution in Mid-Century Culture* (Oxford: Oxford University Press, 2019)

Taylor, Elinor, *The Popular Front Novel in Britain, 1934–1940* (Leiden: Brill, 2017)

Thompson, Edward, 'Notes on Exterminism, the Last Stage of Civilization', *New Left Review* I:121 (1980)

Thompson, E. P., *E.P. Thompson and the Making of the New Left*, ed. by Cal Winslow (New York: Monthly Review Press, 2014)

Thompson, E. P., 'Socialist Humanism: An Epistle to the Philistines', in *E.P. Thompson and the Making of the New Left: Essays and Polemics*, ed. by Cal Winslow (New York: Monthly Review Press, 2014), pp. 49–87

Thompson, E. P., *The Sykaos Papers* (London: Bloomsbury, 1988)

Thompson, E. P., *Witness Against the Beast: William Blake and the Moral Law* (Cambridge: Cambridge University Press, 1993)

Tressell, Robert, *The Ragged Trousered Philanthropists*, ed. by Peter Miles (Oxford: Oxford University Press, 2005)

Wilkinson, Ellen, *Clash*, ed. by Ian Haywood and Maroula Joannou (Nottingham: Trent Editions, 2004)

Williams, Raymond, *Border Country* (Cardigan: Parthian Books, 2020)

Williams, Raymond, *The Country and the City* (London: The Hogarth Press, 1993)

Williams, Raymond, *Culture and Society 1780–1950* (Harmondsworth: Penguin, 1961)

Williams, Raymond, *The English Novel from Dickens to Lawrence* (London: The Hogarth Press, 1987)

Williams, Raymond, *The Fight for Manod* (London: Chatto & Windus, 1979)

Williams, Raymond, *The Long Revolution* (Harmondsworth: Penguin, 1971)

Williams, Raymond, *Loyalties* (London: The Hogarth Press, 1989)

Williams, Raymond, *Marxism and Literature* (Oxford: Oxford University Press, 1977)

Williams, Raymond, *Orwell* (London: Fontana/Collins, 1971)

Williams, Raymond, *Politics and Letters* (London: New Left Books, 1979)

Williams, Raymond, 'The Ragged-Arsed Philanthropists', in *Writing in Society* (London: Verso, 1991), pp. 239–256

Williams, Raymond, *Resources of Hope: Culture, Democracy, Socialism*, ed. by Robin Gable (London: Verso, 1989)

Williams, Raymond, *Second Generation* (London: The Hogarth Press, 1988)

Williams, Raymond, 'The Welsh Industrial Novel', in *Who Speaks for Wales? Nation, Culture, Identity*, ed. by Daniel Williams (Cardiff: University of Wales Press, 2003), pp. 95–111

Winstanley, Gerrard, *The Law of Freedom and Other Writings* (Harmondsworth: Penguin, 1973)

Wolfreys, Julian, *Victorian Hauntings: Spectrality, Gothic, the Uncanny and Literature* (Basingstoke: Palgrave, 2002)

Woloch, Alex, *Or Orwell: Writing and Democratic Socialism* (Cambridge, MA: Harvard University Press, 2016)

Žižek, Slavoj, 'Beyond Discourse-Analysis', in Ernesto Laclau, *New Reflections on the Revolution of Our Time* (London: Verso, 1990)

Žižek, Slavoj, *The Sublime of Object of Ideology* (London: Verso, 2008)

Index

Abensour, Miguel 22, 140, 141, 150, 160
Acland, Richard 91, 92
Addison, Paul 88, 91, 92, 95
affect 19, 25, 27, 29, 54, 56, 65, 67–69, 76, 79, 80, 89, 91, 97, 157
Africa 122, 141, 145, 146
Agamben, Giorgio 70–72, 81, 82, 90, 170
Allison, Mark A. 10, 11, 17
alterity *see* otherness
America 160–171
anarchism *see* anarchy
anarchy
    according to Abensour 140, 141, 160
    according to Levinas 140, 141, 143, 150, 178
    and antinomianism 158–160, 162
    and Gibbon 52, 53, 61
    and Kelman 159–162, 164–166, 173, 175
    and Lessing 139, 140–143, 150, 151
    and Orwell 76–78
antagonism 5, 9, 14, 18–22, 25, 27, 28, 30, 35, 46, 87, 95, 96, 129–131, 133, 135, 173–176, 178, 179
antinomianism 13, 152, 154–160, 162, 164, 166, 168
anti-psychiatry 149, 152
anti-Stalinism 77, 152, 153
anxiety 48, 78, 175, 178, 179
arche (Levinas) 140–142, 146, 148, 149, 151, 155, 159, 173, 177, 178
articulation
    according to Laclau and Mouffe 42, 43, 44, 87

and hegemony 35, 87, 97, 102, 107, 134
and heterogeneity 32, 35, 37, 86
and politics 11, 32, 34, 35, 43, 44, 45, 46, 49, 50, 86, 101, 107, 116, 128, 129, 133
assemblage (Deleuze and Guattari) 3, 65, 68
atheism 64, 161, 166, 169
Attlee, Clement 102

Baker, Timothy C. 54, 55
Baldick, Chris 27
Barrow, Clyde W. 6
Bartley, Paula 46, 47
Bataille, George 6, 7, 21, 182
Bauthumley, Jacob 166
Baxendale, John 88
becoming (Deleuze and Guattari) 52–58, 61, 63, 64, 73, 77, 79, 80, 84–86, 91
    becoming-minoritarian 64
    becoming-revolutionary 77, 85
    becoming-woman 64
Beers, Laura 48
Bellamy, Edward 38
Benjamin, Walter 150, 168
Bercovitch, Sacvan 161
Bergson, Henri 53
Bevir, Mark 2–4, 10, 45, 91
Blake, William 152, 154, 155, 158
Blatchford, Robert 38, 44, 97
Blitz, The 83, 88
body-without-organs (Deleuze and Guattari) 68
Bogue, Ronald 53

Bonapartism 33, 34
bourgeoisie 17, 29, 30, 33, 34, 36, 37,
    47, 49, 69, 75, 77, 121, 128, 147,
    149, 183
Bove, Laurent 89
Braidotti, Rosi 65
Branson, Noreen 101
Brantlinger, Patrick 24
Brome, Vincent 88
bureaucracy 94, 177, 178
Burma 74

Cairnie, Julie 42
Callaghan, John 100
capitalism
    capitalist division of labour 10
    capitalist exploitation 18, 35, 36,
        42, 45, 70, 71, 82, 94, 129,
        163
    capitalist relations of production 1,
        7, 41
    economic contradictions of 43, 45
    and formlessness 70–72, 83, 90
    globalised 160, 163, 164
    industrial 18, 20, 22, 31, 35, 70,
        114
    late 124, 126
    mode of production 6, 9, 72
    and modernity 71, 90
    organised 43
    post-war (1945) 112, 115, 123
Césaire, Aimé 85
Chartism 2, 3, 19, 26, 32, 164, 184
Christianity 16, 29, 30, 36, 58, 62, 91,
    92, 157, 164, 168, 169, 170, 183
Claeys, Gregory 16, 19, 27
Clark, Katerina 8, 99, 100, 102
class
    conflict 15, 17, 27, 32, 33, 61, 101
    consciousness 1, 4, 35, 146
    identity 1, 10, 69, 73, 79, 128, 129,
        179
    reductionism 1–4, 45, 49–50, 183
    struggle 43, 50, 100–102, 119, 128,
        134, 167, 178, 179
    subject 13, 21, 22, 29, 32, 65

to come 44
versus people 1–3, 5–10
see also working class; bourgeoisie
Cold War 131, 133, 139, 141, 155–157
Cole, G. D. H. 94
colonialism 38, 85, 86, 122, 145, 146,
    160, 161, 170
see also imperialism
common 67, 88, 89–91, 95, 108, 110,
    112, 114, 117–119, 123
see also community
Communism 13, 43, 44, 46, 49, 61,
    62, 64, 97, 128–132
    Lessing and 137–139, 141–143,
        145–149
    Lindsay and 99–101, 106–108
    Orwell and 76–78
    Thompson and 152–155
    Wilkinson and 46
Communist Party of Great Britain
    (CPGB) 46, 61, 62, 99–101, 103,
    106–108, 129–132, 138, 139, 152,
    153
Communist Party of the Soviet Union
    (CPSU) 131, 153
community 9, 15, 22, 35, 51, 76, 87,
    89, 93, 94, 97, 103, 104, 109–113,
    115–118, 124, 151, 168
see also common
Connor, John T. 99
conservatism 16, 45, 71, 85, 92, 138,
    149
Conservative Party (Tories) 36, 47, 78,
    86, 97, 106, 135
contemplation (Agamben) 81, 82
contingency 2–5, 11–14, 34, 37, 41, 42,
    45, 46, 50–52, 58, 64–66, 68, 69,
    100, 103, 106, 116–119, 129, 130,
    132–134, 174, 178
Coppe, Abiezer 163, 167
Cranny-Francis, Anne 99
Cripps, Stafford 105
Crockett, Clayton 12
Croft, Andy 100
Crosland, Anthony 112
Cultural Studies 92, 109

D'Albertis, Deirdre 21
Deleuze, Gilles 4, 11–13, 51–54, 57, 58, 64, 65, 67, 68, 73, 78–80, 84, 90, 91, 140, 179
    see also assemblage; becoming; body-without-organs; deterritorialisation; fabulation; nomadism; war machine
democracy 4, 16, 44–46, 76, 92, 93, 95–97, 153, 162, 170, 184
    democracy to come (Derrida) 4, 44, 170
    radical democracy 46, 76, 184
Derrida, Jacques 4–6, 13, 17, 29, 30, 44, 125, 126, 141, 143, 144, 167, 168, 170–172
    see also democracy to come; hauntology; spectrality; trace
deterritorialisation (Deleuze and Guattari) 73–76, 80, 140
Di Michele, Laura 113
dialectics
    and history 6, 7, 35
    and Marxism 5, 7, 8, 183
    see also totality
Dickens, Charles 2, 45, 66, 67, 181, 182
diffusionism 51, 56, 59, 61, 62
Diggers 158
    see also Winstanley; antinomianism
Disraeli, Benjamin 27, 28, 97
Dissent *see* antinomianism
divided society 20, 22, 30, 32, 33, 90, 109, 124
    see also division
division 10, 18, 19–22, 24, 30, 32, 33, 40, 70, 71, 81, 90, 94, 101, 109, 117, 121, 124, 125, 129, 137–139, 141–144, 146–150
Dobrenko, Evgeny 100
Dunkirk 87, 88
Dussol, Vincent 160, 161
Dworkin, Dennis L. 113
dystopia 143, 151, 152, 160, 164, 168, 171
    see also utopia

ecology 156
Edwards, Jonathan 169
Eldridge, John 114
Eldridge, Lizzie 114
empiricism 67, 68, 71
Engels, Friedrich 7–9, 43, 182, 183
English Civil Wars 154, 161
equivalence (Laclau and Mouffe) 42, 87, 128
ethics 30, 44, 65, 91, 92, 140, 141, 144, 146, 149, 152, 158, 168, 172

Fabianism 38, 91
fabulation (Deleuze) 13, 52, 53, 55, 58–60, 64, 84, 85, 90
fascism 59, 75, 79, 85, 87, 89, 90, 93, 96, 128, 129, 131
feminism 46, 48–50, 61, 65, 138
Fink, Bruce 173
Fisher, Mark 125
flight 13, 73–75, 77–79, 81–83
Foucault, Michel 21, 22, 25
Fourier, Charles 22
Fox, Pamela 38, 47
Frankfurt School 92
French Communist Party (PCF) 107

Ganteau, Jean-Michel 160
Gardiner, Michael 177
Gaskell, Elizabeth
    Mary Barton 6, 12, 15–33, 168
gender 20, 26, 30, 71, 121, 138, 150
    see also feminism; masculinity
General Strike (1926) 47, 49, 59, 104, 114, 116
ghosts *see* spectrality
Gibbon, Lewis Grassic
    Cloud Howe (*A Scots Quair*) 51, 58–62, 64
    Grey Granite (*A Scots Quair*) 61–65
    Sunset Song (*A Scots Quair*) 51–58
Gissing, George 2, 3, 9, 10
globalisation *see* capitalism
Gothic 23, 124
Gramsci, Antonio 35, 43

Great Depression 69, 90
Guattari, Félix 11, 51, 53, 65, 68,
    77–80, 140

Hall, Stuart 3, 45, 46
Hardt, Michael 11
Harker, Ben 100, 107, 108
Harker, Dave 37, 38, 44
Harkness, Margaret 8, 9, 182–184
Harvey, David 119
hauntology 17, 28, 125
    see also spectrality
Haywood, Ian 47, 48
Hegel, G. W. F. 5, 7
hegemony 11, 43, 44, 87, 93, 97, 102,
    103, 105, 106–108, 134, 135, 154,
    169
Heinemann, Margot 100
Heraclitus 56, 57
heterogeneity 2, 4–7, 9–14, 21, 33–35,
    37, 40, 41, 44, 45, 46, 49, 51,
    52, 57, 65–67, 86, 88, 89, 102,
    106–108, 113, 129, 132, 143, 144,
    159, 166, 178, 179, 181–184
    see also homogeneity;
        lumpenproletariat
heteronormativity 71
Hill, Christopher 158, 169
history 1, 3, 5–9, 18, 28, 34, 35, 41,
    52–56, 58–62, 64, 65, 79–86, 99,
    100, 102, 103, 106, 114, 116, 119,
    121, 123, 127, 128, 151, 156, 161,
    179
Hitler, Adolf 85, 86, 95
Hoggart, Richard 109
homogeneity 1, 5–7, 9–11, 34, 40, 41,
    47, 50, 51, 67, 105, 107, 112, 129,
    143, 177, 179, 181–183
    see also heterogeneity
hospitality 168, 170–173, 175
Hubble, Nick 65
Hungarian Revolution (1956) 153
Hyndman, Henry Mayers 43, 44

ideology 2–4, 10, 12, 13, 15–18, 20,
    24, 28, 29, 31, 35, 37, 38, 43, 45,
    46, 49, 59, 65, 69, 79, 87, 91–93,
    97, 101–103, 105–107, 111, 112, 128,
    137, 140–142, 146, 147, 149, 151,
    153–155, 165, 175, 179, 181
Idle, Jeremy 51, 52
ILP (Independent Labour Party) 46, 78
immanence 1, 7, 18, 27–29, 32, 42, 45,
    47, 54, 60, 61, 65, 68, 69, 72, 118,
    157
    see also transcendence
imperialism 8, 38, 42, 74, 78, 85, 86,
    160
    see also colonialism
India 42
industrialism 16–23, 27, 31, 32, 35, 38,
    48, 51, 59, 61, 69–72, 90, 93–96,
    105, 107, 114, 116, 124, 145, 181,
    182
International Brigades 76
internationalism 128, 129, 131, 166,
    166
Italian Communist Party (PCI) 107,
    108

Jameson, Fredric 2, 3, 9, 10, 31
jeremiad 161–163, 166, 168–170
Joannou, Maroula 47, 48
Jones, Gareth Stedman 2, 3
jouissance 177
Joyce, Patrick 4
justice/injustice 29, 30, 49, 74, 76, 82,
    106, 167–169, 175

Kafka, Franz 177, 178
Kautsky, Karl 43
Kelly, Aaron 163
Kelman, James 7, 11, 14, 159–179
    God's Teeth and Other Phenomena
        171–174
    How Late It Was, How Late 176–179
    *You Have to Be Careful in the Land
        of the Free* 160, 161, 163–172,
        174, 175
King, Amy Mae 20, 32
Klaus, H. Gustav 1, 52
Knight, Stephen 52

Kohlmann, Benjamin 137
Kondo, Yasuhiro 128
Kornbluh, Anna 8
Kővesi, Simon 164

labour 9, 10, 21, 22, 37, 39–42, 47,
  52, 114–116, 121, 123, 124, 132,
  154
Labour Party 13, 45, 97, 101, 119, 122
  Lessing on the 145–148
  Lindsay on the 102–106
  Wilkinson and the 46, 47
  Williams on the 111, 112, 120, 124,
    130
Labourism 46, 49, 97, 101, 106, 112,
  120, 124, 155
Lacan, Jacques 7, 9, 173–175, 179
lack 4, 87, 93, 171, 174–179
Laclau, Ernesto 4–7, 9, 11, 12, 34, 35,
  41–44, 87, 88, 102, 107, 108, 129,
  131, 174, 175
Lahusen, Thomas 100
Laing, R. D. 149
language 3, 7, 55, 71, 88, 91, 121, 123,
  143, 156, 162, 167, 170, 171, 173
law 159, 165, 168, 170–173, 177, 182,
  184
  moral (Mosaic) law 154, 157, 163
  see also hospitality; justice/injustice
Laybourn, Keith 43, 153
Ledger, Sally 2
Left Book Club 78
Lesjak, Carolyn 8, 15, 66, 67
Lessing, Doris 11, 13, 137–155, 158,
  159, 178
  The Four-Gated City 137, 144–153,
    158, 178
  The Golden Notebook 137–145, 149,
    178
  Walking in the Shade 153
Levellers 162
  see also antinomianism; Diggers;
    Ranters
Levenson, Michael 78
Levinas, Emmanuel 30, 140, 141, 143,
  150, 172, 178

liberalism 36, 45, 131, 163, 182
life 22, 27, 28, 31, 39, 47–49, 51,
  53–57, 59–61, 63–67, 69–73, 80–84,
  88–91, 101, 102, 105–108, 112,
  114, 115, 117–123, 125, 127, 132,
  138–145, 156, 158, 166, 170
  form-of-life (Agamben) 13, 70, 71,
    73, 80, 82, 83, 90
Lindsay, Jack 13, 97, 99–108
  Betrayed Spring 99–107
line of flight *see* flight
logos 141, 144
Lucas, John 30
Lukács, Georg 8, 9, 102, 103, 110, 111
lumpenproletariat 6–8, 33, 34, 39–41,
  65, 164, 176, 179, 182, 183
  see also Laclau; Stallybrass
Lyall, Scott 52, 55

machine 16, 58, 77, 89, 90, 91, 94, 95,
  157
  see also war machine
madness 141, 143, 144, 148–152, 156,
  159, 178
majoritarian 60, 62, 65, 77, 79
  see also minoritarian
Malcolm, William K. 52
Marx, Karl 7, 33, 34, 37, 40, 43
  see also Engels; Marxism
Marxism 2, 6–9, 34, 38, 40, 41, 43,
  44, 47, 52, 53, 76, 91, 99, 107, 108,
  110, 119, 131, 153
  see also post-Marxism
masculinity 17, 30, 148
messianism 44, 58, 59–61, 63, 167, 169
metapolitics 13, 140, 148
Miles, Peter 36
Miller, Henry 78
Miller, Perry 161
miners 72, 103–105, 116, 129, 133–135
Miners' Strike (1984–1985) 133–135
minoritarian 64, 73
  see also becoming; majoritarian
misogyny 62, 63, 71
modernism 8, 38, 51, 54
monarchy 86, 87, 166

monstrosity 17–19, 21, 22–28, 32, 33, 53, 67, 176

morality 15, 16, 19, 22, 23, 32, 36, 40, 41, 53, 54, 71, 78, 89, 90, 93–96, 106, 131, 134, 135, 138, 141, 142, 149, 150, 154, 155, 157, 163, 182, 183

More, Thomas 31, 150

Morris, William 11, 22, 97, 152

Morrison, Herbert 105, 106

Morton, A. L. 162, 167

Mouffe, Chantal 5, 34, 42–44, 175
    see also Laclau

Muggletonians 154
    see also antinomianism; Thompson

Murphy, Dylan 43, 153

Myler, Kerry 148, 149

nation 13, 58–60, 85, 86, 88, 90, 91, 94, 95, 100, 107, 108, 122, 128, 146, 170

nationalisation 103, 104, 111, 130, 155

nationalism 60, 85, 95
    see also internationalism

naturalism 8, 10, 182

Nazism 84, 86, 89, 90, 91, 95, 96, 166

Negri, Antonio 11

New Left 13, 132, 137, 152

Newsinger, John 76, 84, 85

Nietzsche, Friedrich 53–57

nomadism 21, 22, 30, 61, 77, 78, 163

Ó Donghaile, Deaglán 38

objectivity 1, 3–5, 8, 10, 39, 42, 45, 50, 55, 68, 81, 93, 129–132, 134, 161, 175, 176, 182, 183

ontology 4, 12, 17, 19, 23, 28, 30, 35, 52, 55, 56, 62, 77, 91, 119, 139–141, 143, 152

otherness 5, 29, 44, 125, 143, 144, 159, 168, 172, 178, 179

Orwell, George 13, 65–90, 145
    'Charles Dickens' 67
    Coming Up for Air 65, 78–84, 88

Down and Out in Paris and London 65–69

Homage to Catalonia 65, 75–78
    'The Home Guard and You' 87
    'The Lion and the Unicorn' 87, 88
    'My Country Right or Left' 84, 85
    'Notes on the Way' 85, 86
    'Our Opportunity' 86
    The Road to Wigan Pier 65, 69–76, 83, 89, 90, 145

Owen, Robert 10, 15–17, 19, 22–24, 27, 30

Owenism 15, 16, 19, 30

Palmer, Bryan 155

pantheism 166

Partington, John S. 75

paternalism 12, 16–18, 22, 27–29, 32

patriotism 36, 50, 84–87, 95, 164, 165

people 2–7, 10–13, 51, 54, 55, 57, 58, 60–62, 65, 66, 84–87, 89–96, 100, 101, 108, 126–128, 130, 146, 147, 154, 179, 183, 184
    missing people 4, 12, 13, 55, 57, 58, 65, 84, 85, 179

People's War 85, 96

Perrault, Pierre 53

Perry, Matt 46

Pinkney, Tony 124

Plekhanov, Georgi 43

police 62, 74, 77, 78, 90, 160, 169, 170, 176, 178

Popular Front 128, 131, 132

populism 2–5, 9, 12, 13, 84, 87, 88, 92, 95
    see also Laclau; people

post-Marxism 5, 11
    see also Laclau; Mouffe

postmodernism 163, 168

POUM 76

poverty 3, 19, 23, 24, 29, 33, 36, 39–42, 53, 65–69, 72, 84, 120, 147, 162, 164, 165, 183

power 11, 16, 16, 27, 53–55, 60, 61,
  64, 65, 68, 73, 78, 85, 88–91,
  97, 106, 117, 126, 130, 147, 150,
  153–155, 158–160, 164, 165, 169,
  173, 175
Priestley, J. B. 13, 88–97, 111
  Blackout in Gretley 94–96
  Daylight on Saturday 96, 97
  Letter to a Returning Serviceman 97
  Out of the People 92–95
  Postscripts 88–91
proletariat *see* working class
psychoanalysis 6, 138, 141–143
  see also Lacan
Puritanism 161, 162, 166, 169
  see also antinomianism; jeremiad

racism 85, 86, 146, 165, 175
radicalism 2, 3, 5, 12, 13, 15, 16, 21,
  46–49, 76, 78, 79, 88, 91, 92, 95,
  96, 102, 106, 122, 124, 126, 127,
  133, 137, 147, 149, 152, 154, 157,
  160, 161, 164, 166, 168, 169, 184
  see also democracy
Rancière, Jacques 34
Ranters 154, 157, 161–163, 166–170
Real (Lacan) 7, 9, 173
realism 8, 9, 13, 15, 16, 64, 66, 96,
  99–135, 137, 142, 151, 181–184
  see also socialist realism; typicality
reformism 16, 17, 20, 22, 27, 29, 31,
  32, 62, 64, 75, 103, 146
religion 53, 60, 61, 91, 92, 126, 152,
  158, 162, 169
  see also Christianity
revolution 11, 19, 27, 37, 38, 52, 53,
  59, 62, 64, 70, 75–78, 84–87, 91,
  96, 100, 116, 122, 123, 126, 142,
  153, 154, 161, 162, 166
Reynier, Christine 160
Roberts, John Michael 67, 68
Rodden, John 78
Roman, Leslie G. 113

sacrifice 37, 61, 62, 64, 100
Saint-Simon, Henri de 10, 22

Salton-Cox, Glyn 8
Schaffer, Talia 18
schizophrenia 140, 148, 149, 152
Schwarz, Bill 45, 46
Scotland 51–65, 149, 160–179
sexuality 52, 129, 177
Shelley, Mary 24–26
Shiach, Morag 51, 52
Siméon, Ophélie 23
Singer, Sandra 137
slum 66, 71, 182
Smith, Dai 109
Smith, Nigel 162, 163, 166
social democracy 43, 102
  see also Labour Party; socialism
Social Democratic Federation (SDF) 43
social realism *see* realism
socialism
  Christian 58, 62, 91, 92
  democratic 101
  and feminism 46–50, 137
  libertarian 53, 77, 93, 152, 154, 159,
    161
  middle-class 74, 75
  people of 4–6
  revisionist definition of 3
  utopian 10–12, 15–17, 22, 44
  without guarantees 3, 13, 129, 184
  see also anarchy; Communism;
    democracy; heterogeneity;
    Labourism; populism; radicalism;
    social democracy
socialist humanism 153, 154, 157
socialist realism 8, 13, 99–102, 107,
  182
  see also realism; typicality
sovereignty 70, 78, 140, 170, 171, 173
Soviet Union 8, 84, 99, 108, 110, 130,
  131, 148, 153
Spanish Civil War 75–78, 128
spectrality 12, 17, 18, 24, 28–32,
  44, 83, 124–129, 131, 132, 134,
  167–169
Spinoza, Baruch 89, 91, 166
Stalinism 102, 152, 153
  see also anti-Stalinism; Zhdanovism

Stallybrass, Peter 33, 34
State 10, 34, 37, 52, 77, 78, 85, 91, 93,
  94, 97, 126, 133, 141, 152, 154, 160,
  164, 175, 177, 178
Stil, André 100
Stoneman, Patsy 17, 18, 30
strikes 47, 49, 59, 62, 102, 104, 114,
  116–118, 133, 167, 168
  see also General Strike (1926);
    Miners' Strike (1984–1985)
subjectivity 21, 22, 28, 32, 42, 68, 69,
  77, 79–81, 101, 131, 132, 148, 149,
  157, 161, 165, 174, 175, 178
suffragism 46–48
Surridge, Lisa 17
Symbolic (Lacan) 173–177, 179, 182
syndicalism 77, 166, 167

Taunton, Matthew 137
Taylor, Elinor 99
temporality 17, 18, 35, 42, 44, 51,
  52, 54–57, 62, 68, 69, 72, 80, 82,
  90, 113, 114, 116, 119, 125, 126,
  162
Thatcher, Margaret 133, 135, 155, 156
theology 59, 64, 154, 161, 162, 167,
  169, 170
Thompson, E. P.
  'Socialist Humanism: An Epistle to
    the Philistines' 153, 154
  The Sykaos Papers 13, 155–159
  Witness Against the Beast 154, 155,
    157, 158, 162
Togliatti, Palmiro 107
Toryism *see* Conservative Party (Tories)
totality 5, 8–11, 34, 101, 102, 108,
  109, 111, 137, 140, 141, 143, 179,
  181, 182, 183
trace (Derrida and Levinas) 137, 141,
  143, 144, 160
trade unions 16, 21, 26, 43, 46, 47, 49,
  77, 102, 103, 105, 112, 116, 119,
  120, 132, 134, 146, 183
transcendence 10, 17, 27, 30, 31, 53,
  56, 59–62, 64, 79, 80, 167
  see also immanence

Tressell, Robert
  The Ragged Trousered Philanthropists
    6, 12, 35–45
Trotskyism 76, 86, 132
typicality 8, 66, 182
  see also realism; socialist realism

untimeliness 17, 52, 55, 57, 58, 65, 80
utopia 10–12, 15–17, 22, 25, 28,
  30–32, 44, 53, 61, 72, 82, 124,
  126–128, 143, 149–152, 157, 162,
  169, 178
  see also dystopia

Victorian era 2, 15–32, 45, 66, 88, 147,
  176, 181–184
violence 7, 55, 60, 62, 71, 72, 90, 150,
  154, 168, 171, 172

Wales 113–135
war machine (Deleuze and Guattari)
  77, 78
welfare state 45, 120, 177
Welles, Orson 53
Wilkinson, Ellen
  Clash 46–50
Williams, Raymond
  Border Country 109, 113–121, 123,
    125
  The Country and the City 124, 181
  Culture and Society 15, 93, 94, 110
  *The English Novel from Dickens to
    Lawrence* 9
  The Fight for Manod 123–127
  The Long Revolution 109–115
  Loyalties 127–135
  Marxism and Literature 1
  Orwell 76
  Politics and Letters 110, 111, 123, 124
  Second Generation 119–124
Winslow, Cal 154
Winstanley, Gerrard 91, 158
Wobblies (International Workers of the
  World) 167
Wolfreys, Julian 29
Woloch, Alex 74

work *see* labour
working class 1, 2, 6, 12, 15, 17–27, 29, 30, 32, 34, 35, 38, 40, 42–45, 47, 49–51, 62, 65, 71–77, 101–105, 108, 112, 114, 116, 128, 130–132, 134, 145, 146, 153, 154, 163

World War One 46, 49, 51, 58, 81, 95
World War Two 13, 83–97, 145

Zhdanovism 100, 102
Žižek, Slavoj 174, 177–179